Audience–Citizens

Audience–Citizens

The Media, Public Knowledge and Interpretive Practice

Ramaswami Harindranath

⑤SAGE Los Angeles • London • New Delhi • Singapore • Washington DC
www.sagepublications.com

First published in 2009 by

 SAGE Publications India Pvt Ltd
B1/I1 Mohan Cooperative Industrial Area
Mathura Road, New Delhi 110 044, India
www.sagepub.in

SAGE Publications Inc
2455 Teller Road
Thousand Oaks, California 91320, USA

SAGE Publications Ltd
1 Oliver's Yard, 55 City Road
London EC1Y 1SP, United Kingdom

SAGE Publications Asia-Pacific Pte Ltd
33 Pekin Street
#02-01 Far East Square
Singapore 048763

Published by Vivek Mehra for SAGE Publications India Pvt Ltd, Phototypeset in 11/13 Baskerville BE by Tantla Composition Services Private Limited, Chandigarh and printed at Rajkamal Electric Press, New Delhi.

Library of Congress Cataloging-in-Publication Data available

ISBN: 978-81-7829-935-8 (HB)

The SAGE Team: Elina Majumdar, Shinjini Basu and Trinankur Banerjee

Photo Credit: Arvind Jain (The photograph is from flickr.com and under the creative commons attribution license)

Contents

Acknowledgements

A few of the chapters in this book are revised versions of essays published elsewhere. A different version of Chapter 1 was published in the journal *Particip@tions,* vol. 3, issue 2, 2006. A summary of the conceptual framework developed in Chapters 2, 3 and 4 was published in Dickinson, R., R. Harindranath, and O. Linne (eds) (1998) *Approaches to Audiences,* London: Arnold. And finally, the argument developed in Chapter 8 is an extended version of the essays in Cottle, S. (2000) *Ethnic Minorities and the Media: Changing Cultural Boundaries,* Buckingham: The Open University Press, and in *Particip@tions,* vol. 3, issue 1, 2005.

1

Introduction: Media Audiences, Public Knowledge and Democracy

Inspired by the occasion of the sixtieth anniversary of their independence in 2007, several analyses of contemporary political and social formations of India and Pakistan have been published recently. Both academic and journalistic accounts have included, among various points of analyses, comparisons between the two countries in terms of democratic governance, which reveal a stark and startling variation. Whereas India, apart from the two momentous years of Emergency rule during which democratic rights were suspended, has been celebrated as 'the world's largest functioning democracy', Pakistan is seen as lurching between fragile democratic rule and military dictatorship. One of the more plausible assessments of this difference between two countries, sharing a region, provenance and historical trajectory, rests on the divergence in the emphasis on all levels of education. In a recent article in *The Guardian*, for instance, William Dalrymple underlines two related points concerning the continuing problems faced by Pakistan. First, unlike in India, the educated middle class exercises less power in relation to the landowners, which, resulting in the feudalistic control over the electoral process, continues to undermine democracy in Pakistan; and second, the country's 'desperate educational crisis. No problem in Pakistan casts such a long shadow over its future as the abject failure of the government to educate more than a fraction of its people' (Dalrymple 2007: 26). One immediate consequence of the lack of schools with the most basic infrastructure has been the rise in the popularity of *madrasas* or Islamic schools, but the long term effect, according to Dalrymple and others, has been the undermining of democracy. The question can be raised, however, as to what exactly is the role of education in democratic governance and in civil society, particularly in developing societies. The relations between educational capital, interpretive practice and the media in the Indian context, and by extension other developing societies, form the main focus of this book. As the next three chapters will elaborate, examining these links requires a rethinking of the conceptual framework on the relations between media, audiences and socio-cultural contexts.

Among the various terms that have recently assumed a specific global currency, the notion of 'democracy' is arguably one of the most slippery; mutating in significance from being co-terminous with the 'free market', as a marker of difference between a putative 'us' against an alleged 'them', as a lack that undermines development in the African countries and freedom in other regions, to being associated with Western or even occasionally Christian sentiments that can be 'exported', not unlike the crusading evangelists of the colonial period. In each of these manifestations, the notion adopts a particular set of values. As John Dewey once observed, 'democracy' is a word with multiple meanings. In academic literature, 'democracy' as a concept and a term has been scrutinized and debated over for decades, and this scrutiny has spilled over disciplinary boundaries. More recently the lability of the concept has been seen more explicitly as an indication of its status as a floating signifier. Its appearance in various discourses—everyday, political and media—is perceived to represent crucial aspects of the contested terrain of contemporary global politics and culture. For instance, in his influential essay on globalization as constituting various 'scapes', Arjun Appadurai (1996: 37) underlines the fluidity of the term and its links with debates on globalization, identifying it as one of the 'ideoscapes' that has 'clearly become a master term', an example of the 'globally variable synaesthesia' that characterizes the modern 'terminological kaleidoscope'. As Munck argues (2002: 11), the contestation over the meaning of the term is indicative of its centrality to the political discourse, and to the fact that, it takes on different meanings as it is 'appropriated by different social and political forces'.

The media are centrally implicated in discussions of the functioning of contemporary democracies. Most studies on the role of the media in democratic societies have focussed on, the debates surrounding the notions of the public sphere, media texts as the site of contestation and conflict and the ideals of public service broadcasting as opposed to commercial media (Keane 1991). This take is not restricted to the Euro-American context, but it also incorporates other regions, including developing societies (recent examples illustrated in Hyden et al. 2002, Kitley 2003, Cohen 2005, Hackett and Zhao 2005). These are crucial interventions that continue to make very significant contributions to the ongoing debates. For instance, Hackett and Zhao's preliminary remarks, setting out their project on media democratization, include an astute observation on the limitations in the fields of political science and media studies. While on the one hand, the former abounds in publications exploring the links between globalization and democracy, it largely neglects the dimension of the media. On the other hand, media or communication studies contain elaborations on media and democracy or media and globalization, 'few combine these problematics... Moreover, there is little dialogue between cultural and political communication dimensions of the debate about media globalization' (Hackett and Zhao 2005: 1). Following Cees Hamelink, they seek to explore 'both democratization through the media ... and democratization of the media' (Hackett and Zhao 2005: 2).

In a useful summary of research on media and democracy, particularly in the field of political communication, Dahlgren

(2004) argues that, there have been two productive alternatives to the traditional political science approach to communication, which has 'evoked criticisms over the years, for being too formalistic, too bound to the prevailing political/institutional arrangements, too wedded to constrictive methodologies' (2004: 15). The first of the two challenges he identifies to the political science tradition, which he refers to as the 'public sphere approach', has, as he rightly observes, contributed to the examinations of the role of the media in democratic societies. Influenced mainly by the theoretical edifice constructed on the philosophical insights provided by Habermas, this perspective engages with notions such as deliberative democracy and communicative rationality. Using a normative idea of democracy, this perspective has been used by communication scholars to investigate, for example, the role of public service broadcasting. We will return to Habermas in later chapters, but Garnham's (1993, 2000) argument, regarding the globalization of political power and the corollary need for a global public sphere in the shape of a unitary global media system as opposed to a plural media public, is worth noting here. Intrinsic to this argument is the notion that a global power-bloc requires a system of accountability of similar scope, and that the media offer the best means of achieving that.

> If the impact [of economic and political decisions] is universal, then both the political and media systems must be universal. In this sense a series of autonomous public spheres is not sufficient. There must be a single public sphere, even if we might want to conceive of it as made up of a series of subsidiary public spheres, each organized around its own public political sphere, media system, and set of forms and interests. (Garnham 1993: 264)

As Barnett (2004) has noted, Garnham identifies the lack of a symmetry between contemporary global politics and a fragmented media system, and the consequent lack of democratic political participation leading to the emergence of a politics of identity. This position takes for granted a connection between a common media system and democratic functioning in the form of deliberative democracy, without taking into account the sheer variety, intrinsic to the practices of consumption among audiences. In other words, what is emphasized here is the democratic potential of cultural production over the socio-cultural variables that are characterized in the audiences' appropriation of media material. It presumes a knowledgeable citizenry, possessing the social, political and cultural means to guarantee accountability from those exercising political and economic power. The differentiated access to specific symbolic resources and the disproportionate distribution of cultural or political knowledge—specifically through education—is largely ignored in this formulation. Akhil Gupta's (2000) examination of how the state is imagined by the rural populace in India through their everyday experience of the intermediaries of the state is indicative of a need to rethink citizenship and knowledge. His argument is suggestive of a new direction of research on media and citizenship, bringing anthropology as an approach to the study of the political process, particularly in developing countries.

The other alternative to the traditional political science approach to media and democracy that Dahlgren points to is the 'culturalist' approach which examines communication and the media from the perspective of citizenship, 'which in turn offer frameworks for analysing and assessing features of political communication.... Themes such as meaning, identity and social agency are highlighted' in this approach (Dahlgren 2004: 16). A recent special issue of the *European Journal of Communication* (Hermes and Dahlgren 2006),[1] a collection of essays seeking to explore citizenship in cultural terms, attempts to begin a reconceptualization of citizenship through an engagement with the ways in which meaning-making, belonging and the exercise of power are linked in important ways. This

---

[1]This issue of the *European Journal of Communication* (Hermes and Dahlgren 2006) contains essays examining the notion of cultural citizenship from different perspectives such as political philosophy, the politics of the everyday, gender and the sociology of news.

includes an emphasis on the everyday rather than on the governmental. As the editors declare, 'citizenship can be found both above ground as parliamentary politics... and as the "underground" reflection on what binds us, what we expect from life and of what we are critical. We need to broaden and deepen our efforts to understand this' (Hermes and Dahlgren 2006: 260). For the purposes of the arguments in this book, the crucial point here is the idea of meaning-making and its relation to citizenship, in particular to the media. If we agree with Hartley (1999) that television plays a pivotal role in shaping the ways in which we consider difference and identity, the centrality of the audience becomes evident.

The audience, as public, is the central concern of this book in its attempt to present a theoretical frame with which to examine media audiences in relation to the diversity of their responses to media, and how that might reflect on participation in the practices of deliberative democracy. Crucial to this are the ideas of mediated knowledge and representation, and inequality of access to symbolic resources and cultural capital, both of which are essential components to the conception and nature of democratic dialogue and debate that constitute public spheres. The premise underlying the argument in this book is that, while debates on the role of the media in democracy continue, the audience's perspective remains relatively under-explored in such studies (one of the exceptions here is Madianou 2005). Thus, there is a need bring to the discussion the audience, by way of refocussing the arguments on media and democracy along the lines of citizenship, the audience–public, and public knowledge.

Barnett (2003) explores the wider implications of the forms of governmental and disciplinary power for the media audience. He sees the media as 'crucial sites for contested struggles over the conditions for the formation of new subjectivities' (2003: 102), and argues that, a crucial component of this politics is 'the production of knowledge through which audiences are made knowable'. Significant for him is the knowledge of audiences–however spatially dispersed they may be–which challenges the notion of them as completely autonomous, and presents them as 'objects of policy in public and private media institutions' (Barnett 2003). The knowledge of audiences contributes to the governing of media audiences, 'characterised both by an acknowledgement of a high degree of autonomy of dispersed subjects, and by a countervailing imperative to protect audiences, not least from their own worst inclinations'. He argues that, in contemporary neo-liberal socio-cultural contexts, this ambivalence is demonstrated in the dual treatment of audiences: on the one hand, as embodying consumer sovereignty that underpins privatization, commercialization and media liberalization, and on the other hand, a simultaneous attempt to resuscitate conservative values and regulatory regimes that promote the 'protection' of citizens from the perceived excesses of media representations. The implied or overt moral imperative that drives such conservative agendas, in particular those relating to sex and/or violence, has been explored in other studies (Barker et al. 2001). What is significant in the present context is Barnett's concern regarding the governance of audiences in neo-liberal moral regulation that seeks to simultaneously celebrate their perceived autonomy as evidence of consumer 'freedom'. Implicated in this formulation is the idea that consumer sovereignty is directly related to identity formation. The knowledge of the audience consumption practices, therefore, becomes crucial for both commercial enterprises as well as governmental organizations. Accordingly, research data on audiences are seen as contributing to their governance and regulation.

Interpretive practices of audiences, the frames of understanding employed by them and how these reveal broader socio-cultural contexts form the main concerns of this book. It attempts to explore the relations between the media and citizenship from the perspective of audiences, in particular the ways in which discrepancies in cultural capital impact upon citizenship as an active engagement with the civil society. This requires, it will be argued, a phenomenological hermeneutic conception of audience participation, that is, an investigation of the nature of interpretive practices of audiences and how these relate to particular socio-cultural contexts. The main theoretical arguments are based on an empirical investigation of the differences in the interpretations of non-fictional television programmes among audiences in India. Considering alongside arguments relating to television and consumerism in contemporary India, the conceptual and the empirical aspects of the argument in the book present a way of grasping the nature of mediated citizenship in the country. The 'consumer–citizen' is a useful concept with which to negotiate the complex entanglements that constitute the current formations of national political culture, and India presents a particularly interesting case study as, through the 1990s and until the 2004 elections it navigated the precarious waters of economic liberalization simultaneously with the rise of Hindu fundamentalist politics.

Citizenship requirements for democratic participation

In reformulating the question of audiences and democratic citizenship, I draw on Murdock's (1999) examination of public discourse and cultural citizenship, in which he negotiates the complex territory of identity, media and consumerism. Murdock defines the fundamental prerogative of citizenship as 'the right to participate fully in social life with dignity and without fear, and to help formulate the forms it might take in the future' (1999: 8). The formations of citizenship in contemporary, market-oriented societies are, for him, complicated by the apparent paradox between liberty and fraternity, or what Tocqueville referred to as constituting the tension between empathy and mutuality on the one hand, and competitive individualism on the other. The paradox, inherent in the multicultural liberal democratic states, has been identified by Mouffe (2000) as symptomatic of the antagonism intrinsic to the values that constitute such states:

> ...on the one side we have the liberal tradition constituted by the rule of law, the defence of human rights and the respect of individual liberty; on the other the democratic tradition whose main ideas are those

of equality, identity between governing and governed and popular sovereignty. (Mouffe 2000: 3)

One of the consequences, for Mouffe, is the creation of a barrier that identifies those that belong to the 'demos' ('us'), as against those who do not ('them'). This, combined with the fact that in liberal democracies, limits are imposed on the exercise of the sovereignty of the populace, brings to the fore the question of representation and the assertion of cultural difference.

To Murdock, the right to participate in the formation of democratic societies includes the rights of expression, constituted by the rights of listening as well as of speaking. Given that contemporary politics 'is increasingly centred on the politics of identity–the struggle over forms of belonging, loyalty and solidarity' (Murdock 2000: 8), the burgeoning of identities within contemporary cultures 'poses particular problems,' specifically the limits to free expression in the domains of public discourse. As a primary arena of public discourse, he argues, the media ought to be concerned with the complex negotiations implied in the politics of difference. This is further compounded by current cultural politics that revolves around the central figure of the consumer: 'the notion that identity and fulfilment can be purchased in the marketplace, and that the good life is to be found through total immersion in the world of goods' (Murdoch 2000: 10). He sees this promotion of private spending as undermining political participation, and the privileging of life styles as personal choices as undermining citizenship by negating 'any attempt to arrive at a conception of the 'common good', based on the negotiations of differences in their full complexity'. The dynamics of capitalism preclude the arbitration of the tension between consumer sovereignty and the rights and responsibilities of citizenship that are fundamental to the requirements of a functioning democracy.

Murdock's argument is central to the examination of audiences as participating citizens in a democracy, intrinsic to which is the notion of social and political inclusion that enables and encourages participation. The two basic requirements for this participation are: access to material and symbolic resources, and public knowledge, including knowledge of the functioning of the state. His thesis regarding the proliferation of identities and the mediation of difference is particularly relevant in the current, post 9/11 political climate, in which citizenship in multicultural societies, both in the West and elsewhere, is being negotiated in complex ways, alongside concerns regarding national security. The politics of difference involves, consequently, much more than the expressions of diverse cultural and moral discourses, as it entails perceptions of and by the ethnic minorities in relation to the dominant discourses on terror. This underlines, even more strongly, the centrality of the media and the contestations over public knowledge. The idea of audiences as active participants in the democratic discourse, therefore, assumes a particular resonance. In this respect, Murdock's argument regarding state intervention becomes even more important: '[I]n addition to guaranteeing basic material conditions for participation, full citizenship also required access to relevant symbolic resources and the competences to use them effectively' (Murdock 2000: 11).

Exploring the political formations in the subcontinent demands the acknowledgment of its cultural, religious, linguistic diversity and the multiple loyalties these inspire. Both historically and currently, separatist politics within India, drawing on such loyalties, has continued to threaten the notion of national cohesion and state authority. While India's cultural diversity is often commented upon and included in the analyses of its political and social processes, the role of the disparities in state provisions such as education, are less often recognized as relevant to the discussions of citizenship and political participation. It is worthwhile making a slight detour here to include Benhabib's (2002) proposal on participatory democracy in our contention regarding the media, audience participation and public knowledge. The notion of participatory or deliberative democracy is a central component of the discussions of the media and the public sphere, in which the media are envisaged, in an ideally functioning democracy, to contribute to public participation and deliberation. Benhabib's formulation, her plea for dialogue as fundamental to democratic practice, can be seen as crucial, specifically to nations constituted by as much diversity as India. Allegiances to the essentialist notions of identity privilege the local and the particular, and consequently conceive of collective identity as a unitary whole—what Appiah (1994) has referred to as 'tightly scripted identities'—thereby disavowing the possibility of change through encounters with other groups.

Benhabib's plea for a dialogue between cultures, considered not as complete and coherent wholes, but as unstable, hybrid and 'polyvocal', in the place of what she considers the unproductive explorations of the alleged tension between relativism (which privileges the local and the particular) and universalism (which promotes theses of incommensurability and untranslatability), is linked to her notion of participatory democracy and cultural difference. 'Politically, the right to cultural expression needs to be grounded upon, rather than considered an alternative to, universally recognised citizenship rights' (Benhabib 2002: 26).

Benhabib's vision includes a participatory democracy, involving a dialogic relationship between different perspectives, inspired by diverse cultural formations and value systems. Benhabib's argument is clearly significant in terms of the debates on multiculturalism and representation, raising as it does, questions regarding cultural politics and the issue of who speaks for whom and in what context (Harindranath 2006). The fundamental requirement for such a dialogue, and the key aspect of her critique, is the equality of access to the symbolic capital that provides for equal powers of enunciation among the diverse groups. This formulation goes some way towards addressing the objections raised to the propositions presented by Habermas (2001) on deliberative democracy in pluralistic societies, specifically, his distinction between demos and ethnos and his consequent emphasis on the abstract notions of rights and sovereignty and underestimation of cultural identity. Nevertheless, the insistence by Habermas on the intersubjective basis of identity maintenance, and the structures of recognition and reciprocity that it entails, are indispensable to his notion of communicative action. What are significant in the present context are the Indian audience groups, socio-cultural contexts and the perception of the 'Other'. Examining the role of the media in the democratic functioning of the Indian society demands the inclusion of the audience perspective.

Audiences, public knowledge and citizenship

Radway's (1984) call for 'radical contextualism' in audience research is indicative of a shift in focus in the conception of the media audience that occurred at that time. Ten years or so since that reconceptualization of audiences as 'actively' engaged in meaning construction, and the consequent rethinking of the text–audience relationship particularly through the investigations of internet users and participants in Multi-User Domains (MUDs) and Computer Maintained Communities (CMCs), there has recently emerged a more direct engagement with the politically constitutive role of audiences. In her attempt to transcend the unproductive binarism of 'audiences' and 'publics', Livingstone (2005) argues that audiences

> ...sustain a modest and often ambivalent level of critical interpretation, drawing upon—and thereby reproducing—a somewhat ill-specified, at times inchoate or even contradictory sense of identity or belonging which motivates them towards but does not wholly enable the kinds of collective and direct action expected of a public. That after all, is the point: it is precisely such context-dependent yet under-determined, plural and hybrid identities, understandings, practices that must and do shape people's engagement with others, in private and public. (Livingstone 2005: 31–32)

She suggests that a third concept—the 'civic'—allows for grounded, empirical research on phenomena such as gender politics and the relevance of talk show debates. Crucially, it enables the reconceptualization of audiences as 'citizen–viewers', as Corner (1995) has argued.

As Livingstone usefully demonstrates, Dahlgren's (2003) argument regarding the productive use of the concept of the 'civic' to redraw questions of political communication to include audience participation is valuable here. Dahlgren sees the 'civic' as 'a reservoir of the pre or non-political that becomes actualised at particular moments when politics arises' (2003: 155). Crucial for Dahlgren are the 'cultural factors that can impinge on the actions and communications of people in their roles as (multifarious) citizens' (2003: 152), and consequently, the empirical study of audience life-worlds, including quotidian experiences and cultural contexts, becomes relevant. This appears to be a productive move towards incorporating audiences in everyday contexts into the examination of media and democracy.

Public participation in deliberative democracy presumes a knowledgeable citizenry. In an earlier exploration of media and citizenship, Dahlgren (1995) underlines the significance of the concepts of civil society and citizenship to the analysis of the role of the media in democracy. Central to linking these two concepts, for him, is the process of television reception. Civil society offers for him 'a way to conceptually gather up the sites of reception and recontextualize them to a larger theoretic horizon which has relevance for both democratic theory and the public sphere' (Dahlgren 1995: 120). On the other hand he argues that the category of 'audience' alone is far too media-centric and, consequently, inadequate for the examination of the public sphere: 'the public sphere requires "publics", in the sense of interacting social agents. The category of audience becomes too constricted in this regard. We need to move, in our theoretic vistas, from audience members to citizens' (Dahlgren 1995: 120). While reception research continues to provide useful insights into the socio-cultural aspects of television viewing, he recommends the reformulation of audience activity and viewership as a 'potential moment of citizenship', as it allows the productive exploration of media reception in its everyday context and thereby its relation to civil society. This is because the 'television has a significant impact on the public/private distinction. It scrambles the distinction in such a way that reception as an activity potentially transcends the geography of the private by discursively

positioning the viewer as a citizen, as a member of the public'
(Dahlgren 1995: 123–124). Dahlgren's thesis raises several issues that are pertinent to the recasting of audiences as 'publics' and citizens, crucial to which are the concepts of public
knowledge and the centrality of the access to the symbolic
resources of cultural capital.

Entangled in the network of audience, knowledge and symbolic resources are the politics and experience of difference.
Morley (1999) argues succinctly that 'Knowledge is always
a matter of class, race, and gender positioning, among other
things' (1999: 139). As demonstrated in Harindranath (1998,
2000), the other complicating factor, in particular in developing societies, is education, which acts as a conduit to certain
kinds of knowledge, predispositions and expectations in relation to the media, as well as to the perceptions of democratic
rights and the role of the state. Education is significant in this
context, not only in terms of literacy, but because it also relates to the processes of imaginings of the state, knowledge of
rights and responsibilities, the inbuilt hierarchies that characterize everyday life in both rural and urban areas, and in terms
of social mobility. Madianou (2005), arguing the case for the
significance of the distinction between comprehension and in-
comprehension of news media, supports Morley's (1999) argument that the audiences' failure to make 'dominant' readings
of television news need to be distinguished from the lack, on
the one hand, of specific forms of media literacy, and on the
other hand, of cultural resources with which to initiate alternative perspectives on events presented in the news reports.

Madianou (2005) underscores the importance of the notion
of 'experience' to her study, arguing that the diverse perceptions and evaluations by different people of different events
promote a revaluation of ideas and perspectives, which, in
turn, contributes to a reformulation of experience. This circularity between experience, interpretation and re-evaluation is,
as we shall see in a later chapter, a central feature of Gadamerian hermeneutics. For the time being, however, Madianou's
point regarding experience as providing a 'personal dimension' to the notion of collective identity is worth noting.

The notion of 'experience' and how it informs identity, agency and resistance has been much debated, particularly in relation to the significance accorded to 'immediate' or 'raw' experience. This privileging of the allegedly unmediated experience as providing a unique perspective runs the risk of essentializing cultural identity, and thereby providing the basis for ethno-nationalist assertions of uniqueness. And therein lies the dilemma: recourse to allegedly prediscursive, concrete experience, while it provides the vocabulary for cultural and collective identity, is simultaneously susceptible to the vagaries of fundamentalist politics. As we saw earlier, Benhabib's (2002) contention regarding the requirements of a dialogic relationship among diverse communities in deliberative democracy presumes a willingness by such communities to forestall any attempt at presenting themselves as unequivocally unitary and closed, which leads to an unproductive form of relativism. Madianou, too, is aware of this risk. She argues, however, that it is important to recognize that differences in perceptions and experiences of events, far from being arbitrary, are closely tied up with both the material and symbolic structures and resources. 'Resources, the symbolic and material means through which people make sense of the world, are an important parameter in the mediation process.... Resources include education and access to media and information' (Madianou 2005: 139).

If public knowledge is a constituent of democratic participation, and knowledge and interpretation of the media as the arena of public discourse are related to experience, then audience evaluations of what constitutes valid knowledge become crucial. Livingstone (1999) asserts that what audiences gain from specific media genre derives from what they consider valuable:

If experts are considered to be lacking in personal experience while ordinary people are seen as authentic, the value of what each says will be regarded differently than it will be by those who consider that experts are more credible and more knowledgeable than ordinary people. (Livingstone 1999: 92–93)

This underpins one of the research questions in the project that she describes, 'Whose knowledge is being (re)produced?' (Livingstone 1999: 94), which is an indispensable component of the exploration of the functioning of the media in democratic states, in particular regarding issues concerning mediated knowledge and its regulation, as well as its relations with the private and the public, with the public sphere and with cultural and political elites and marginalized communities. In news and current affairs programming, as well as in the documentary genre, the role of the experts and their perceived credibility are centrally implicated in the audiences' response to the programme. As we shall see in Chapter 5, the veridicality of the documentary genre, its truth claims that sets it apart from the fictional genres, is, in most forms of the genre, linked to the knowledge of the experts that is provided as part of the evidence constituting the argument.

Consumption and public participation

As Canclini (2001) has argued in his examination of consumers and citizens, research on audiences has contributed to the reconceptualization of the audience–text relations, which has paved the way to conceiving communication as being not one of domination, but a much more complex 'collaboration and transaction between both parties' (2001: 38), as against the earlier conception of media consumption as being determined by corporations and texts. This is a well-known and established conception of audience activity, although, as argued earlier, celebrations of audience autonomy do occasionally go to the other extreme, not taking into account the broader socio-cultural dimensions of audience engagements with the media.

What is specifically of interest to us, however, is Canclini's point regarding the study of consumption 'as a marker of difference and distinction between classes and groups', which 'has led to a focus on the *symbolic and aesthetic aspects of the rationality of consumption*. There is a logic to the construction of *status* markers and in the ways of communicating them'

(Canclini 2001: 39–40). Drawing on the work of Bourdieu and Appadurai, Canclini advocates the notion that, in contemporary liberal societies, social relations are constructed more in terms of the struggle over the means of symbolic distinction rather than for the means of production and the mere gratification of material needs. This permits him to reformulate the dichotomy of the state and civil society in terms of reconsidering, simultaneously, both policies as well as forms of participation, which to him requires understanding ourselves as both citizens and consumers.

Canclini's reformulation of the state–civil society relations, in turn, involves a reconceptualization of the idea of the public sphere: 'Neither subordinated to the state nor dissolved in civil society, it is reconstituted time and again in the tension between both' (Canclini 2001: 154). He is, consequently, sympathetic to Alejandro's (1993) efforts to conceive of the public sphere by taking into account not only Habermas's well-known thesis on it, but also Bakhtin's notion of 'heteroglossia'. Alejandro's hermeneutic re-evaluation of the public sphere builds on and expands both Gadamer's hermeneutics and Bakhtin's assessment of language: the public sphere is 'a space of heteroglossia', 'a field of competing traditions and languages', and 'a terrain in which meanings and traditions are enforced but, in the process, new forces can pose different meanings or emphases... thus challenging existing ones' (Alejandro 1993: 206). Canclini's and Alejandro's reformulations of the public sphere is useful here in several ways: they underline the necessity of dialogue in a democratic public sphere, thereby supporting both Habermas's notion of the (contrafactual) ideal speech situation as well as Benhabib's forceful argument for the case of a dialogic relationship between different communities as a requirement for participatory democracy; they recognize the dimension of power inherent in the public sphere, which is predicated upon unequal access to the symbolic resources and distinctions in cultural capital; and finally, Alejandro's exploration of hermeneutics and citizenship allows for the exploration of audience activity through Gadamerian hermeneutics, as revealed in the phrase 'field of competing traditions and languages'. The latter, in particular, enables an assessment of the ways in which cultural capital, access to education, media literacy, the every day, and socio-cultural contexts impact on the ways in which audiences interpret and respond to mediated knowledge as citizens and how that may have consequences for their participation in democratic dialogue and deliberation.

As I will elaborate in Chapter 3, Gadamer's (1975, 1976) hermeneutics emphasizes the role of the fundamental 'thrown-ness' of human life–that is, our ordinary, everyday situation–as well as its temporality and historicity, in which understanding and interpretation are inescapably embedded. In other words, the audience–citizen's historicity, their specific socio-historical and cultural context, is crucial to their engagement with mediated forms of knowledge. Gadamer considers this historicity to be the consequence of both a biographical past as well as a cultural past, both of which fashion the 'hermeneutic situation' of the audience, that is, the context of the audience's interpretive activity. Crucially for him, understanding involves the anticipation of the meaning of the whole text, based on prior knowledge of the nature of its constituents, as for instance, of its generic features. He refers to this as 'the horizon of expectations', a set of assumptions that we take to the text. These assumptions however, are not fixed, but are modified constantly as we encounter texts. In other words, we continually revise our expectations of the whole text on the basis of our understanding of parts of it. It is useful to note here that this idea can be applied to other situations, for example, the culturally, historically situated set of 'prejudices' also undergo constant revision. In other words, we constantly revise our cultural resources–and therefore our prejudices and prejudgements–as we encounter new experiences in the form of real and/or mediated events.

To extend this further, cultural differences can be construed as the specific hermeneutic 'horizons' that contribute to the differences in the engagement of the audience–citizen with mediated and public knowledge. Notions of deliberative democracy as facilitated by the media, therefore, presume dialogic participation between different 'horizons' and 'prejudices'. The public sphere, as 'a space of heteroglossia' and 'a field of competing traditions and languages', ought to provide the necessary means for such dialogue, premised on an ideal speech situation. This involves addressing the inequality of resources, cultural and symbolic, that underlies unequal relations in power, and constitutes the difference between the elites and the marginal. However, the notion of cultural difference needs to be interrogated further, by way of avoiding the conceptual trap of structural determination as well as of engaging analytically with patterns of difference that emerge in the audience's interpretive activities. As demonstrated by Barker, Arthurs, and Harindranath (Barker et al. 2001), audience engagement with media texts such as cinema, (with particular reference to Cronenberg's *Crash*), involves issues such as prior knowledge of the film or film-maker and prior preparation in terms of reading reviews, as well as the pleasures derived from watching the film. Notions of taste and ethical stances are also significant here, mobilized in audience evaluations of the media material. For our present purposes, however, the challenge is to explain the sociology of the patterns of difference in interpretations of documentaries. As I shall argue in Chapter 4, the ideas of Alfred Schutz present an opportunity to link Gadamerian hermeneutics with the evidence of socio-cultural difference that avoid being confined within tight structural compartments.

Media and democracy in India

Sen (1999) has argued that '[d]emocracy has to be seen as creating a set of opportunities, and the use of these opportunities calls for an analysis of a different kind, dealing with the practice of democratic and political rights'(1999: 154). Both the availability and the use of such opportunities, however, are predicated upon state intervention to promote equal access to public knowledge in terms of policies that countervail the logic of the market and oppose the values reinforcing consumer practice as a form of individual identity formation. Beteille (2003), in his analysis of contemporary Indian civil society and citizenship, declares that despite the achievements of the Constitution, under which all Indians are formally citizens of the country, the 'public' as a politically significant entity remains dormant. The reason for this, he argues, is that, although the social restrictions to active political participation have been removed by the constitutional guarantees,

> ...the abilities essential for effective citizenship have not been created. There has been a quantitative enlargement of citizenship without much qualitative advance...It hardly need to be emphasised that the substance of citizenship is outside the reach of millions of Indians. Apart from the divisions of caste and community...society is deeply stratified by income, occupation, and education. Poverty, hunger, disease and illiteracy are widespread. If there is a public domain in which decisions relating to the major institutions of society are made, it is inaccessible to very many Indians. (Beteille 2003: 107–08)

It is well known that, in the 1990s, India liberalized its hitherto regulated market, thereby entering the global economy in such a fashion that it has resulted in a spectacular annual growth rate. Alongside the liberalization of the economy has been the removal of restrictions in the media sector, in which, for instance, the staid state run television channel *Doordarshan* has had to compete for audiences with privately run domestic and global channels since the early 1990s.

To take the example of the complicitous relations between the media, the market and Hindu extremism, Rajagopal's (2001) well known study of the complex ways in which the Indian television was the site for the revival of Hindu nationalism as well as the espousal of neo-liberalism and the apparent merits of globalization is perhaps the most comprehensive analysis of this seemingly contradictory development in contemporary Indian political culture. Others, such as Nandy et al. (1997), Ludden (1996) and Jaffrelot (1999) provide extensive and occasionally provocative analyses of the emergence and rise of Hindu nationalism within the democratic process in India. In terms of the media, the market and religious nationalism in the context of globalization, however, the works of Fernandes (2000), and Chakravarty and Gooptu (2000) are exemplary attempts at tracing the complicated lines of connection. Fernandes is interested in shifting the terms of the debate on the apparent failures of the state in order to examine 'how the nation is being reformed through the processes of globalization to the question of how the production of "the global" occurs through the nationalist imagination' (2000: 611). The transformation of the national political culture from the post-independence Nehruvian vision that included industralization and a steadfastly secular state to the economically liberalized contemporary India is, for her, marked by the deepening of the culture of consumption. Fernandes argues that, in a culture that has subscribed increasingly to the visible indicators of wealth in the form of 'foreign' products, the adoption of the global within the purview of the national is evident in the 'visual representations of newly available commodities [that] provide a lens through which we can view the ways in which meanings attached to such commodities weave together narratives of nationhood and development with the production of middle-class identity' in India (Fernandes 2000: 615). Her essay presents a convincing analysis of television and print advertisements of the consumer goods that draw on images and narratives from a nationalist and Hindu tradition as instances of advertising strategies that successfully combine the global, in the form of the products that they sell, with the idiom of the national. The conclusion that, 'the aesthetic of the commodity does not merely serve as a passive reflector of wider social and cultural processes but instead becomes a central site in which the Indian nation is re-imagined' (Fernandes 2000: 619), presents a different conception of the apparent paradox of economic liberalization and cultural nationalism that has been a characteristic of contemporary India, in which both developments combine to produce a particular national imaginary. Chakravarty and Gooptu (2000) see the consolidation of Hindu nationalism in India as an antidote to the presumed perils of subsumption by 'Western culture, on the one hand, and on the other the apparent threat to national security presented by the Muslim "other"'. However, this essay too, focuses on the mediation of consumption and consumerism, linked to the specific constructions of family and national community. 'With the market driving the growth of the media', they argue, 'and the middle class forming its primary target audience, not surprisingly, media productions not only drew upon, but also reproduced and magnified middle class notions of the "Hindu" nation in a bid to promote consumerism among these classes' (Chakravarty and Gooptu 2000: 97).

In the complex multicultural and multi-religious formation of the contemporary Indian national imaginary, the construction of the Hindu consumer–citizen is a cause for concern. Related to this is the notion of the state as an imagined community, as proposed by Gupta (2000), whose ethnographic analysis encompassed the practices of the lower level bureaucrats in a small town in North India and was complemented by an investigation of the representations of the state in the mass media. Central to his analysis is the discourse of corruption, which he sees as 'a key arena through which the state, citizens, and other organizations and aggregations come to be imagined. Instead of treating corruption as a dysfunctional aspect of state organizations, I see it as a medium through which "the state" itself is discursively constituted' (Gupta 2000: 333). His focus is on 'the "multiply mediated" contexts through which the state comes to be constructed' (Gupta 2000: 335), which include engaging with the ways in which discussions with the villagers concerning the state were refracted through the lenses of the everyday encounters with corruption, as well as with the mediated forms of state functions. For our concerns, what is crucial here is the ways in which this impacts upon the self-perceptions among his respondents regarding their roles as citizens, and the validity of their claims. What emerges as significant in his study is the continuing marginalization of certain communities, whose voices are absent in the public dialogues that constitute the Indian state.

As will be evident in the following chapters, the results of my own study that compared interpretations of documentaries and audience evaluations of their truth claims between groups in the UK and India were strongly suggestive of the role of higher education in the diversity of interpretations between different audience groups in India. Briefly, the similarities between the interpretive frames used by Indian groups with higher education qualifications and those used by British audiences, and equally the differences between the frames used by these Indian groups and their compatriots without university education are revealing of the role of education in interpretations and evaluative judgements of media content. Evidently, the data undermine the conflation of culture with geographical or national space. Even at a preliminary level of analysis, the data is indicative of the fundamental error in assuming that all Indians share the same cultural resources. On the contrary, the Indian respondents with university education share similar cultural resources—or, to use Gadamer's terms, 'historicity' and the 'hermeneutic situation'—with the British groups. Consequently, what emerges as significant is not the racial or national difference but the difference prompted by university education. The importance of higher education as a constitutive aspect of a person's biographical history, with the potential of creating a 'culture' of its own, providing a demonstrably effective 'hermeneutic horizon', is indicative of a hybrid culture that is simultaneously removed from the local communities without university education, and bridges the gap between indigenous Indian and Western cultures. The historical origins of university education in India that links them to its colonial past are not directly relevant here. What is pertinent is the issue of how higher education in India contributes to gaining access to specific cultural and symbolic resources that determine whether or not a person or community has a voice in the contemporary Indian polity.

In this chapter I have attempted to present an argument for the re-fashioning of audience research in such a way that it takes into account questions concerning the media, public knowledge and the enduring inequality of access to the cultural resources that are fundamental to conceptions of deliberative democracy. Existing studies on the relations between media and democracy–with their focus on policy, texts or ownership and control–present valuable but incomplete arguments, as they largely neglect the audience dimension. This book is a preliminary effort at tracing the outlines of a conceptual framework with which to redress this lacuna in media research.

2

Audiences and Socio-cultural Contexts

Frames of reference, though, seem to belong less to what is described than to systems of description .... If I ask about the world, you can offer to tell me how it is under one or more frames of reference; but if I insist that you tell me how it is apart from all frames, what can you say? We are confined to ways of describing whatever is described. Our universe, so to speak, consists of these ways rather than of a world or of worlds.

Nelson Goodman, *Ways of Worldmaking*

This chapter aims to perform a propaedeutic function of preparing the ground by presenting a clarification and elaboration of the research problem which is being examined in the book. It does so not only by bringing the relevant questions into sharper focus, but also by signposting the conceptual route that I take in my attempt at answering some of these questions. Such preliminary indications are important, especially in the light of my intention to provide critical, theoretically complex arguments in the chapters that follow.

The broad concern of the project can be stated simply enough: the examination of the differences in the interpretations of television programmes by audiences from different cultures, and how the employment of the interpretive frames, and the different meanings that they engender, are intimations of the diverse modalities of engagement with mediated knowledge. But even such a simple statement of the task stands on certain crucial assumptions. To take the cross-cultural interpretation of television as problematic is to acknowledge, among other things, that the televisual texts are open to more than one interpretation; that audiences, functioning as members of socio-culturally motivated interpretive communities, actively construct meaning out of texts; that the interpretation of programmes could vary from one culture to another; and most crucially, that sociological factors, such as cultural background, somehow affect interpretation. The first two ideas, that texts are open to multiple interpretations and that audiences are active constructors of meaning, have been established in a number of research projects—some of which are discussed later in the chapter—and accepted by the academic establishment long enough for them to be almost self-evident. As we shall see later, the main criticisms against such conceptions have more to do with the way in which the active audience has been conceptualized, and with the degree of autonomy accorded to audiences, rather than with the basic idea in itself. The third aspect of the present research problem, that there could be differences of interpretation among different cultures, has been empirically demonstrated by studies such as (Liebes and Katz 1990). It is the last proposition that forms the focus of this book—how do the sociological, cultural factors affect the signifying practices? What are the mechanisms by which the structural features both facilitate and constrain the process of meaning-making? And how do differences in the audience engagement with the television reflect diverse attitudes to mediated knowledge and democratic citizenship?

Active audience theory not only freed the audience from the tyranny of the text by transferring the locus of control of meaning production from the text to the audience, but in doing so, encouraged examinations of the actual processes of signification, and the ways in which demographic variables affected–and indeed shaped–the frameworks that the audience took to the text. The Centre for Contemporary Cultural Studies at Birmingham was in many ways a pioneer, its study of culture reflecting and contributing to the concept of the active audience. In keeping with its political orientations, a majority of the work influenced by the Centre initially sought to examine the mechanisms by which the dominant ideology sustained its dominance through the use of the mass media, and, subsequent to Hall's (1980) oft-cited article on the possibilities of the media texts being perceived differently by different persons, also studied the ways in which the audience reacted to these media messages. As I hope to indicate later in this chapter with my comments on Morley's (1980) study of the *Nationwide* audience, much of the work, emphasizing the active audience theory, suffers from conceptual weaknesses which are symptomatic of an under-theorization of the fundamental issues.

The notion of active meaning construction implies a tension between textual features and social factors. This reconceptualization of the audience, as Jensen (1991) observes, 'suggests that both the audiences and contexts of mass communication need to be examined as socially specific, empirical objects of analysis' (1991b: 137). In other words, the sociology of interpretive activity involves the recognition of the viewer as acting as a member of a culture or society. Underlying this assertion is the belief that mediated meaning is neither completely in the subjective domain, generated by the idiosyncratic interpretive strategies the viewer employs and demonstrated through the laborious cognitive research in strict laboratory conditions, nor is it contained entirely within the objective domain of the text, whose semiotic mechanisms are open to structural analysis. More is said about this subjective–objective divide later in this chapter. What is of interest now is that, we are not to be caught between the extremes of textual exegesis on the one hand, and the 'banal, unproductive truisms about individual uniqueness on the other' (Corner 1991: 18) on the other. The resolution of the 'text–context problematic' (Ang 1985) is central to the understanding of the complexities of television and meaning construction.

Recent accounts of audience research (Barker et al. 2001, Strelitz 2002, Harindranath 2006) have extended, in new directions, the analyses of audiences' interpretive practices mobilized in the late 1980s and 1990s. Studies investigating the signifying practices with regard to the television have included those with a social psychological perspective (Livingstone 1990, Hoijer 1992), as well as those interested in the hermeneutics of television reception (Dahlgren 1985a, Jensen 1986). While these have gone some way towards clarifying certain fundamental issues, other essential concerns about the nature of television interpretation, I want to argue, necessitate a search outside these perspectives. As Dahlgren has observed, in order to study

> ...the social reality of meaning...I think we should wade in the currents and test the waters. It is essential that media research continually renew its intellectual tools; this requires that we look beyond the confines of our own field, but with a selective eye. Idea development is central to research. (Dahlgren 1985b: 14)

Approaching audiences—the swinging pendulum

The metaphors used by three scholars in relatively recent assessments of audience research in the field of mass communications perhaps capture the extreme oppositional positions that have characterized a lot of work in this area. Livingstone (1993), Morley (1993) and Silverstone (1994) make use of surprisingly similar images to demonstrate the proclivity of much of the audience research to swing between two extremes: 'the recent convergence, actual and potential, between administrative and critical schools of mass communication plays a key role in changing the pattern of oscillation—from a history of oscillating active and passive audiences to a dialectic process of theory development in the field' (Livingstone 1993: 6); 'It certainly seems that, over the last few years, the pendulum has swung again in the world of audience research'

(Morley 1993: 13); and more recently that 'the pendulum has swung between competing positions' with regard to 'the question of the medium's influence' on the audience (Silverstone 1994: 132). The history of audience research has seen the pendulum oscillate continually from passive to active audience, from administrative to critical perspectives, from the study of texts to the study of audiences and from quantitative to qualitative methodologies.

While it is difficult to draw a history of research without suggesting a linear progression or development that belies the simultaneous, sometimes chaotic presence of opposing theories and approaches, it is not impossible to follow the pattern of dominance of various conceptions of the audience. For instance, while contemporary research does include a recalcitrant strain of quantitative, textual studies aimed at assessing the effects of certain media texts on passive audiences, there is little doubt that the accepted wisdom in current research work is that audiences actively interpret meaning from potentially pluralistic television texts (Evans 1990). That audiences actively construct meanings was demonstrated as early as in the 1920s and 1930s, when psychological studies investigated 'the way individual personalities and social factors influenced interpretation' (Hoijer 1992). In their review of the five traditions of audience research–effects studies, the uses and gratifications approach, literary criticism, cultural studies and reception analysis–Jensen and Rosengren (1990) claim that 'in all the five traditions the audience members have come to stand out as increasingly active and selective in their use and interpretation of mass media messages' (1990: 218). But the new approaches are characterized by 'methodologically unconventional (qualitative rather than quantitative) and theoretically fresh (emphasising the social and cultural engagements of audiences with the medium rather than the traditional interest in effects and effectiveness) studies' (Ang 1991: 12). These have paid attention to such diverse topics as the ways in which people make sense of news and documentary programmes (Morley 1980, Jensen 1986, Corner et al. 1990), a few of which have attempted to correlate audience decodings with specific socio–economic backgrounds such as class; the gender specific pleasures that underlie the popularity of television genres such as soap opera (Ang 1985, Seiter et al. 1989); culturally or ethnically motivated reception of popular television (Liebes and Katz 1990, 1991, Lull 1988); ethnographic analyses of the dynamics of television viewing within everyday family life (Morley 1986, Silverstone and Hirsch 1992, Silverstone 1994); audience interpretations and censorship campaigns (Barker et al. 2001); audience preferences and cultural identity (Strelitz 2002); and ambitious multi-regional analyses of film reception (*Lord of the Rings* Project led by Martin Barker).

The new conceptualization of audience activity, and the concurrent idea that texts are open to multiple meanings, are not, however, without their critics. As Curran (1990) notes, the active audience theory is by no means a novel idea–the pendulum has been there before, and to him this signifies a 'new revisionism' which invokes the results of psychological research, conducted in the 1940s and 1950s, in a reaction against the concept of the dominant media. That the over-emphasis on audience creativity undermines studies of the ideological force of the media has been suggested by some scholars. Schiller, for instance, arguing against the claim of the arrival a 'postimperialist era', observes that 'there is much to be said for the idea that people don't mindlessly absorb everything that passes before their eyes. Yet much of the current work on audience reception comes uncomfortably close to be apologistics for present-day structures of cultural control' (quoted in Biltereyst 1995: 260).

Schiller's reservations are particularly apt in the context of the assertions made from a postmodernist, post-structuralist position by writers like Fiske (1987), that the polysemy of the mediated texts and the cultural practices of the audiences combine to produce, through pleasure, a 'resistance' to the dominant media. Critiques of this stance have been trenchant. Gripsrud (1995), for example, laments the fact that some 'overarching theoretical perspectives' in recent audience research have become 'mixed with elements of trendy "postmodernist" theories. Banalized bits and pieces of post-structuralist thought ('deconstruction') have led to misunderstood over-rating of the instability of meaning and a disregard for how all communication is constrained by material, social and semiotic conditions' (Gripsrud 1995: 8). There have been a number of dissenting voices (as, for instance, in Allor 1988, Erni 1991, Seaman 1992) that have queried the easy formulations of the text–audience dialectic.

In the context of these debates, a caveat is required. The notion of audience activity posited in this study is that, it is markedly social, which denies the ultra-relativistic formulations of approaches like that of Fiske (1987). Audiences function as members of a socio-cultural community, which constrains their power as interpreters. To reiterate, this study recognizes both the media texts as well as the audience as being socially embedded, and is therefore interested in discovering the ways in which sociological or cultural factors influence interpretive activity. Given the remit of this present project, a brief assessment of the *Nationwide* study becomes pertinent, especially since it has been more closely studied, followed, critiqued and built upon than the others, not least because its success at changing the text–audience relationship has been celebrated as liberating the audience (Ang 1989, Corner 1991, Wilson 1993).

More to the point, it would be useful to briefly discuss Morley's (1980) study not only because of its path breaking contribution–a role that calls for the examination of both its merits as well as its faults, some of which have encouraged skepticism of the active audience concept, but also since, as Hoijer (1992) points out,

...of all the most frequently cited examples [...] Janice Radway's (1984) study of some women's reading of popular romances, Ien Ang's (1985) analysis of the relationship obtaining between the TV-serial, *Dallas* and its viewers, Dorothy Hobson's (1982) study of women who watch the British soap, *Crossroads*, and last, but certainly not the least, David Morley's (1980) study of how members of different social strata interpret items in the BBC news magazine, *Nationwide*, [...] only Morley's study may be said to treat meaning construction as it occurs during reception. The others focus on readers' and viewers' attitudes and what they get out of the texts in question.

It would be fair to say that the position in which the pendulum currently finds itself in audience research owes much to the seminal study, *The Nationwide Audience* (Morley 1980). Prior to Morley's pioneering work, critical discourse concerning film and television in Britain had been caught within the structuralist framework. Originating in the formalist film criticism, and developed and popularized in the 1970s as 'Screen theory', this conception of moving image viewership was restricted to that 'inscribed' by the text (see Moores 1990, 2005 for a detailed summary of this development). Eschewing any dialogical relationship between the text and the audience, this tradition had theorized meaning as residing solely in textual features. In other words, texts determined audience consumption and interpretation. For all practical purposes, therefore, the real audience did not exist in Screen theory; in this conception, 'the subject-in-the-text tends to collapse with "real" social subjects' (Ang 1989: 98). Dissatisfied with this textual determinism, Morley 'decided to undertake an empirical investigation of how different groups of viewers with different social positions read or interpret one particular text, an episode of the television programme, *Nationwide*' (Ang 1989: 99).

Morley's (1980) study and others influenced by it were reacting against the use of semiotics and close textual analysis in order to not only discern the 'deep' meaning of the text, but also to detect the ideological force embedded in the text (Glasgow University Media Group 1976, Morley 1976, Brunsdon and Morley 1978). These studies argued that the dominant set of social determinations, which the texts contained, was consumed unproblematically by the audience. As Connell (1985) observes, such emphasis on the text and the assumption that political bias could be so discerned in the media content led to these studies either ignoring or taking for granted the audience who received the messages.

The reconceptualization of media texts and audiences, formulated by Morley, engendered other qualitatively inflected empirical studies (for example, Radway 1984, Hobson 1986, Lindlof 1987, Livingstone 1990, Philo 1990 apart from those already mentioned) which have continued the tradition of 'reception' research, and emphasized the notion of interpretation as socially motivated rather than textually determined, underscoring the fact that audiences use and make sense of the media content in different, sometimes unexpected ways. In explaining the variations in audience interpretations of the media texts, reception research has normally stressed the social determinations of these responses. This emphasis is on the basis of empirical research, positioning the member of the audience in quite traditional variables such as class, gender, occupation or race. Use of the term 'reception' in this context has been critiqued. Fiske in 'Semiological struggles' (1991) claims that 'those working in the post-Saussurean tradition, however, tend not to use it, preferring terms such as reading and production, which emphasize the active role of the media user in the production of socially pertinent meanings from the text' (1991: 34).

Morley anchored his study on Parkin's (1972) theory of the relationship between class position and 'meaning systems',[1] and the corresponding account of the three positions that are allegedly available for the receiver of the media content, drawn out by Hall's (1980) classic paper which 'amplifies' and clarifies Parkin's model. Morley employed

> ...two distinct modes of analysis (semiotics and sociology) to analyse two distinct types of constraints on the production of meaning. These are: (a) the internal structures and mechanisms of the text/message/

---

[1]Parkin's claim is that, 'so far as class stratification in Western societies is concerned it seems that we can usefully distinguish three major meaning-systems... These are: the dominant value system ...the subordinate value system...the radical value system' (1972: 81). This echoes Engels observation in *The Condition of the Working Class in England* in 1844 that the bourgeoisie and the working class represented interests so different that they inhabited 'two nations'.

programme which invite certain readings and block others (and which can be elucidated through semiotics); and (b)the cultural background of the reader/recipient/viewer, which has to be studied sociologically. The interaction of these two constraining structures will define the parameters of a text's meaning–thus avoiding the traps of either the notion that a text can be interpreted in an infinite number of (individual) ways or the formalist tendency to suppose that texts determine meanings absolutely. (1992: 75)

Significantly the *Nationwide* study treated the textually privileged meaning as the 'preferred' meaning, whereby the structural elements of the text worked towards narrowing, but not entirely abolishing, the range of potential meanings that could be read in it, that is, 'the notion of textual closure operating on the polysemic potential of the sign' (Morley 1992: 119). Morley uses the concept of 'preferred reading' to retain both the creativity of the reader as well as the determinate conditions of the text. This narrowing and yet not complete closure of meaning allowed the audience room to manoeuvre (albeit to only three possible reactions), and thereby undermined the text's 'positioning' of the subject. The other factor that the study examined was 'the determinations of meaning, produced by the effectivity of traditional sociological/structural variables–age, sex, race and class–in terms of the way a person's position in these structures may be seen to determine that person's access to various discourses in play in the social formation' (Morley 1992: 119). This concern rested on Bernstein's and Bourdieu's conceptions of cultural competence and its distribution across cultures.

Projected in such a way, this study attempted to avoid both simplistic textual determinism, as well as sociological determinism, but at the same time tried to link different interpretations to different socio-economic structures. In other words, the assumption that formed the basis for Morley's project was that, if differences in social positions and experiences produced differences in interpretations, then it is surely inadequate to simply analyze the textual structures of a programme to arrive at its meaning: 'to raise this as a problem for research is already to argue that the meaning produced by the encounter of text and subject cannot be "read off" straight from textual characteristics' (Morley 1980: 18). Developing his theory on the Althusserean concept of 'ideological problematic', Morley placed the study firmly within the cultural studies tradition. The concern was the same–the operations of dominant ideologies:

> The problematic is importantly defined in the negative–as those questions or issues which cannot (easily) be put within a particular problematic–and in the positive as the set of questions or issues which constitute the dominant or preferred 'themes' of a programme. (Morley 1980: 139)

The problematic, thus defined, set up an agenda of issues which can be 'visible' or 'invisible'. However, the presence of this problematic within a programme–in this case, *Nationwide*–does not necessarily produce uniformity of interpretations or universal acceptance:

> For some sections of the audience the codes and meanings of the programme will correspond more or less closely to those which they already inhabit in their various institutional political, cultural, and educational engagements, and for those sections of the audience the dominant readings encoded in the programme may well 'fit' and be accepted. For other sections of the audience the meanings and definitions encoded in a programme like *Nationwide* will jar to a greater or lesser extent with those produced by other institutions and discourses in which they are involved–trade unions or 'deviant' subcultures for example–and as a result the dominant meanings will be 'negotiated' or resisted. (Morley 1980: 159)

The 'visibility' or the 'invisibility' of the programme's problematic, thus, corresponds to the social 'engagement' of the audience group; to the conservative groups, whose interpretations approximate the 'preferred' reading, the problematic will largely be 'invisible'.

Both in its aim and in its method, *The Nationwide Audience* broke new ground. Employing 'an ethnography of reading' (Morley 1981: 13), in other words, qualitative empirical research, Morley tried to demonstrate the ideological operations of television programmes and the audience's varied responses to these. This was a pioneering effort, not only in its methodology, but also in its confirmation of the audience as wide awake and active. There have been, however, critical voices which have raised objections to his formulations: Hoijer (1992) points out the 'missing link' between social determinations and the activity of reception, whereas Corner (1991) is concerned with the concentration on the micro-processes of reception in audience studies, which he feels, blunts their critical edge. Morley himself was not unaware of some of the problems with his study–his 'critical postscript' (1981) anticipated many objections. Mindful of his respondents' decodings which refused to correspond to the objective variables he had initially set for them, he comments elsewhere, that,

> It is simply inadequate to present demographic and sociological factors such as age, sex race or class position as objective correlates or determinants of different decoding positions without any attempt to specify how they intervene in the process of communication. The relative autonomy of signifying practices means that sociological factors cannot be 'read in' directly as affecting the communication process. (Morley 1986: 243)

Allor (1988) suggests that although the audience studies approaches influenced by Morley locate the audience in the dichotomy between 'individual realism' and 'social determinism', they finally privilege the social which subsumes the subject. Erni (1989) subscribes to this view, going to the extreme of even questioning the presence of a 'real' audience who can be studied using sociological methods. Such scepticism about the effectiveness of ethnographic methodology is shared by Seaman (1992) who regards the empowerment of audiences in the appropriation of meaning as 'pointless populism'.

The emphasis in most reception research has been towards the demonstration of audience interpretations as socially motivated. In studies whose empirical aspects include comparisons of interpretations or attitudes of audience members/subjects residing in structurally different social or cultural spaces (Morley 1980, Liebes and Katz 1990), such data have been used to demonstrate the links between social/cultural positions and interpretation. The audience members themselves are assumed to be socially constructed subjects whose view of reality is consequently contingent on their class or culture. So far so good. But despite the intrinsic merit of this formulation, a refusal to treat the audience as uniform or textually controlled is evident in such a stance. In their haste to prevent the audience from 'disappearing' (Fejes 1984), or being completely subsumed by textual characteristics, researchers have made assumptions which are at the least grossly under-theorized; and despite the use of ethnographic methodology with its non-positivistic connotations (see Jensen 1987), the problem that becomes immediately identifiable is that, these scholars attempt to make ingenuously straightforward cause and effect connections between social positions and audience responses. As Morley is aware himself, in seeking to explain causal connections between nominally distant areas of social structure and sense-making activities, his *Nationwide* study was only partially successful, as was demonstrated by data that contradicted his initial hypothesis. In his attempt to investigate the structures and processes that might affect the sociality of interpretative action, Morley had positioned his respondents within various 'discursive spaces' corresponding to clear 'objective' demographic variables, and then tried to squeeze the respondents' 'subjective' accounts of their interpretations into the preconceived patterns relating to these variables. Corner (1991) suggests that other than class, gender and age, there are 'also those easily plottable yet often highly significant variations of disposition and "cultural competence" (including familiarity with particular linguistic and aesthetic conventions) which occur within as well as between the conventional sociological categorizations' (Corner 1991: 18). This is a valid point. However, there is a more fundamental, conceptual difficulty in Morley's conflation of both the objective and subjective categories, motivated by the belief in the simple correlation between social position and cognitive structures. The explanatory inadequacy of such under-theorized, easy correspondence between a subject's position in society (along 'classical' variables) and his or her interpretation of political or economic reality (as encountered either in every day existence or in a mediated form) was manifested in the 'aberrant decodings' that Morley faced.

But while such data undermined his project when audience positions in response to the projected ideological problematic refused to fit neatly within a class-differentiated grid, the problem seems to lie less with him grouping his respondents according to class, and more with the inadequately theorized stance that he adopted with regard to the sociology of interpretive action. I believe that attempts to map out the ways in which persons in socially differentiated categories interpret televisual texts need a much more fundamental conceptualization of the process of sense-making and the ways in which social factors impinge upon it. Quite apart from overt political and economic standing, but connected to them in important ways, is the question of a rudimentary sociology of knowledge, which Morley does not consider in any great detail. This was a crucial omission in his attempt to fit subjective accounts of television interpretations to objective structural criteria, and the simple utilization of Parkin's tripartite 'meaning systems' proved insufficient for an explanation of the prodigal decodings. In a sense, Morley had merely substituted Parkin's 'positions' to that 'inscribed in the text', and had therefore been unable to account for the creative interpretations which escaped the structural fencing. It must be made clear at this point that, while I concur with Morley's basic contention that an audience's signifying practices are socially motivated, I disagree with his attempts to categorize audience activity along normative, conventional variables. This touches upon the recurrent structure–agency debate in sociological research.

Bourdieu's work is a case in point. As demonstrated brilliantly and with painstaking clarity in his *Distinction* (1984), the relations between knowledge and social position cannot be denied. His combination of empirical work on cultural consumption with attempts at theorizing the role of structural determinants is unique even among critical sociologists (see Murdock 1989). In his effort to overcome the seemingly incompatible opposition between objectivism and subjectivism, Bourdieu utilizes his theory of 'constructivist structrualism, or structuralist constructivism':

> By structuralism or structuralist, I mean that there exist within symbolic systems (languages, myths, etc.), objective structures independent of the consciousness and will of agents, which are capable of guiding and constraining their practices or their representations. By constructivism, I mean that there is a two-fold social genesis, on the one hand of the schemes of perception, thought, and action which are constitutive of what I call habitus, and on the other hand of social structures, and particularly of what I call fields and of groups, notably those we ordinary call social classes. (Bourdieu 1989: 14)

This marriage of unlikely partners–subjectivism and objectivism–is consummated in the formulation of the idea that social reality is constructed by the subject, but this construction takes place under structural constraints. Bourdieu is thus able to transcend the artificial distinction between structure and representation and complete the move 'from social physics to social phenomenology. The social "reality" that objectivists speak about is also an object of perception. And social science must take as its object both this reality and the perception of this reality' (Bourdieu 1989: 18).

Bourdieu is mentioned here not only to demonstrate the possibility of the closure of the subjective–objective or psychologism–physicalism rupture, and the productivity of such an exercise, but also to present the preliminary steps towards repairing the critically orientated reception research, such as Morley's (1980), whose edifice threatens to crumble under the weight of data standing on weak theoretical foundations. Bourdieu's clarification of his stance is instructive at this juncture:

> ...the social world does not present itself as pure chaos, as totally devoid of necessity and liable to being constructed in any way one likes. But this world does not present itself as totally structured either, or as capable of

imposing upon every perceiving subject the principles of its own construction. The social world may be uttered and constructed in different ways according to different principles of vision and division for example, economic divisions and ethnic divisions. (Bourdieu 1989: 19)

This proposition is useful to the present study in two ways. The idea of social reality as both subjectively constructed as well as structurally controlled is analogous to my conception of the interpretation of television as active meaning construction from within the textual and socio-cultural constraints. Thus, the text is neither completely polysemic, to the point of nihilism, nor capable of presenting itself as a unified structured totality to the reader/viewer; textual interpretation then becomes neither a case of 'anything goes' (to borrow Feyerabend's phrase), nor of the projection of a single, unproblematic meaning. Similarly, while the audience practices are socially embedded, deterministic conceptions of this relationship between audience and society proffering a cause-effect dichotomy is problematic.

Bourdieu's observation is also pertinent in the present context as a prolegomenon to the core of my theoretical framework in its attempt to identify and to develop the links between interpretation or understanding of mediated communication and the construction of everyday, commonsense 'reality'. It is my basic contention that the investigation of socially or culturally situated cognitive processes involved, in the interpretation of television requires such theorizing. The issue, therefore, is one of providing an adequate theoretical map which locates centrally the social perception of reality–both experiential and mediated.

The nature of understanding and society

Concerns of such a fundamental nature necessitate an exploration of the assumptions that underlie social scientific research, and especially those that underpin studies concerning media and audiences. With the risk of sounding unduly revisionist, or worse still, pretentiously iconoclastic, I would argue that the most pertinent of these concepts that need to be examined are those concerning, on the one hand, the person–society relationship with its corollary, subordinate questions regarding structure and agency, and the other notorious bug-bear of many a social theorist, the subject–object interface; and on the other hand, theories about the nature of understanding itself. It should be made clear that, such attempts at raising and answering questions of a more fundamental nature are themselves hardly neutral or value free. Indeed, one of the basic assumptions this study stands on is that there is no Archimedean point outside a value-laden environment from which to fashion a neutral, 'objective' stance. Every perspective is defined by its philosophic core, by its epistemic and epistemological presuppositions that colour the entire edifice. This, of course, is by no means a startling or novel position. Debates about the relationship of the researcher to the subject have polarized social scientists and herded them into camps that have flying as their pennants the flags of various 'isms'–both philosophical and methodological. Indeed, even within the most exact of sciences, physics, in its modern preoccupation with the quantum world, questions have been raised regarding the influence of the researcher on the experiment. Both relativity theory and quantum mechanics challenged the enthronement of linearity–the idea that events unfolded in a predictable, rigidly predetermined manner–which was the basis of Newtonian physics, the apotheosis of Western culture. Non-linear equations of Einstein's theory of relativity pointed towards a reality that was more complex, unpredictable and less causally controlled (Komesaroff 1986). Mechanistic theories of matter have had to be replaced in the face of the 'queer and sometimes mutually contradictory properties' of atomic particles (Hesse 1954: 92). Pushing the argument even further towards fundamental issues, one can see that the problem at hand involves even essentials such as the constitution of reality and the determinism versus freewill dilemma–issues that have been perennial in Western philosophy–and their corollaries, topics of power and emancipation and the nature of human collectivities.

Without, at this point, getting entangled in the complex philosophical jungle that characterizes the debate about whether
or not the human phenomena can be studied using methods
of natural sciences, and without necessarily taking the extreme
Nietzschean position that there are no facts, only interpretations (Nietzsche 1968), it is possible to argue that causal laws
are inappropriate while studying some aspects of existence,
such as the meaningfulness of much of the human phenomena
and the cultural diversity of the human societies. Nevertheless,
scholars within the naturalist and realist schools have coun-
tered this argument using different means. Papineau (1978),
for instance, uses a Lakotosian account of the natural sciences,
which he claims, shows natural science to be an objective, rational and critical enterprise without the simplicities of positivism, while some realists (Keat and Urry 1975) have questioned
the assumption that causal explanations require general laws.
Such positions, however, lead to problems, some of which
are manifested in the analysis of meaningful phenomena. It is
difficult to see a positivistic natural science model being useful in elucidating what understanding meaning actually entails, since the notion of 'the structure of linguistic practices'
(Papineau 1978: 137) of a society–which, incidentally, echoes
Taylor's (1971) 'intersubjective meanings' and Geertz's (1973)
notion of culture as 'structures of signification' which will be
used in later chapters–does not comprise a causal factor in itself,
but a realm in which causal factors operate. Shared conceptual
frameworks are not events which are observable, and are consequently exempt from being causes. It makes more sense, therefore, to conceptualize them spatially, as in the *Tractatus* (1921),
Wittgenstein's metaphor of 'logical space' to discuss the worlds
of meaning, and Bourdieu's concept of 'social space'.

Inextricably linked with the debate surrounding natural
science versus human science models are two diametrically
opposed philosophical positions which underlie the whole
of social science: the issue of 'objectivism' and 'subjectivism'
which represent broad ways of seeing the social world, of essential conceptions of the social itself, and the various schools

that subscribe to them–naturalism, empiricism and positivism on the one hand and existentialism and phenomenology, among others, on the other. As Natanson (1963) notes, quoting Coleridge: 'Every man is born an Aristotelian or a Platonist', this division has separated philosophers and social (or 'human') scientists into two apparently irreconcilable conceptual positions.

> I am suggesting that the philosophical dimension of social science theory is located in its *Weltanschauung*, its primordial way of looking at the world and trying to see it entire [...] The essential struggle between 'objective' and 'subjective' ways of seeing the world rests partly on the hopes one places in the development of science and the stress given to the unique possibilities of human consciousness. A naturalistic conception of consciousness places the individual within a world that promises to explain him in the course of its general business of explaining the natural order. A phenomenological view of social reality considers the intersubjective world as constituted in the activity of consciousness, with natural science being one aspect of the productivity of consciousness. (Natanson 1963: 14–15)

But as we saw with Bourdieu, these *Weltanschauungen* are not as irreconcilable as was assumed. Indeed a reconciliation is necessary in order to not only include research problems that would have been precluded by the division, but also to be able to build a conceptually adequate social theory for the problems which, when examined by either 'camp' under this 'artificial' separation, could not be sufficiently explained. Nor is Bourdieu alone in this: Goldstein (1961) mediates between the two positions, arguing that naturalism and phenomenology are not conflicting theories of the same reality, but are complimentary in their different levels of description and analysis.

My own stance is not dissimilar to these unifying tendencies. With Sartre (*The Critique of Dialectical Reason,* 1960), I am wary of the diachronic determinism of the dogmatic Marxist as well as the synchronic pattern of Levi-Strauss (*The Raw and the Cooked,* 1969), but at the same time I find the existential concept of 'freedom' unacceptable. Social praxis, including active citizenship, is, therefore, neither entirely up to the subject nor is it determined by social structure and consequently beyond the choice of the subject. It should be noted here that the position I advocate is not a conveniently neutral sitting-on-the-fence, but a philosophical repudiation of both the constraints of determinism as well as the postmodernist, nihilist reduction of any form of given knowledge to mere discourses. In this book I use phenomenological concepts to explore, like Bourdieu, the essential connections between the subject and society, between his/her construction of reality and that which holds the social structure together. It will be seen, however, that the impulse behind this exercise is the desire to explain these structures as intersubjectively held systems of meaning, which makes my stance slightly ambivalent. I adopt this position because of the difficulty, as pointed out earlier, of studying meaningful phenomena using natural science conceptions, and also because I want to avoid Morley's mistake of using the conventional, normative categories which privilege social structures and neglect the scope for individual variations.

Audiences and cultural spaces

The next three chapters present, clarify and explore my theoretical intervention, but at this juncture it would be useful to make another contribution towards the propaedeutic by indicating a few landmarks in my conceptual framework. It is worth emphasizing that the present project includes fashioning a theoretical frame with which to understand and explain the empirical data generated through qualitative audience research. With the intention of excavating and examining the assumptions that underlie most projects belonging to the tradition of reception research–as a prolegomenon to exploring the relations between audiences and citizenship–I would identify three key areas which have been so glaringly under-theorized that they have either been ignored or taken for granted, resulting in the inability to explain 'startling' data or unexpected results. The three crucial concepts that I isolate for close scrutiny are: understanding, social collectivities and genre. The reason for this is obvious enough, since the focus of interest in this study is the socially generated understanding of media texts. Conceptual confusion surrounding these and other areas have persistently undermined reception studies. Corner (1991) similarly identifies three areas as meriting closer attention:

> ...'meaning', 'genre', and 'context'. Around each one, it seems to me, there has clustered not only a number of conflicting accounts, but also confusions. One of the results of this is that although overviewing commentators may talk boldly of a thriving new 'ethnographic' tradition, there is in fact a good deal of deconstructive work to be done if significant further progress is to be made.

What he suggests is definitely a step in the right direction—conceptual clarification is absolutely vital for the continuation and development of the tradition. But while his concern is with the domination, in current research, of micro analyses and the neglect of the examination of cultural and media power, my interest is in a more fundamental clarification of theoretical issues in order to give them more explanatory adequacy. To that effect I focus on a slightly modified version of Corner's three key areas: in the place of 'meaning', I examine the concept of understanding; 'context' in this study alludes to the socio-cultural collectivity and its relation to the individual; and 'genre' has been narrowed down to the exploration of documentary television and film. The next three chapters that follow examine these three concepts.

To reiterate, the concern in this book (Erni's objections notwithstanding) is with the investigation of the ways 'real' cultural and social spaces affect the manner in which 'real' audiences, situated within them negotiate meanings received from the televisual texts, especially documentaries. The philosophical grounding that this investigation draws its inspiration from is, as the title suggests, phenomenological hermeneutics. The conceptual framework, thus, shares similar interests with Wilson's *Watching Television* (1993), which uses key concepts from phenomenology and hermeneutics to examine 'the relationship between television programmes and television audiences. In asserting the polysemic status of television textuality, it seeks to integrate a study of programme form with an investigation of forms of viewing' (Wilson 1993: 4). However, there are significant differences too. While most of these emerge during the course of the presentation of the argument in the next two chapters, two dissimilarities between the studies suggest themselves immediately. Despite our common philosophical platform, we take different routes from it: whereas Wilson, placing his 'theoretical alignment with post modernism' (1993: 9), takes the post-structuralist way, my guide is Schutz's phenomenological sociology with its Heidegerrean emphasis. This conceptual difference is also indicative of another dissimilarity, that is, our attitudes to empirical work: my more sociological grounding allows me to make an empirical case study, while Wilson's (more literary orientated) interests lead him towards 'an anti-empiricist phenomenology of reading' (Wilson 1993: 8).

The chapter that follows contains an analysis of the process of understanding. Given the remit of this project, what is called for is, broadly, the understanding of the audience's understanding of the text. And bearing in mind that one of its main concerns is the link between the construction of everyday reality and the construction of meaning from television, the social nature of understanding is foregrounded throughout. Philosophically this draws upon post-Heidegerrean hermeneutics, using such notions as Gadamer's 'fusion of horizons'. The attempt is to make the connection between the subject's historical location and his or her signifying practices. What is promoted, therefore, is a philosophical hermeneutics that is very different from the nineteenth century version with its emphasis on textual exegesis.

The next chapter carries this argument forward to an exploration of the individual situated in an intersubjective horizon. The attempt here is to examine the common sense of reality that unites and holds together a collective, creating and maintaining 'ways of world-making', significatory practices that tie the subjects to the collective, in the present case, a culture. This examination is informed all along by phenomenological sociology, especially the ideas of Schutz. Crucial among these is the Husserlian concept of the *Lebenswelt*, or the life-world, revised by Heidegger and brought to the sociological debate by Schutz.

The phenomenologist's concern with the *Lebenswelt* as a theme for social science is twofold: To begin with, the typifications of the social world are aspects of the life-world in so far as the individual caught up in daily life utilizes them naively with no realization that daily life itself presupposes such philosophical problems as that of intersubjectivity and that of there being a social world. Apart from this, however, the *Lebenswelt* is seen as a constituted structure, that is, a vast network of meaningful relationships which have a developmental history in the activity of the consciousness as much as they do in historical genesis. (Natanson 1963: 188)

I shall argue that Schutz's ideas—especially that of 'multiple realities' and that of the individual life-world as containing both the values and norms that have been handed down in his/her existential situation as well as those encountered in the individual's experience of daily life—are particularly pertinent to the concerns of this study.

It is worth reiterating that the sense in which the concept of 'culture' is used in this study is—following Geertz (1973)—a semiotic one, as a 'web of significance'. With its emphasis on audiences and sense-making practices, the present project differs from the political preoccupations which, motivated by its preoccupations with the workings of ideology, was used and popularized by the British Cultural Studies tradition. This is not to deny the presence of power relations in a meaning-laden world. It would be naive to be blind to the ideological structuring of the construction of the social world and its maintenance. As argued in the previous chapter, the notion of power is unavoidably constitutive of differences in interpretive practice, and is consequently revealing of differences in access to public knowledge, and to whose knowledge is circulated in the public sphere. Issues of power do crop up, both in the theory chapters, in which it is suggested that ideological power is the elevation of a particular meaning system over others, as well as in some of the responses of audiences who perceived a certain weighted meaning in the programme and 'resisted' it. What is called for then, is not a temporary suspension of the 'hermeneutics of suspicion' that characterizes most work on ideology, but a more nuanced engagement with the manifestations of societal power relations in audience responses, considering that the overall emphasis of this study is the investigation of the differences in interpretation of television by audiences inhabiting different cultural spaces.

The next two chapters set out to provide the 'missing link' which Hoijer identifies between the macro and micro analyses of social structure and television reception, or to put it differently, the connection between collective, intersubjective representations of reality and individual perceptions of it. The argument is returned to the consideration of media in Chapter 5 which examines the notion of the documentary genre's truth claims. I argue that the social acceptance of the genre as non-fiction, together with its rhetorical strategies, increases its 'veridicality' (Wilson 1993). While documentary's mode of address retains fictive elements, the logic of information which drives the rhetoric underlines its claim to depicting profilmic 'reality'.

This project is thus an attempt to examine both conceptually and empirically some of the processes which form part of 'the complexity and the dynamism of the social, cultural, psychological, political and historical activities that are involved in people's engagements with television' (Ang 1991: 13), particularly in cross-cultural interpretation of television documentaries. The assumptions which underlie such a formulation need to be unpacked and examined at some length in order to clarify the ways in which sociological factors affect interpretive activity. One way of accomplishing this is to inquire into the concept of understanding itself, and its relationship to culture; and second is to bridge the gap between the macro and the micro, the socio-cultural environment and the individual, for what is being called into question is the manner in which the cultural (the object of the study) impinges on the individual (the origin of the data and the space where the potential differences are actualized).

3

Understanding 'Understanding': The Hermeneutics of Audience Reception

Since the thoughts an individual can think and the mental opera-
tions he can perform have their source in some or other interpretive
community, he is as much a product of that community (acting as
an extension of it) as the meanings it enables him to produce.

Stanley Fish, *Is There a Text in This Class?*

In the last chapter I argued that an adequate theorizing of the terms 'understanding', 'context' and 'genre' is essential in order to examine the nature of the relationship between interpretive activity and socio-cultural context. Using concepts from contemporary phenomenological hermeneutics, this chapter deals with the notion of understanding, asserting that understanding is irretrievably linked with the interpreter's historicity. The first section rehearses some of the debates in audience research, particularly those pertaining to viewers' reception of television; the subsequent sections present a brief history of hermeneutics, starting from the nineteenth century writings of Scheiermacher, before going on to discuss the complex notion of understanding presented in Heidegger and Gadamer's philosophies.

Debating audience activity

As we saw in the last chapter, recent work on television audiences, especially that which falls under the broad rubric of 'reception studies', has demonstrated with sufficient clarity and sophisticated data ((Morley 1980, Livingstone 1990, Jensen 1986, Liebes and Katz 1990) the undeniable connection between textual interpretation and the social situation of the viewer. The works of Gillespie (1995), Mankekar (1999) and Strelitz (2002) are examples of a more ethnographic approach to the study of audience activity, designed to examine the relations between interpretive practice and cultural identity. Although, attempts at drawing a causal link between specific socio-economic groups and constructed meanings have not proved successful (as in Morley 1980), such studies do serve to underline the situatedness of signifying practices. As such, I have no quarrel with such a stance. Nor is there any dispute regarding the type of methodology favoured by reception analysis: in keeping with the subject matter they seek to examine, qualitative methods of data gathering and analysis are entirely appropriate. However, as Silverstone (1994: 32) observes, while recent reviews of audience research have debated extensively the merits of various methodologies, they seem to have lost sight of the audience itself. Ang's (1991) contention, that the audience is problematic from within both academic and commercial concerns, serves to underline the limitations of the ways in which the audience has been conceptualized so far. Despite the amount of research into audience behaviour, viewing habits, decoding practices and so on, the quest for the 'real' audience in its entirety, or failing that, its true representativeness, continues in both commercial as well as academic research. As we saw in the last chapter, Erni (1989) also raises a similar issue in his query of the concept of a 'real' audience.

I would argue that given the concern with the relationship between television and the viewer, the actual practices by which meaning is appropriated by differentially situated viewers needs special attention. There is no denying the support that the data, generated by these studies, provide to the concept of active audience, and to the corollary underprivileging of the tyrannical hold of the text over the audience. And yet, the audience, though loosened from the bondage to the text which Screen theory had kept them under, are not completely free–they are herded, as outlined by Morley (1980), into class-orientated straitjackets. As mentioned in the last chapter, the causal chain, linking meaning-making to texts, has been replaced by another, linking meaning to tightly defined class variables. While it is harsh to claim, with Seaman (1992), that Morley's attempts were generated by a populist impulse to draw the political economy perspective into audience research which renders his work 'pointless', or that these studies are conceptually flawed from the outset because the 'audience exists nowhere' (Erni 1989) and are therefore impossible to pin down and examine, the paradox cannot be denied: even while demonstrating that meaning-making is socially derived, Morley failed to make the causal connection between class and meaning, which he had set out to do. As Morley himself acknowledges (1981), this failure was prompted not only by his efforts to squeeze audience interpretations into predetermined patterns, but also because of inadequate theorizing; by placing his entire conceptual framework within Parkin's tripartite division, and trying to draw connections with carefully controlled class demarcations, Morley made his own position indefensible. As Silverstone (1994) points out, despite contributing to our improved understanding of audience activity,

> ...none of these reception theorists and researchers has provided entirely satisfactory explanations of the relationship between sociological and psychological variables in the audience's relationship to television. The elements of the dialectic of the socially situated yet individual reader and his or her relationship to texts and social structures remain problematic. (Silverstone 1994: 151–52)

Members of an audience certainly do not function in a social vacuum, as the earlier effects studies, with their behaviourist orientations suggested. Their socio-cultural situatedness can and must be assumed. They function as social subjects of a particular class, society or culture, as family members, and it is not difficult to see their behaviour, including media consumption and interpretation, being shaped by this membership. The question here is how rigid are these compartments divided along 'classic' sociological variables, and are there, as Corner (1991) argues, other areas operating within and between these variables which have to be considered if a theory concerning signifying practices is to be meaningfully articulated? More significantly, can audiences–who have been acknowledged to inhabit several intersecting social spaces simultaneously (Silverstone 1994)–be unproblematically reduced to just one variable or position? It follows that the subjectivity of the audience member who confronts the text is shaped by all these intersecting identities, and to privilege a socio-economic position over the others is to be reductionist. As Dyer (1977) contends, it is doubtful whether the knowledge of a person's class, age, gender, and so on, is enough to predict their interpretation of a text. It could be argued, following Bourdieu, that this socio-economic position is fundamental, transcendentally shaping the subjects' horizons of knowledge and behaviour, but even to do that is to reduce a complex web to a relationship of linear causality. We are therefore faced with a dilemma: how to conceptualize the audience and its socially motivated interpretive activities without subscribing to deterministic, cause–effect notions?

It follows that what is being called for is essentially a humanistic enterprise: first, an exploration of the ways in which social factors help create and maintain interpretive frameworks, bearing in mind the multi-dimensional nature of the audience's subjectivity and without pushing the audience into watertight compartments; and second, an investigation of the interface between the private and the public, between biography and history, in other words, the individual–collective dialectic. The enterprise is humanistic in the sense that, what is required is an ontological rather than an epistemological investigation; it is an attempt to understand rather than to explain. To this end, the conceptual framework in this book is built around Heideggerean and Gadamerian hermeneutics and phenomenology, with their anti-scientist discourse and the predominantly qualitative methodologies that they have inspired and informed.

This chapter gives the central role to a concept that has remained, at best, on the periphery in the debate concerning audience and media: the notion of understanding. While this debate has, as mentioned in the previous chapter, swung between the extremes of textual determinism and audience autonomy, little has been said about what it is to understand a programme or a news story. Wilson's (1993) work on the hermeneutics of television is but an exception that proves the neglect of this dimension in the evaluation of audience–media relationship. And yet, an understanding of the essential nature of understanding mediated texts is surely crucial to the significance, if any, of the structural features to signifying practices. An allied question is with regard to whether understanding these texts is connected to understanding in general, to every day understanding of the common sense existence, and if so, in what way. How else to explain the differences in interpretation by audiences occupying different structural spaces–be it class-oriented, cultural, or educational? In other words, this research problem requires a connection, to be made between hermeneutics and ontology.

Theories of meaning

What is being advocated here is the taking of a step or two back from the immediate research concerns of television and audience interpretation, to extend focus as it were, in order to accommodate sufficient theoretical arguments concerning meaning and understanding, and their relation to the individual in his/her social space. An objective stated in such vague and general terms projects a picture which contains only the faintest of outlines of the original research agenda, but it should be borne in mind that the nature of the problem, as stated in Chapter 1, necessitates such an excavation of an abstract discussion of the terms 'interpretation/understanding' and 'culture'. This task is further complicated by the presence of the theories of meaning and interpretation which stand on opposing philosophical traditions. Nevertheless, a study aimed at clarifying the ways in which social factors affect understanding ought not to accept, without adequate theorizing, the idea that meaning construction is socially motivated, especially when the task at hand is to explore this idea whilst simultaneously avoiding deterministic notions. The concept of understanding that we are concerned with here is not the methodological means of unearthing the meaning of a text, as construed by logical semantics, or the notion of understanding as linked to 'truth conditions', as put forward by such theorists as Quine and Grice. According to Platts (1979), theirs is a 'readily empiricisable theory of meaning. The securest data upon which to found an empirical theory of meaning, because the least theoretically loaded, are assent and dissent behaviour; the connection with truth is obvious' (Platts 1979: 57). Rather, the concern here is the idea of understanding as similar to and connected with the common sense existence of everyday life. This is where Heidegger's phenomenology, and the hermeneutics it inspired, I would argue, become pertinent. Logical semantics, through the use of rational methodology, seeks to control the excess of meaning, seeking to dissolve the constraints on a 'correct' understanding of a text–constraints imposed by the very human existence of the reader. Its projection of methodology is, simultaneously, a denial of the historicity and the sociocultural locatedness of the subject: the method, based on logic, embodies attempts to rise above these controls. In its preoccupation with method and content, semantics projects the text as the object, knowable to a subject only through the utilization of methodological tools. Semantics does go beyond language in order to thematize our relationship with the external world, but the emphasis is different from that of hermeneutics:

> ...semantics appears to describe the range of linguistic facts externally, as it were, and does so in a way that has made possible the development of a classification of types of behaviour with respect to these

signs.[...] Hermeneutics, in contrast, focuses upon the internal side of our use of this world of signs, or better said, on the internal process of speaking, which if viewed from outside, appears as our use of the world of signs. (Gadamer 1976: 82–83)

However, the task here is not the unveiling of the meaning of a text, indeed, it could even be stated as a denial of the possibility of such meaning. It is to explore the ways in which the very cultural and societal embeddedness, which semantics tries to subsume under the rules of procedure, can actually facilitate understanding.

The principal theories of understanding and interpretation represent, broadly, the analytic and hermeneutic schools of philosophy.

The specific difficulty we have in understanding understanding itself is difficult to understand, because we do not have a clear idea of the nature of the obstacles that stand in the way of understanding in a case of this sort, nor do we have a point of comparison from which to measure the difficulty of the task. (Parret and Bouveresse 1981: 1)

The difficulty in understanding something could arise for two very different reasons: on the one hand, it could correspond to the particular complexity of the object and consequently require scientific, rule-bound analysis in order to unveil its meaning; on the other hand, it could stem from the every day, taken-for-granted transparency of the object, along the lines of the difficulty that Augustine finds with respect to time: 'What is time? If no one asks me, I know what it is; if someone asks me, I no longer know' (quoted in Ricoeur 1991: 6). Wittgentstein, in *Culture and Value*, echoes this view while making a slightly different point about the intransigence of received knowledge:

What makes a subject hard to understand–if it is something significant and important–is not that before you can understand it you need to be specially trained in obstruse matters, but the contrasts between understanding the subject and what most people *want* to see. Because of this the very things which are most obvious may become the hardest of all to understand. (quoted in Taylor 1971: 9)

The excess of ordinariness that precludes the understanding of the mundane and familiar requires, what could perhaps be termed as a philosophical explanation of the object–for instance, as in Augustine's case, time.

Is the difficulty with understanding the concept of understanding due to a lack of proper scientific explanation of a complex problem, or is it because it is similar to our understanding of time: something that we 'know' without being able to explain it adequately? It has been suggested by Parret and Bouveresse in the introduction to their work (1981) that the problem with understanding understanding could contain both a 'philosophical' and a 'scientific' side to it. This of course, recalls the old split between philosophy and science and their attitude to the familiar and the strange:

> According to one classical view, philosophy consists, first of all, of an astonishment at what goes without saying, and thus the generation of a certain type of non-understanding of those very objects that seem to be the best understood.... The difference between scientific and philosophical astonishment is supposed to be that in philosophy we try to understand in another mode the objects that we already understand in a certain way, whereas in science we should endeavour to explain objects that we do not really understand at the outset. (Parret and Bouveresse 1981: 2)

In the present context, the 'scientific' side is represented by the analytical philosophy of language, and the opposing 'philosophical' side by the modern phenomenological hermeneutics.

Thus, for Ziff, understanding is essentially an analytic process, 'a matter of analytical data processing' (1972: 18). To understand an utterance, therefore, is to perform

> ...in effect a morphological analysis of the utterance; the utterance is segmented, decomposed into its morphological constituents. The data processing that can culminate in understanding has a specific character:

it is an analytic process. Understanding, not surprisingly, is akin to figuring out, deciphering, decoding, and the like. (Ziff 1972: 19)

In this conception, the difficulty with understanding an utterance or text is related to the complexity of the structure–to increase the structural complexity of an object is to correspondingly increase the difficulty of understanding it. However, as Rosenberg (1981) notes, this is not always evident even in instances of understanding sentences, where often it is not the peculiar complexity but the 'singularity' that renders them difficult to comprehend. In the case of literary works, although Henry James's prose can be said to be more difficult to understand than say Hemingway's, because of the former's syntactic complexity, the same cannot be true of a Shakespearean sonnet (complex) and a Japanese haiku (simple). For Rosenberg, the impediment to understanding in the latter case is not structural complexity, but contextual: the lack of familiarity with Japanese culture. Contrary to Ziff's formulation, it is the very simplicity of the poem (as in a Mondrian, or an elegant mathematical proof) that stands in the way of our understanding it.

What is called for in such cases is not some sort of analytical data processing. Here understanding appears to be a matter not of analysis but rather of interpretation. Understanding, in such cases, seems to be a matter of finding a context for what is otherwise somehow anomalous. It is not a question of 'segmenting' or 'decomposing' something into 'parts' or 'constituents', but rather of bringing things into relation, of building up a network of connections, interdependencies, and affinities. (Rosenberg 1981: 32–33)

The pre-requisite of an adequate familiarity with a sociocultural or historical context, in order to understand a text originating in that context, is precisely what contemporary hermeneutics problematizes and theorizes. In its manifestation as phenomenological hermeneutics, it questions the notion of a 'perfect' understanding of a historically and/or culturally different text, undermining the scientistic project of the 'objective' investigation of meaning. In the next section, I present a brief account of the ideas of the precursors of modern hermeneutics, before discussing Gadamer's philosophy.

The hermeneutic tradition

Contemporary hermeneutics has moved beyond its subsidiary role where it was 'a regional and occasional necessity–a subdiscipline in theology, archeology, literary studies, history of art, and so forth' (Howard 1982: xiii) and has now attained a philosophical status in its own right. Moving beyond the confines of rule providing, modern hermeneutics sees its task as exploring and explaining the very conditions for the possibility of understanding. As Howard argues, the practice of philosophical hermeneutics comprises of two broad schools, springing from two different fountainheads of inspiration and following different paths.

One school, originating from a Kantian form of rationalism, is found in the linguistics of Saussure and Chomsky, and in the structuralism of Levi-Strauss and Barthes, and in this guise, 'structuralist hermeneutics' disperses the role of the individual foregrounding, in stead, the transcendental generative 'grammars', as in Chomsky's universal grammar, Levi-Strauss's cultural patterns and Barthes' stylistics.[1] The other branch of philosophical hermeneutics, however, promotes the individual and his/her historicity, and gathering momentum in Heideggerian phenomenology, emerges in Gadamer's version.

The Kantian origins of structuralism are not difficult to locate. As Howard (1982) points out, they lie in Kant's attempt to answer his epistemological question: looking for the conditions necessary for the occurrence of reliable knowledge, Kant identifies two main features–the normative role of science, and the subject–object relationship in the activity of knowing.

---

[1] Seung (1982) argues that Levi-Strauss presents an anti-Cartesian thesis through his argument that the primitive and advanced cultures project different mental structures, and that, therefore, he takes a stance against 'innate psychological structuralism', since 'innate psychological structuralism is the thesis that all human minds have the same innate structure whether they are nurtured in primitive or advanced cultures.' (Sueng 1982: 19). However, this does not detract from Levi-Strauss's essential structuralism with its a priori categories.

In the *Critique of Pure Reason* (1781), he gives a clearly privileged role to reason as the logic of inquiry in the natural sciences, and consequently as the necessary condition of all reliable knowledge:

> ...reason...must itself show the way with principles of judgement based upon fixed laws, constraining nature to give answers to reason's own determining...[Reason must play the role] of an appointed judge who compels the witnesses to answer questions which he himself has formulated...It is thus that the study of nature has entered on the secure path of science, after having for so many centuries been nothing but a process of random groping. (quoted in Howard 1982: 4)

Formulated this way, the methods of the natural sciences become the touchstone for true knowledge, and all other forms of knowledge, achieved through non-scientific methods are, as a consequence, untenable, an idea that still holds currency—through the advocacy of Comte, and more recently, Hempel and Popper—and underlies the ongoing 'explanation' and 'understanding' controversy. We shall have occasion to return to this later in the chapter.

Kant's idea is given further support by his formulation of the clearly defined roles of the subject (the knower or the self) and the object (the apprehended reality). Kant's 'subject' contains two elements: one, the concrete, historical being, the corporeal existence; and the other, the transcendental subject, which is possessed of the 'rules which I must presuppose as being in me prior to objects given to me, and therefore, a priori' (quoted in Howard 1982: 5). These a priori pre-given rules are essential for the ordering of the diverse sensations into a systematic form that becomes a person's experience.

> As omnipotent these rules are transcendental: they apply, not to diverse regions of thinking, but to thinking as such. They are the a priori necessary conditions of 'pure' reason. The constructivist role which Kant assigns to the subject, then, is what marks his second Copernican revolution in epistemology, his 'new method of thought, namely that we can know a priori of things only what we ourselves put into them.'...

Kant located in transcendental consciousness the rules that determined all other forms of knowing. (Howard 1982)

The two elements, which formed important part of Kant's epistemology, triggered reactions both from the empiricists and the logical positivists on one side, and the metaphysicians and the phenomenologists on the other. These positions are evidenced in the nineteenth century and twentieth century hermeneutics; in other words, the works of Dilthey and Gadamer offer positions different from that of rationalism. The opposition between what has been called ontological hermeneutics (Bleicher 1980), and its rational or critical counterpart is brought out with sufficient clarity in the famous debate between Gadamer and Habermas, which centres around the question of Gadamer's notion of 'tradition', whose authority he accepts, and Habermas's belief that the concept of Reason could (and should) be used to undermine tradition in the interest of fashioning an ideological critique. Despite their disagreements, Habermas and Gadamer share similar conceptions of understanding (Bleicher 1980, Mueller-Vollmer 1985, Howard 1982), confronting in similar ways the positivistic theories in human sciences.

Before going into an exposition of Gadamer's hermeneutics, however, it would be worthwhile to examine the contributions of Schleiermacher and Dilthey to hermeneutics, both by way of providing the pertinent features within the historical development of hermeneutics and also contextualizing and delineating the way in which Gadamer's philosophy differed from, and at the same time improved on, the ideas and the main concerns of his predecessors. Nineteenth century hermeneutics is characterized by its belief that perfect understanding is a case of empathic reconstruction—a reaching across the temporal divide by the interpreter, to understand the 'real' meaning of the author by following strict methodological rules. Reconstruction, therefore, is essentially a psychologistic bridge, propped up on sustained and methodical effort, and spanning the temporal distance between the reader and the author; and reconstruction, thus formulated, achieved true understanding of what the author had intended to communicate. This psychologistic aspect of hermeneutics is sometimes referred to, dismissively, as the 'cup of coffee' view of hermeneutics.[2] Understanding, as psychological reconstruction continues to exert its influence in the twentieth century, as for instance in Hirsch's contention in *Validity of Interpretation* (1967), that the basic object of any interpretive exercise is the intention of the author. The validity of the interpretation is, according to this view, to be measured by its approximation to the intended meaning. It is this contention that lies at the basis of his efforts to establish the criteria of validity to protect against the tendency towards relativism:

> The fact that these criteria all refer ultimately to a psychological construction is hardly surprising when we recall that to verify a text is simply to establish that the author probably meant what we construe his text to mean. The interpreter's primary task is to reproduce in himself the author's 'logic', his attitudes, his cultural givens, in short, his world. (quoted in Hoy 1978: 12)

Hirsch's claim that the original intention of the author is the only measure with which to match and validate an interpretation, suggested as a guarantee against the slide towards interpretive relativism, has itself been characterized, along with the reader-based, 'affective' theory (which focussed on readers' responses to a text), as containing 'relativistic fallacies.' The major critique of both these theories comes in one of the classic texts of the American literary New Criticism–*The Verbal Icon* (1954). Wimsatt and Beardsley's formalist theory, which presupposes meaning to be the property of the text, condemns any movement away from the confines of the text

---

[2]This gained currency after 'the positivist philosopher Otto Neurath, who remarked in 1930 that such empathic understandings enter into the actual explanation or rational appreciation of an event about as much as does a good cup of coffee, which also awakens or at least sustains a researcher's mental powers.' (Howard 1982)

in search of meaning—in the direction of either the reader or the author— as unproductive and fallacious.[3]

It was Schleiermacher who initially gave hermeneutics its psychologistic turn. Synthesizing the major trends of the hermeneutics of the older schools, while at the same time providing foundations for a new direction, the combination of the philological and the philosophical in Schleiermacher's work represents a true beginning of modern hermeneutics. The origins of this departure can be found in two significant features of his hermeneutics which were to influence Dilthey. The first was the reformulation of the task of hermeneutics: before Schleiermacher, the work of hermeneutics was conceived as that of removing the impediments that came in the way of true understanding, a pedagogic aid to eliminate the blocks that promoted a lack of understanding in exceptionally complex texts. For Schleiermacher, however, it is not just the lack of understanding that is of primary concern, but misunderstanding; and hermeneutics ought to be a scientifically controlled methodology designed to reveal the author's meaning directly to the reader. Gadamer himself recognizes the importance of this contribution:

> Schleiermacher defined hermeneutics as the art of avoiding misunderstanding. To exclude by controlled, methodical consideration whatever is alien and leads to misunderstanding—misunderstanding suggested to us by distance in time, change in linguistic usages, or in the meanings of words and modes of thinking—that is certainly far from an absurd description of the hermeneutic endeavour. (Gadamer 1976: 7)[4]

---

[3]There have been a number of responses to this contention. For instance, Stanley Fish (1980), using the concept of 'interpretive communities', in his provocatively titled 'Is There a Text in This Class?', proposes the social determination of the individual reading and interpretation as a corrective to the relativistic tendency present in the affective theory of reading.

[4]Gadamer, of course, is concerned with more than preventing possible misunderstandings: 'But the question rises as to whether the phenomenon of understanding is defined appropriately when we say that to understand is to avoid misunderstanding. Is it not, in fact, the case that every misunderstanding presupposes a "deep common accord"?' (1976: 7)

In Schleiermacher's hands the hermeneutical task moves beyond the mere philological considerations of textual exegesis and towards a more philosophical concern with the possibility of understanding. By grounding hermeneutics on the concept of understanding, Schleiermacher initiated the shift of the problem of hermeneutics to its present philosophical level. This shift contains, in his conceptualization, echoes of the Kantian impulse in its attempt to reach beyond particular interpretations in order to comprehend the general, universal act of understanding, which Kant construes as an expression of reason in his *Critique*.

This transcendental turn towards the process of understanding in Schleiermacher is complemented by his linguistic interpretation of it. Conceiving understanding as analogous to the act of speaking, he underlines the linguistic basis of both the activities. Linguistic competence underpins the ability to understand and to speak, and the act of understanding is the reverse of the act of speaking. But 'proper understanding' is a coalescence of two 'moments': the grammatical, aimed at the comprehension of the language of the utterance but excluding authorial intentions; and the psychological, which is geared towards identifying the speaker's individuality, intentions within the utterance, which operates on a deeper, 'divinitory' level than the merely verbal:

1. Psychological interpretation is higher when one regards language exclusively as a means by which a person communicates his thoughts. Then grammatical interpretation is employed only to clear away initial difficulties.
2. Grammatical interpretation and language, because it conditions every thinking person, are higher only when one regards the person and his speaking exclusively as occasions for the language to reveal itself. Then psychological interpretation and the life of the individual become subordinate considerations.
3. From this dual relation it is evident that the two tasks are completely equal. (Mueller-Vollmer 1985: 75)

The two most significant insights of Schleiermacher—that the hermeneutical problem was profoundly epistemological, and the identification of the meaning of the text with the subjective intentions of the author—were borrowed and modified by Dilthey in his endeavour to fashion a methodology for the historical analysis of human life. Dilthey's theories of the historicity of meaning apprehension provided one of the bases for Heidegger's *Being and Time* 1927, and consequently Gadamer's concept of 'effective history'.

The initial impulse to Dilthey's ideas came in the form of a desire to bring to, what he considered Schleiermacher's Romantic, metaphysical vision, an empirical corrective, in order to provide a firm, objective footing for the human sciences (Howard 1982, Palmer 1969: 91). But while he was dissatisfied with the unscientific basis of historical enquiry, he was equally wary of borrowing positivistic methods from the natural sciences. Dilthey's attempts at tackling this problem have their echoes in modern hermeneutics, and also in Heidegger's anti-scientism stance.

Dilthey's basic question can be framed in Kantian terms: if reliable knowledge can be said to occur in the field of human sciences, what are the conditions of this occurrence? His ideas differed in one fundamental aspect from those of Kant's: his methodology for the human sciences rejected Kant's concept of the static, ahistorical self. 'No real blood flows in the veins of the knowing subject constructed by Locke, Hume, and Kant; it is only the diluted juice of reason, a mere process of thought' (quoted in Howard 1982). Such a formulation was inadequate because of the nature of the subject matters of the natural and the human sciences, a distinction which Dilthey elaborates in his *Critique of Historical Reason*:

> The human sciences are distinguished from the natural sciences in that the latter take as their object features which appear to consciousness as coming from outside, as phenomena, and as given in particulars; for the former, in contrast, the object appears as coming from within, as a reality, and as a vivid original whole. It follows therefore that for the natural sciences an ordering of nature is achieved only through the ordering of a succession of conclusions by means of linking by hypotheses. For the human sciences, on the contrary, it follows that the connectedness of psychic life is given as an original and general foundation. Nature we explain, the life of the soul we understand. (quoted in Howard 1982)

This distinction is crucial for Dilthey, and is based on his observation that while the ahistorical, mathematical methodology of the natural sciences could adequately tackle the impersonal 'out there' reality, the nature of our experience of cultural phenomena–not as 'non-self' but as meaningful to us– requires a refining of methodology that takes account of the cultural phenomena's meaningfulness for a historically situated self. Human sciences must fashion a methodology which transcends the reductionist objectivity of the natural sciences in order to understand the special quality of 'connectedness' which links cultural objects, in an intuitive relationship, to the fullness of human life.

On the basis of this distinction, Dilthey attempted to formulate a methodology for understanding human expressions. The success or failure of his efforts is not at issue here. More significant is the influence on Heidegger of his suspicion of the mechanistic and reductionist attitude of the natural sciences. As Palmer (1969) observes, his sharp critique of creeping scientism in the human studies was one of the aspects of his hermeneutics which Heidegger was to radicalize in his attempts to move beyond Husserl's scientific phenomenology.

The other aspect of Dilthey's ideas, which was used and extended by Heiddeger and by the hermeneutics to which his philosophy contributed, was Dilthey's concept of *Erlebnis*. As has been argued elsewhere (Palmer 1969; Gadamer 1975; Howard 1982; Mueller-Vollmer 1985), Dilthey resurrected the term *Erlebnis* from the German Romantic tradition to signify 'lived experience'. The 'lived' aspect of experience is what gives it meaning, following patterns of significance, fashioned through our lives–both personal and that within a particular collectivity. To Dilthey, human understanding of everyday situations (which he called 'lower' forms) is reflected in the human behaviour, and is derivative of more complex, 'higher' reflexive forms of understanding, like the human sciences. Mueller-Vollmer (1985) rightly points to the affinity between Dilthey's concept of this 'category of life' and the later Wittgenstein's formulation of the meaning of expressions as deriving primarily from their use in everyday situations. But more significant is the affinity between Dilthey's idea of the significance of the immediate lived experience itself as a manifestation of life, and Heidegger's concept of pre-understanding.

Thus, in Dilthey are seen the first signs of the move away from the exclusive concerns with the text of traditional hermeneutics, and from its corollary role, as conceived by Schleiermacher as 'the science of linguistic understanding', towards a more ontological concern with everyday reality. His concept of *Erlebnis*, moving over and beyond his self-appointed task of fashioning a methodology for the human sciences, suggests a more phenomenological argument, positing a connection between experience and understanding. Yet his attempts carry forward the strong psychologistic overtones of earlier hermeneutics:

> ...while understanding may be initially concerned with objectified expressions, its final task remains the 'rediscovery of the I in the Thou'. Thus, in spite of Dilthey's attempt to establish a firm foundation for the human sciences, the philosophy of life to which he adhered tends to return this attempt to the Romantic medium of experiential empathy. (Thompson 1981: 38)

Understanding as the empathic reproduction of authorial intentions - a notion severely criticized, as we have seen, in literary studies, continues to imply the presence of specific rules and methods which are to be used to achieve this empathy. Moreover, it also suggests objectified meaning, and the idea of the recognition of the 'I in the Thou' positions Dilthey in the Kantian subject-object divide (Thompson 1981). Understanding as the 'fusion of horizons', as an existential encounter rather than a methodological discovery, receives its impetus from Heideggerean hermeneutic phenomenology, which, as we shall see, conceives of understanding not as a specialized, trained activity, but as the very basis of ordinary, everyday life. It is worth noting at this juncture the threads that link Heidegger's work to Gadamer's concepts, both by way of clarifying a few of the important, peculiarly idiosyncratic, and therefore difficult concepts and labels, and also as a more direct prolegomenon to the phenomenological sociology that is used to bridge the subject–object divide in the subsequent chapter.

Gadamer's phenomenological hermeneutics

It is in Heidegger's ontological hermeneutics that we find the initial ideas which were to be formalized later into philosophical hermeneutics by Gadamer, and into the phenomenological branch of sociology by Schutz and Merleau-Ponty, among others. Heideggerean phenomenology and hermeneutics affected a definite break from the earlier Husserlian version in its call for the examination of common sense, everyday reality–the very properties of human existence which Husserl had attempted to 'bracket' away in his quest for a presuppositionless philosophy. Indeed, in his insistence on the 'groundedness' or 'situatedness' of human existence, Heidegger undermines both Husserl's project as well as Dilthey's attempt to seek a point outside history in order to facilitate the objective understanding of history. It has been argued (Bleicher 1982, Komaseroff 1986) that Heidegger's proposals seek to cut the ground from under the feet of the objective, 'natural' science enterprise. For Heidegger, understanding is 'not simply a way of knowing, nor even a method of investigation distinctive to the human sciences. Rather, understanding is an ontological characteristic of *Dasein's* being-in-the-world. To understand, in Heidegger's primordial sense, is to understand one's position within being' (Thompson 1981). Palmer (1969) suggests that Heidegger's choice of the word 'hermeneutics' to explain his project in *Being and Time*–as a 'hermeneutic of *Dasein*'–with its etymological associations with philology and theology points towards Heidegger's anti-scientific bias contra Husserl, a bias carried over into Gadamer's hermeneutics.

Heidegger's anti-scientism stance is also evident in one of the formulations that underlie his hermeneutics: his concept of 'world'. In his influential *Being and Time*, which, as Eagleton (1983) points out, 'addresses itself to nothing else than the question of Being itself–more particularly, to that mode of being which is specifically human' (1983: 62), he expands this concept into the ontological conditioning of human life: 'world', in Heidegger's sense, does not mean the physical environment encompassing humans, but the always present, transparent, presuppossed, precognitive life-world, in which humans are inevitably immersed in society. Unlike the Husserlian conception of the 'world', which could be bracketed away through pure contemplation, Heidegger's 'world', as Eagleton puts it, 'is never something we can get outside of and stand over against. We emerge as subjects from inside a reality which we can never fully objectify, which encompasses both "subject" and "object", which is inexhaustible in its meanings and which constitutes us as much as we constitute it' (Eagleton 1983: 62). Thus this 'world', which includes and simultaneously situates a human being, as well as his/her fellow humans, is not out there at a measurable distance, and therefore eludes empirical investigation. Not unlike Santayana's notion of happiness, the unobtrusive, unnoticed world in which we are existentially suspended comes to the forefront only when the ordinary and the mundane does not occur or is disrupted.[5] In Heidegger's view, this world and the 'Being' that it represents, is obscured by the dominant categories of Western metaphysics, which, with its epistemological concern with the 'beings', overlooks the a priori, primordial understanding or orientation of humans. Heidegger's 'world' undermines scientism also because the life-world, thus conceived, does not support the subject–object divide which underpins objective description. Indeed, this very division could arise from within the life-world itself. As Palmer observes, 'World is prior to any separation of self and world in the objective sense. It is prior to all objectivity, all conceptualizing; it is therefore, prior to subjectivity, since both objectivity and subjectivity are

---

[5]To use Heidegger's own example, explicated with characteristic lucidity by Bauman (1978), the qualities of a hammer are grasped and understood almost only when it is broken in use, when its 'hammerness' gets noticed.

conceived within the subject–object schema' (Palmer 1969: 132). This world is fundamental to all forms of understanding, from the most complex to the simplest.

Heidegger thus extends Dilthey's idea of understanding as experience-oriented and projects it on to the ontological realm. While doing so, he also repudiates the Cartesian notion of the Ego as a foundational category, and consequently 'rejects the Romantic notion of the sovereignty of the author as the subjective creator of his work, as well as that of the reader who, through the work, "understands" the author' (Mueller-Vollmer 1985). The 'thrown-ness' of human existence–its situatedness in an existing, and developing tradition of customs and beliefs–denies us the Cartesian project of valueless analysis of the external world. Heidegger's life-world thus usefully breaks with both the concept of the objective understanding of a text, as well as understanding as a psychologistic reappropriation of the authorial intention. It is precisely this transparent, taken-for-granted world which characterizes normal everyday life, that is, I shall argue in the next chapter, the chief concern of phenomenological sociology; it also bears similarities with Geertz's concept of culture (collectivity) as a system of meanings.

The fundamental 'thrown-ness' of human life, its temporality and historicity, is also the situation in which understanding is inescapably embedded–the category of historicity, which is 'the distinctive ontological mark of man, whose existence is always temporarily and historically situated. Historicity is an essential feature of the hermeneutic circle, and of a philosophy as well' (Hoy 1978). The notion of the hermeneutic circle, which, according to Seung (Seung 1982), originated in the old German hermeneutic tradition, is the idea that the whole can only be understood in terms of its parts, and vice versa. Heidegger's version of this concept both undermines Schleiermacher's preoccupation with the retrieval of the original meaning, and rejects the idea of presuppositionless knowledge. While for the earlier theorists, 'The circular movement of understanding runs backwards and forwards along the text and disappears when it is perfectly understood' (Howard 1982), a conceptualization of understanding that culminates in Schleiermacher's theory of the divinatory act of intuitively knowing the speaker's mind, 'Heidegger describes the circle in such a way that the understanding of the text remains permanently determined by the anticipatory movement of fore-understanding' (Howard 1982). Extending the idea further, it is possible to see the impossibility of 'pure' understanding. In Heidegger's phenomenological hermeneutics, understanding is inextricably connected to the human temporal being-in-the-world, which provides the 'prestructure' of all understanding. This prestructuredness of understanding 'is not simply a property of consciousness over and against an already existing world. To see it in this way would be to fall back into the very subject–object model of interpretation which Heidegger's analysis transcends' (Howard 1982); and it underlies his preoccupation with

> ...how things themselves come into view through meaning, understanding, and interpretation. He is discussing what might be called the ontological structure of understanding [...] Hermeneutics in Heidegger, then, is a fundamental theory of how understanding emerges in human existence. His analysis weds hermeneutics to existential ontology and to phenomenology. (Howard 1982)

Heidegger's *Being and Time*, undermining in this way the preoccupation of earlier hermeneutics with methodology and objective understanding, opened up the ontological character of all understanding by positing understanding as fundamental to human existence and not merely an exercise of a particular mental faculty (Palmer 1969). Moreover, confined, as it is, within the finitude of human life, understanding is also finite and temporal. This is a crucial point, developed further in Gadamer's revision of hermeneutics and its premises on the nature of understanding.

Gadamer took up Heidegger's historicism in his radical reappraisal of hermeneutics in *Truth and Method* (1989), emphasizing the situatedness and boundedness of a subject's understanding, which precludes any attempt to rise above his/her own historical horizon. In stressing the context-dependence of the interpreter, Gadamer is clearly going against the neo-Kantian orientation, which posits a situationless, ahistorical subject; and contra Schleiermacher and Dilthey, who, while recognizing the relevance of the historical distance between the interpreter and the text, conceived of understanding as a method to overcome this temporal divide. Gadamer stresses the inevitable historicity of understanding itself, which no amount of methodological rigour can possibly overcome. He 'claims that the context-free or context-independent subject is neither desirable nor possible' (Seung 1982). The present–in which the subject is existentially situated–is the result of a combination of both a biographical past as well as a cultural past (tradition), and as such, fashions the 'hermeneutic situation' of the interpreter.

To Gadamer, however, this boundedness is not a negative phenomenon, to be broken down in order to understand a historical phenomenon, but quite the contrary, it is the very fertile ground that makes understanding possible. He gives this enabling condition the name 'prejudice' or 'prejudgement', perhaps one of the most controversial aspects of his philosophy:

> It is not so much our judgements as it is our prejudices that constitute our being. This is a provocative formulation, for I am using it to restore to its rightful place a positive concept of prejudice that was driven out of our linguistic usage by the French and the English Enlightenment. It can be shown that the concept of prejudice did not originally have the meaning we have attached to it. Prejudices are not necessarily unjustified or erroneous, so that they inevitably distort the truth. In fact, the historicity of our existence entails that prejudices, in the literal sense of the word, constitute the initial directedness of our whole ability to experience. Prejudices are biases of our openness to the world. They are simply the conditions whereby we experience something–whereby what we encounter says something to us. (Gadamer 1976: 9)

Gadamer uses the concept of prejudice in this modified sense to push forward his theory of understanding in two ways: first, to demonstrate the impossibility of the 'objective' understanding of a historical phenomenon–understanding can occur only within a set of prejudgements, therefore the

Enlightenment ideal of a context-free subject is not only a misconception, but is also unnecessary. Prejudices and prejudgements are both inevitable and indispensable to understanding, fashioned by the 'tradition' to which one belongs–a tradition that is bound up with history, as Being with Time. 'Understanding is not to be thought of so much as an action of one's subjectivity, but as the placing of oneself within a tradition, in which past and present are constantly fused' (Gadamer 1975: 258). His other contribution is in his account of the actual operation of prejudices, where Gadamer extends the phenomenological discussions of both Husserl and Heidegger and uses, as his starting point, the idea that all understanding is understanding something as something (Warnke 1984). Intrinsic to Gadamer's notion of 'prejudice' is the idea that the understanding of an event or experience goes beyond its immediate constituents, the perspectival aspects of which require a projection of meaning that takes account of this phenomenon and anticipates the meaning of the whole. In other words, one understands a given part of something in terms of a projected whole. This projection of meaning is grounded in a network, or "'horizon'", of expectations and assumptions. ...On this view, any apprehension of the immediate data of experience is theory-laden; the apprehension reflects the experience and values of the culture and society to which one belongs' (Warnke 1984: xiv).

Thus, understanding is a 'fusion of horizons' (Gadamer 1975: 273)–the horizons or prejudices of the interpreter and those of the text. The part–whole aspect of textual understanding involves the projection or anticipation of the meaning of the whole, and the revision of this projection in terms of the actual interpretation of the parts. The initial projection of meaning is therefore not fixed and final, but flexible and ever-changing. This idea can be applied at different levels: the culturally and historically situated set of prejudices or horizons also undergo constant revision:

> We started by saying that a hermeneutical situation is determined by the prejudices that we bring with us. They constitute then, the horizon of a particular present, for they represent that beyond which it is

impossible to see. But now it is important to avoid the error of thinking that it is a fixed set of opinions and evaluations that determine and limit the horizon of the present, and that the otherness of the past can be distinguished from it as from a fixed ground. (Gadamer 1975: 272)

For Gadamer, therefore, while all understanding is a projection of a horizon of anticipation, the prejudgements that underlie these projections, themselves undergo changes as a result of the act of interpretation. Thus, the process of interpretation is dialogic. According to Hoy (1978), this notion of an interpretive dialogue between the text and the interpreter, involving the anticipation of the intentions of the text (as opposed to those of the author) and its disclosure, avoids the 'traditional vocabulary of the Cartesian philosophy of consciousness and hence the antinomies of subject–object language' (Hoy 1978: 40). It is important to bear in mind that the Gadamerian dialogue is significantly different from the Romantic conception where dialogue is a perfect correspondence between the speaker and the hearer, and involves the intuition, through language, of the speaker's intended meaning. In the modern conception, meaning originates in 'some source other than the intuitive immediacies of subjectivity or even intersubjectivity. Meaning always remains irreducible to the immediacy of the speaking subjects, coexisting in a homogeneous time or space' (Kearney 1984: 128).

By repudiating the notion of the 'proper' understanding of a text as the reproduction of authorial intentions, and undermining the concept of objective understanding, Gadamer's theory, regarding the groundedness of understanding and interpretation in 'effective history',[6] also points towards the

---

[6]The term 'effective history', according to Bleicher (Bleicher 1980), 'eludes short definitions.' However, its 'structural elements are: the awareness of one's hermeneutic situation and the "horizon" that is characteristic of it; the dialogical relationship between interpreter and text; the dialectic between question and answer; openness for tradition.[...]Effective history represents the positive and productive possibility of understanding.' (Bleicher 1980: 111).

presence of multiple meanings in a text. The reader, acting from within his/her socio-historical context, understands a meaning which is coloured by his/her experience in that context. The life-world shapes world view, which in turn fashions the understanding of an act, an expression, or a text. The reader, as a social agent, undermines the idea of the text as the carrier of a single (set of) meaning: the 'fusion of horizons', depending as it does on the prejudices or prejudgements of the reader, could, in effect, differ from one reader to the other, connected as it is to their historicity.

This idea of the possibility of a multiplicity of meanings, all equally valid[7], together with his denial of any method of testing the validity of a particular interpretation and the consequent privileging of one meaning over others, have encouraged Gadamer's critics (Hirsch 1967; Habermas 1988) to accuse him of fostering a rabid form of relativism. Grondin (1990) offers a spirited defence of Gadamer prefering to see the philosophical turn of contemporary hermeneutics as a move towards pluralism:

> Whereas traditional hermeneutics, which was normative, had a tendency to think that a text could have only one meaning, hermeneutics, which has become philosophical, seems entirely disposed to accept the plurality of meanings that a single text can receive. A hermeneutics open to only one meaning seems to have changed into one that is open to pluralism. (Grondin 1990: 44–45)

Grondin celebrates this move as the typically hermeneutic virtue of tolerance. In Gadamer, this tolerance, though it allows him to refuse to rank the available interpretations of a text, stops short of supporting Valery's claim that 'my verses have whatever meaning that is given them' (quoted in Gadamer 1975: 509)–a stance that Gadamer considers 'untenable hermeneutic nihilism' (Gadamer 1975: 85).

---

[7]'Valid' should not be taken to invoke the argument for the objective standards of evaluating interpretations. In this context it is used to mean the exact opposite, that any interpretation is as valid as another.

Although Gadamer emphasizes his concept of 'effective history' to make a case for the impossibility of an 'objective' understanding of a historically different period, the ontological foundations of this idea can also be seen to support a similar impossibility of understanding a different culture. The historicity of the reader/viewer and his/her situatedness in the present, together with the development of tradition up to that present, act as forces operating 'from behind his/her back', unnoticed and unacknowledged, but nevertheless potent and inevitable. The past can only be looked at through the eyes of the present; texts from the past are always interpreted from a historical perspective. But the same constraints that militate against the bridging of the temporal divide–a time-conquering act which would enable the understanding of a text from its contemporaneous position–can be seen to be equally effective in restricting the bridging of the spatial distance which would facilitate the 'perfect' understanding of a different culture, and consequently, the texts of a different culture. I use the terms 'objective' and 'perfect' here to mean the approximation of the meaning that a text has for the people of that period or culture–in other words, the replication of their signifying practices.

Such a stance has the potential danger of not just relativism, but more insidiously, of the sealing off of different cultures and races (indeed, any form of collectivity) into mutually incomprehensible camps–a stance that is intellectually unacceptable and politically suspect. However, the threat is magnified and made more real only from within the predominantly epistemological, 'scientific' paradigm, since it undermines any attempt at a valueless empirical observation of an alien culture. The more ontologically paved road that we have been travelling on takes us not only to the recognition of the validity of different world-views (and the 'tolerance' that accompanies this recognition), as in Whorf's example of the Hopi and Castenada's work with Yaqui Indians, but also, and more importantly, to a self-reflexive orientation in methodology, interpretation of data (even the acknowledgement that it is an 'interpretation') and theory construction. The move towards *verstehende* social science, with its recognition of the meaningfulness of beliefs, norms, practice, and so on, and its affinities with the humanities, coincided with 'the rise of hermeneutics' (Baumann 1978), and is more evident in the recent debates in anthropology, as in the works of Rosaldo (1993). The essential features of this debate are discussed in a later chapter as part of the rationale for the methodology adopted for this project, which also discusses the empirical significance of the producers, the texts, as well as the audience for this project.

Hermeneutic 'horizons' and television viewing

From within the perspective of phenomenological hermeneutics, however, the examination of the role of the author (producer), and the texts (documentaries) is not unproblematic. With the denial of the psychologistic reconstruction of the author's intended meaning, contemporary philosophical hermeneutics appears to subscribe to the Barthesian idea of the 'death of the author'. Risser argues persuasively that, despite Barthes's claim that post-structuralism initiates a move beyond hermeneutics, Gadamer's version echoes deconstructive criticism's erasure of the author's signature:

> For Gadamer, the normative notion of the author's intention represents only an empty space, for what is fixed in writing always frees itself for a new relationship. The author is always decentred in the act of reading, and the reader, in turn, is decentred in the act of textual production.[...] The reader participates in an event in which the text is made to speak again. The act of reading becomes, as it does for post-structuralism, an act of production. (Risser 1991: 94)

Similarly, the objective analysis of the text is inimical to Gadamerian hermeneutics, since the very notion of objectivity is called into question through the evocation of the authority of tradition. In the present case, however, the project is not the examination of interpretation in relation to a text, but a comparison of interpretations across different 'traditions' or 'effective histories', and is therefore Gadamerian in its impulse.

Reading, or in this context, viewing, as a productive sense-making exercise, not only emphasizes the act of generation of meaning as an active, creative act, but at the same time, underlines the essential mismatch between intended and interpreted meanings, as Wilson (1993) argues: '"overcoming" semantic difference never reaches fruition in a final act of perfect understanding' (1993: 46). Using the Gadamerian concept of understanding as a 'fusion of horizons', Wilson attempts to repudiate the structuralist claim of the act of interpretation as the reader's reproduction of the ideological positions inscribed in the text. Although the process of understanding involves the attempted closure of the cognitive distance between the text and the reader, this process is 'imperfect' and would inevitably fall short of complete fulfilment because of the difference in the 'horizons' of the viewer and the textual subject. However, this semantic gap also embodies, to Wilson, an emancipatory power: the interpretive framework that the reader brings to the text enables the 'distanciation', necessary for an adequate ideological critique.

> To theorize the relationship of a programme and viewer as a 'fusion of horizons' allows both for different audience readings of the text's cognitive perspectives and for different positions of distanciation from its definition of the 'real'. Reading permits resistance, never finally producing a loss of subjective autonomy for the reader. (Wilson 1993: 47)

Once the rhetoric is removed, Wilson's claim, that the hermeneutic avowal of the process of understanding as a creative act makes possible the doubting of the veracity of textual content by the viewer, becomes clear. The active, creative utilization of the semantic practices implies the generation of a multiplicity of meanings—polysemy, which in turn indicates the possibility to resist the text's ideological 'hailing'.

Despite a commendable exposition and insightful use of Gadamer's hermeneutics in his exploration of the dynamics of television viewing, the power that Wilson ascribes to the reader is problematic. In his anxiety to provide a conceptual position oppositional to that of structuralism, he appears to have given the reader an unduly privileged space, and overlooked the equally important hermeneutic concept of 'tradition' and its role in the formation of the prejudgement or prejudice that a reader takes to a text. That the interpreter does not operate from a valueless position is one of the fundamental arguments of contemporary hermeneutics. Human situatedness in a cultural, historical tradition informs the prejudgements, and consequently the prejudgements themselves betray ideological positioning. To put it another way, the individual reader, when facing the text, is already socio-culturally embedded, and this embeddedness is surely not ideology-free. Recent commentaries linking Heidegger's philosophy to his political affiliations is a case in point, as is Seung's (1982) critique of Gadamer:

> If everybody is trapped within his or her own historical horizon, so must be Gadamer and his theory of interpretation. In that event, there is every reason to believe that his theory is determined by the unique character of his own historical context; his historical relativism may simply reflect the gradual loss of confidence in European rationalism. (Seung 1982: 204)

Wilson does recognize that 'reading is always from a pre-existing point of view. Understanding does not disengage itself from the presupposition of the reader or investigator' (Wilson 1993); but he appears to see in this very nature of pre-understanding the emancipatory power of reading, while being blind to the ideological structuring of these horizons.

Wilson's adroit use of Gadamer's notion of the 'horizon of expectations', in order to theorize the understanding of television, on the other hand, is particularly useful. In relation to television, these horizons represent 'an audience's assumptions about generic practices, routine camera work and appropriate ways of behaving, assumptions they bring to the context of viewing.[...] Horizons of expectation are constituted by the audience's anticipations, which arise in turn from a long history of viewing' (Wilson 1993). Building on Gadamer's idea that 'all understanding presumes a living relationship between the interpreter and the text, his previous connection with the material that it deals with' (Gadamer 1975: 295), Wilson enumerates the importance of genre recognition in successful television viewing. Knowledge of generic features produces a series of expectations which enable the viewer to understand the text. During an evening's viewing, an audience's horizon of expectations brings

> ...together items and programmes as instances of types.[...] Raymond Williams's concept of 'flow' can be read as drawing attention to the way in which one section of programming influences the horizon of expectations brought to bear on another. Continuity announcements, for instance, offer appropriate descriptions of impending textual activity. (Wilson 1993)

Crucially, these expectations, deriving from the knowledge of and familiarity with the generic properties, in turn support television's 'veridical effect': 'an apparently unmediated and reliable presentation of how things are' (Wilson 1993), making transparent the constructedness of the programme.

These expectations, specific to television, and by extension, film, are part of the hermeneutic horizon of the viewer in more ways than Wilson's reference to the familiarity with a particular genre. Most significant is the link between the horizon of expectation or pre-understanding, and the socio-culturally constituted 'tradition' of the viewer. As we shall see later in the book, generic expectations with regard to documentary, particularly in connection to its truth claims, appear closely bound up with the viewer's cultural context.

The role of the reader/viewer and his/her socially defined signifying practices are thus important, and particularly crucial to this thesis. This is elaborated in the next chapter while exploring the links between the individual and the social, but an intriguing issue suggests itself in the present context: granted that a particular interpretation results from a particular pre-structuring, which itself is shaped by a particular socio-cultural situation, a justifiable assumption is that individuals, inhabiting the same collectivity, interpret texts in a similar fashion. This is obviously one of the presuppositions of Morley's *The Nationwide Audience*, which he himself criticized later. As suggested earlier in this chapter, a problem with such an assumption is that, its reductionist attitude fails to acknowledge the multiple intersecting spaces that make up an individual life-world. The intrigue is when the question is turned around: can persons, whose interpretations exhibit similar orientations, but who occupy different spaces geographically, economically, etc., be construed as belonging to the same 'interpretive community' and therefore the same collectivity? Such a scenario, given the argument presented in this chapter, would require a reworking of the concept of 'culture'.

The notion of understanding, presented in this chapter, offers a possible explanation of the link between socio-cultural situatedness and the signifying practices. As we saw, Heidegger's concept of understanding differs from his predecessors in its recognition that understanding is not a specialized activity aimed at retrieving a text's meaning, but the very basis of the human being-in-the-world. Understanding as a central element of human life assumes an ontological character, and, restricted as it is to human historicity, is also temporal and bounded. 'Tradition', a fundamental aspect of Gadamer's hermeneutics, builds on Heidegger's concepts and posits understanding as, first, an exercise of creative 'prejudices'; and second, as the future-oriented 'projection' of expectations. From the perspective of the phenomenological hermeneutics of Heidegger and Gadamer, therefore, understanding is inevitably and irretrievably anchored to one's historical and cultural situation. In the next chapter, I explore the Heideggerian foundations of Schutz's ideas of intersubjectivity and 'multiple realities' which, I argue, offer a particularly useful alternative to the conventional sociological categories.

4

Exploring 'Context'

> *To entertain the idea that the diversity of custom across time and over space is not a mere matter of garb and appearance, of stage settings and comedic masques, is to entertain also the idea that humanity is as various in its essence as it is in its expression. And with that reflection some well-fastened philosophical moorings are loosed and an uneasy drifting into perilous waters begins.*
>
> Clifford Geertz, *The Interpretation of Cultures*

If the explanations of the social embeddedness of understanding were the only task in this project, the previous chapter would go some way towards fulfilling that. However, the argument, as it stands thus far, suggests a degree of determinism which is guilty not only of raising the spectre of irredeemable relativism, but also of falling into the very trap to which Morley, in his self-reflexive account of the *Nationwide* study testified: that of employing classic sociological variables without taking into account the fact that while, for instance, class stratification could justifiably affect a person's outlook and behaviour (including interpretive practices), the unthinking employment of these variables, as causal categories with which to understand and explain social behaviour, is inadequate and unsatisfactory. And therein lies the difficulty. It is worth reiterating, at this point, the theoretical problem which this project seeks to address. In recognizing the act of interpretation as socially embedded, I acknowledge the viewer as acting, not in a socio-cultural vacuum, but as an individual whose behaviour (in the wider sense of the word), or 'world' is inevitably shaped by his/her society and culture. But in doing so, I seek to circumvent the conception of the social variables as straitjackets controlling the individual's behaviour. Exploring the reception of mediated knowledge and its contribution to democratic formations requires accounting for the socio-cultural contexts in which the reception takes place. This chapter deals with the idea of 'context' on this wide, socio-cultural level. I argue, that in place of the one-dimensionality of these classic variables, phenomenological sociology, as proposed by Schutz (1964, 1972, 1973), offers a sufficiently complex elucidation of the individual's world with which to avoid these deterministic straitjackets. Schutz's links with Heidegger offer an additional advantage for this project in the sense that it ties in with the Gadamerian hermeneutics presented in the previous chapter.

The individual and the collective

Almost ever since its conception and birth as a 'scientific discipline', sociology has had to contend with the problem of the relationship between the individual on the one hand, and society on the other. Conceived as a science of society (whose birth has generally been attributed to Comte) along the lines of the certainty offered by Newtonian physics, its primary function was to observe and record the general 'laws' of human collective life. Behind this rubric was the assumption that societies worked on fundamental, immutable principles, analogous to the 'laws' on which the natural world functioned; and, similar to the physical laws, these fundamental principles, once discovered, would enable the accurate mapping and prediction of the behaviour of humans in the industrial societies. Comte's visions were given a slightly different shade by

Durkheim's proposition of treating social behaviour as 'facts', dealt with as objectively as natural or physical facts (Giddens 1982:13). While this conception of society and human behaviour continues to exert its influence on the positivistic version of the social sciences with its insistence on the examination of society using methodology which approximates those employed by the disinterested neutral observer in natural scientific research, it has generally been recognized that the social sciences differ from the natural sciences in important ways.

However, the split between the individual and the collective remains intransigent and almost intractable. Reflections on the nature of these two categories have spawned disputes in social philosophy, involving questions about the subjective and objective nature of reality, action and structure, and freedom and constraint; and through all of them, blows the wind of Cartesian dualism. It has been argued (Wuthnow 1989) that the Cartesian split between the subject and the object, between the thinking self and the external world, and the resulting epistemological issues form the basis of the arguments made by writers as different and as influential as Marx, Weber and Durkheim. Though framed in different ways, the concern for the subject's sense of alienation from the external world runs through their work (Wuthnow 1989: 23). This conception of distinct 'worlds' has generally been the norm both in classical sociology as well as in the challenges to such reification of external reality.

There have been attempts, by contemporary sociologists, to transcend this divide: Elias's (1978) 'figurational sociology', Giddens's (1976, 1984) 'structuration theory' and Bourdieu's (1977) 'constructionist structuralism or structuralist constructivism' are some of the conceptions which have attempted, not so much to ignore the classic distinction, but to emphasize the dialectic nature of the relationship between the two categories. Layder (1994) labels some of these attempts as 'breaking free and burning bridges' (Part 3, *Passim*). 'For these writers, the elements involved in the dualisms are so neatly and completely interwoven with each other that we need to capture this quality in our theories and the analytic language we use to describe them' (Layder 1994: 91). However, none of these reconciliations has resulted in a happy marriage. Morawaska and Spohn (1994), for example, deem Bourdieu's concept of 'habitus' and the Eliasian 'figurations' as deterministic, while Thompson (1984) finds that 'Giddens manages to preserve the complementarity between structure and agency only by defining agency in such a way that any individual in any situation could not be an agent' (1984:169). More recently, Bennett (2007) has critiqued Bourdieu's use of 'habitus' on the basis of a study exploring the relations between cultural capital and social inequality in contemporary Britain.

Culture has been a problematic issue in terms of structure and agency. Indeed, its very definition has been problematic, despite contemporary sociology's reawakening to the relevance and significance of culture. Whereas Wisdom (1987) wonders 'whether there is anything to be gained by giving it any very precise use' (1987: 19), Wuthnow laments the fact that it lacks a properly rigorous definition: 'Culture remains, by many indications, vaguely conceptualized, vaguely approached methodologically, and vaguely associated with value judgements and other sorts of observer bias' (Wuthnow 1989: 5–6).

Williams (1981) identifies a convergence between what he calls the 'idealist' and the 'materialist' conceptions of culture. This convergence contains elements common to either position, but goes beyond them: with the 'materialist' position, it emphasizes a whole social order, but unlike it, insists 'that "cultural practice" and "cultural production" [...] are not simply derived from an otherwise constituted social order but are themselves major elements in their constitution'; with the 'idealist' position it shares the conception of cultural practice as 'constitutive, but [...] sees culture as the signifying system through which necessarily (though among other means) a social order is communicated, reproduced, experienced and explored' (Williams 1981: 12–13).

In the context of the present study, in which my intention was to compare the interpretations of documentaries by audiences in India and Britain, the implicit assumption was that, geographically distanced people inhabit cultural spaces which are similarly distant. While these spaces are not hermetically sealed compartments since there are intersecting areas of commonality, my original conjecture, on which I based my fieldwork, included the notion that audiences in India and Britain resided in cultures sufficiently distant and different as to allow for different interpretive practices.

By constructing the problem of the investigation of interpretive practices in terms of Gadamerian hermeneutics, my position—in relation to Williams's tripartite division of the sociology of culture—is made clear: I conceive of culture as a signifying system, or to use Geertz's memorable phrase, as 'webs of significance' spun by humans in their effort to understand, come to terms with, and live as a collective in, the world. As mentioned in Chapter 2, these webs of significance and their links to behaviour are redolent with issues of power and inequality. It follows that the view of communication that I espouse is what Carey (1989) categorizes as 'a ritual view of communication [which] conceives communication as a process through which a shared culture is created, modified, and transformed' (1989: 43). Such a stance has obvious theoretical and methodological significance. Theoretically, I would argue, this combines the merits of the conceptions of both verstehen and 'observational' sociology (Williams 1981: 16), and goes some way towards dissolving the unproductive dualisms discussed earlier. This is not an ecumenical enterprise; nor is it an attempt at constructing a grand theory, capable of subsuming within its rubric the various dualisms and their concomitant theories and methodologies. Construing the task of the sociology of culture as the understanding of the ways in which human collectivities make sense of their world suggests the operation of two complementary forces—the reification or objectification of the cultural system, that is, the signifying system of meaning, as well as the interpretive practices constituting the individual constructions of reality which function within this system. The complexity of this process needs to be acknowledged: on the one hand, since 'what persons create is not merely one reality but multiple realities. Reality cannot be exhausted by any one symbolic form, be it scientific, religious, or aesthetic' (Carey 1989: 63); and on the other hand, on the collective level, culture as a system of signification is similarly not a monolithic or singular entity. The theoretical underpinning to this claim, in the form of phenomenological philosophy and sociology, is elucidated in the rest of the chapter, but first my invoking of Geertz's conception of culture needs some elaboration.

Geertz's approach to anthropology, indeed to social sciences in general, is decidedly interpretive. The claim that the 'cultural phenomena should be treated as significative systems posing expositive questions' (Geertz 1983: 3) is, according to him, no longer 'alarming' to social scientists; since the earlier 'laws-and-causes social physics' was replaced by a cultural hermeneutics, social scientists discovered that

> ...they did not need to mimic physicists or closet humanists or to invent some new realm of being to serve as the object of their investigations [...]; and many of them have taken up an essentially hermeneutic [...] or 'interpretive' approach to their task [...] The woods are full of eager interpreters. (Geertz 1983: 21)

Along with this recognition and acceptance of their new role was a recasting of the human being—away from the Enlightenment view of 'man as the naked reasoner that appeared when he took his cultural costumes off' (Geertz 1973: 38), to a 'more viable concept of man, one in which culture, and the variability of culture, would be taken into account' (Geertz 1973: 36). To step away from a 'uniformatarian' view of the human nature towards the realization of cultural diversity is to step in the direction of cultural relativism, but to Geertz that is not a problem. In stating categorically that 'there is no such thing as a human nature independent of culture', Geertz is not admitting to either the competitive man of Hobbes or to Rousseau's noble savage, but that

> ...we are, in sum, incomplete or unfinished animals who complete or finish ourselves through culture—and not through culture in general but

through highly particular forms of it [...] Between what our body tells us
and what we have to know in order to function, there is a vacuum we
must fill ourselves, and we fill it with information (or misinformation)
provided by our culture. (Geertz 1973: 49–50)

For Geertz the relationship between culture and meaning is
fundamental to the understanding of the kinds of behaviour of
various people, and he demonstrates this through his distinction between 'thin' and 'thick' descriptions of the cultural and
behavioural practices, treating them as texts which portray the
sense of reality which the people of that culture possess. What
is significant in the present context is the idea that culture is
made up of shared patterns of meaning which provide the
frame of reference for everyday life. This conception is useful
in so far as it provides a foundation to elaborate upon culture
as the thread that unites and holds together an intersubjective
world by furnishing the individuals who comprise it with a
common sense of reality, in other words, a common world-
view or set of values. However, there is little in Geertz's work
that enumerates the percolation and infusion of this idea of
culture as the meaning from the collective level into that of
the individual behaviour, the processes through which this
web of significance affects and defines the lives of individuals
suspended in it. For this, I would argue, that phenomenological sociology, especially some of the ideas of Schutz, would
be useful.

Schutz's phenomenological sociology

Perhaps the most crucial of Schutz's ideas—certainly the most
relevant in the present context—is that of the life-world, or
Lebenswelt, a concept fundamental to phenomenological sociology, and originating from Husserl. Within Schutz's phenomenology, however, the emphasis in and use of *Lebenswelt*,
perhaps influenced by Heidegger's interpretation of it, is
markedly different from that of Husserl's. As Gurswitch (1970)
defines it, this is

...the world as encountered in everyday life and given in direct and immediate experience, especially perceptual experience and its derivatives like memory, expectation, and the like, independently of and prior to scientific interpretation. [...] As the universal scene of our life, the soil, so to speak, upon which all human activities, productions, and creations take place, the world of common experience proves the foundations of the latter as well as of whatever might result from them. (Gurswitch 1970: 35)

This formulation of the concept of the life-world captures the primary preoccupation of phenomenological sociology, both as a subject matter to be studied and described, as well as a philosophical repudiation of the other social sciences which, in their desire to replicate the methodological foundations of the natural sciences, not only ignore this 'world' but worse, take its existence for granted. Philosophers generally classified as 'existential phenomenologists', like Heidegger, Sartre and Merleau -Ponty have focussed on this life-world for their analyses, but as Roche (1973) points out, these writers, along with Schutz, 'contributed different versions of man's existential condition to the phenomenological school in a general reaction against Husserl's emphasis on essence' (1973: 19). They replaced the idea of the transcendental consciousness with the concept of consciousness as lived experience: 'Consciousness is personal experience, not impersonal essence, as Husserl asserts' (Roche 1973), and with this displacement, human consciousness and the life-world it operated in became the subject of study.

Husserl's initial conception of the 'world of natural attitude'– expressed in *The Idea of Phenomenology* and *Ideas: General Introduction to Pure Phenomenology* (1913) (which he was to modify in his later writings)–with all its mundane and commonsense solutions and interpretations, employed by humans in everyday life, was the Platonic cave which had to be escaped from or 'transcended', in order to encounter and understand the equally Platonic 'essences' of human existence and consciousness. The impulse behind Husserl's quest for the invariant properties of 'pure' consciousness derived from his strong anti-empiricist stance against the positivistic, empiricist psychology prevalent at the turn of the century (Dallmayr and McCarthy 1977: 219). To achieve this end, he advocated rigorous epistemological procedures, which involved the employment of a philosophical 'epoche' or 'bracketing', fashioned to enable the 'scientist' to transcend the mundane world of perceptions and empirical proof, that is, the world of 'natural attitude' which enables humans to overcome their potential Cartesian doubt and solipsism in order to live with others in a profoundly 'intersubjective' existence. For Husserl, the understanding of 'pure' subjectivity is impossible without a radical disentanglement from the world of daily life and its taken-for-grantedness. The initial task of the philosopher, therefore, is to place 'in brackets' this world and his or her 'naive belief' in it, in their investigation of the 'essence' or eidos. Schutz (1964) rightly marks this as 'radicalising the Cartesian method of philosophical doubt', but the 'suspension of our belief in the reality of our world' that this calls for, is to him mirrored by an epoche, utilized effortlessly by humans in their daily lives: 'He [sic] does not suspend belief in the outer world and its objects, but on the contrary, he suspends doubt in its existence. What he puts in brackets is the doubt that the world and its objects might be otherwise than it appears to him' (Schutz 1962).

Husserl, realizing the problems with the applicability of his conceptions, was to later attempt to rectify the difficulty with his transcendental approach by trying to fill the gap that he had created between consciousness and the life-world.[1] However, as Bauman (1978) points out,

> …having once settled down in the phenomenologically reduced world, he could only articulate his task as finding the way of 're-building' the full-blooded social and cultural world while using only the bricks and

---

[1]As Morris (1977) suggests, although the concept of the life-world was central to Husserl's later work, his failure to clarify it fully could be the reason 'that phenomenology, as it continues to develop, is a moving philosophy, comprising several currents that have a common point of departure but move out at different speeds and in different directions. (1977: 10)

mortar permitted in his purified world. [...] The task, no wonder, has not been accomplished. (Bauman 1978: 127–28)

Despite his new found interest in the investigation of the life-world itself, Husserl could not successfully resolve the relation between a concern for the essences or 'pure' meaning and the fundamentally intersubjective nature of *Lebenswelt*.

The general configuration of the life-world, as defined by Husserl, laid the foundation from which Schutz and later phenomenologists were to design their sociologies. But in transforming the mundane, common world from being seen as the impediment to the understanding of the transcendental Ego, to the very object of inquiry, the later writers turned the early Husserlian world on its head. The concern of phenomenology was no longer with the fashioning of a presuppositionless philosophy, aimed at interpreting the invariant, fundamental properties of existence, or 'essences'. In Schutz, for instance, phenomenology takes on the role of clarifying the philosophical foundations of the social sciences. For him, the life-world is predominantly a social world, 'the "naive natural stance" was an eminently social stance' (Wagner 1983: 288), and it thus became the goal, rather than the starting point of his analysis. Contrary to Husserl's attempts to 'bracket' away the 'naively, pre-reflexively given' world, Schutz sees it as 'the field which the student of social phenomena should never abandon' (Bauman 1978: 175). In his formulation of the life-world itself, as well as the understanding of it, Schutz's social philosophy is 'a hermeneutically conscious sociology which operates within the Heideggerian framework of life-world as the ultimate foundation, and the only habitat, of meanings and of the activity of understanding' (Bauman 1978: 21).

Heidegger's crucial break with Husserl came in the form of his anchoring everything in existence: meaning and interpretation as firmly founded within the life-world, within existence, and not arising as a result of pure contemplation; truth (and, as we saw in Chapter 3, meaning and interpretation) was therefore contingent upon tradition and context. In Heidegger's framework, presuppositionless philosophy in

search of an interpretation of a transcendental reality was neither possible nor desirable, since existence, including that of
the philosopher/scientist, is inextricably grounded in *Dasein*.[2]
Thus, while Heidegger shares Husserl's belief that the sciences
are one way of interpreting reality, his locating science within
Dasein inverts the Husserlian project of a transcendental analysis of science. To Husserl, this denial of phenomenological
reduction was an indication of Heidegger's reluctance to transcend the 'naive' attitude, and his insistence on the priority of
the existential aspects of human life amounted to, for Husserl,
a transformation of phenomenology into a 'philosophical anthropology' which had all the failings of the earlier forms of
psychologism (Kockelmans 1967: 274).

Heidegger's rejection of Husserl's transcendental philosophy[3] comes in the wake of his conviction that understanding
is a fundamental feature of being and existence, and not an
aspect of knowledge. To him,

> ...the activity of understanding can be grasped solely as an aspect of
> being, as an essence of existence. As Ricoeur put it, instead of asking
> what is to be done in order to obtain correct understanding, Heidegger
> took another question as his major concern: what, in the human mode
> of being-in-the-world, determines both the possibility and the actuality
> of understanding? (Bauman 1978: 148)

As a consequence, the question of understanding becomes
an ontological rather than an epistemological concern.
Heidegger's phenomenology is, therefore, profoundly hermeneutic. Not only is the task an interpretation of *Dasein*, but this
task is to be carried out under the rubric that understanding

---

[2]Bleicher (1982) sees *Dasein* and *Lebenswelt* as congruent concepts,
but that they 'emerged in different universes of discourse.' (1982: 154.),
whereas Bauman (1978) interprets *Dasein* simply as 'existence typical of humans.'(1978:158).

[3]Ironically, some of the reviewers of *Being and Time* found it lapsing into
'windy mysticism', and the logical positivists of the Vienna Circle thought
it a perfect example of the meaninglessness typical of metaphysical writing.
(Roche 1973: 29)

and interpretation are features of everyday life. Far from being a philosophical feat, understanding is an act carried out by humans in their existence with other humans and objects. One of the tasks of phenomenology is consequently to examine the interpretive procedures employed in 'normal' life.

Heidegger makes a distinction between everyday understanding and 'theoretical' understanding. Everyday understanding papers over the incongruities and lack of harmony present in the world, since *Dasein* entails objects dissolving 'in our daily existence so completely that in our ordinary circumstances they do not appear as opaque objects which invite questioning as to their meaning. We take them for granted' (Bauman 1978: 158). In other words, we seldom reflect on our lives or on the objects we encounter and use; we also take for granted the existence of others about whom we rarely 'theorise'. To return to the example of the hammer mentioned in chapter 3, the qualities of the hammer are pointed to us only when our act of using it as a tool is disturbed. The process leading to theoretical knowledge is triggered off when things reveal that their 'givenness-to-hand, their readiness to be handled, their obedient fitness, are not qualities which can be taken for granted' (Bauman 1978: 159). The 'thrown-ness' of human life, the fact that we are born into a world which already contains objects, rules and people means that we are born into a meaningful world where things are encountered, 'naturally' as it were, as parts of the totality of pre-reflexive existence. In 'normal' life, reflection arises only when this 'natural' quality is threatened or disturbed.

The Cartesian subject–object dualism is undermined in this formulation since it claims that such distanciation does not occur in everyday life. To use Descartes' example, the qualities of wax are seldom reflected upon in the everyday context; the question 'what is wax?' and the theoretical reflection it entails require that the piece of wax be treated as something other than for what it is unthinkingly (pre-reflectively) used in the life-world. That is, questions about the essence of things arise only as a result of their removal from their natural context to a purified but artificial world. This examination of objects, independent of their everyday context is, according to Heidegger, symptomatic of the fundamental flaw in epistemology grounded in an artificial distinction between subject and object. Heidegger's insistence on the pre-reflexive understanding of Being explicitly rejects Cartesian foundations. An isolated 'I' without a given world is impossible, since the thrown-ness of life, with its pre-reflexive understanding, precedes any epistemological question. In effect, *cogito* presupposes the *sum*, the thinking subject is already embedded in existence, and is therefore not a primary datum: 'With the *cogito sum* Descartes claimed to provide philosophy with a new and certain foundation. But what he leaves undetermined within this "radical" departure is the kind of being characterising the res cogitans, or more precisely stated, the ontological *meaning of the "sum"*' (*Being and Time*, quoted in Schrag, Bauman 1978: 283; emphasis in the original).

Any separation of the subject and the object, or the internal and the external reality is inimical to the core of Heidegger's philosophy, in which the fundamental a priori of human existence, the 'thrown-ness' of 'being-in-the-world', contains a primeval unity of consciousness and 'external' nature:

> ...to 'prove' the existence of an external world is to overlook the a priori nature of Being-in-the-world...Rocks and trees do not depend on man for their occurrence in the universe, but reality, which is merely a mode of man's interpretation of the world, does depend on man's existence. (quoted in Bauman 1978: 153–54)

To Heidegger, *Dasein* was very much a case of 'being-in-the-world', which, in turn, meant 'being-with-others'. Here we have the concept that offers a preliminary attempt at answering a problem which Husserl could not resolve: that of intersubjectivity. Even Husserl's later attempts to take into account the features of the life-world were insufficient for rectifying the quandary of the intersubjectivity of human existence, since his 'insistence on "egological" premises threatened to confine phenomenology in a solipsistic straitjacket, blocking access to intersubjective meanings and experiences' (Dallmayr and McCarthy

1977: 220–21; Bauman 1978). Heidegger solved this dilemma by claiming that one of the fundamental characteristics of 'being-in-the-world' is being with others: 'Yes, ultimately, this is the most trivial and empty thing we can say; it simply means that [human existence] is found amidst other beings and so can be met with there' (quoted in Bauman 1978: 152). However trivial, this formulation undermined conceptions of interest-free pursuit of knowledge as well as knowledge without presupposition, and in turn inspired non-positivistic social philosophies.

This admittedly sketchy account of Heidegger's basic precepts hardly does justice to the complexity of his philosophy, but the intention here was to indicate the shift in emphasis in twentieth century Western philosophy from epistemological concerns to questions of a more ontological nature. Concomitant with this shift in emphasis and the critique of positivistic foundations of the human sciences that it entailed, was the development of an 'alternative' sociology which emphasized the significance of the subjects' life-worlds and their analysis. Phenomenological sociology's focus on everyday life has resulted in an increased 'sociological interest in the taken-for-granted world of social reality wherein everyday accounts take on a natural appearance and situations are constructed such that it appears that they could not be otherwise' (Bauman 1978). One of the consequences of this refraining of the social world as being constituted by the activities of its members during the course of their being-in-the-world has been the development of ethnomethodology and its concern with the manner in which people make sense of and act in their worlds. Schutz has been generally acknowledged as having provided the bridge between phenomenological philosophy and sociology (for example, Bauman 1978; Layder 1994), and it is to Schutz that we must now return to relocate our bearings within this chapter.

The pre-reflexive, intersubjective world

The task here is to explicate the nature of being-in-the-world and being-with-others, or to put it in a non-Heideggerean fashion, the understanding of the individual in his/her collective

situation, be it society or culture, and of the patterns of meanings that make up the individual's reality. In terms of Schutz's
work, this amounts to the cognitive setting of the life-world and
its intersubjectivity. The primary concern in Schutz's phenomenology is the elucidation of the structures of the life-world,
and the individual's or 'subject's' action within them. While
Husserl (and later Heidegger) provided the phenomenological
baseline for Schutz's sociology, Weber's notion of *Vertsehen* and
meaningful action played a significant part in his argument that
'meaning had to be found in lived experience or internal time-
consciousness and more specifically in the reflective glance of
the ego upon such experience' (Dallmayr and McCarthy 1977:
220). In combining the insights of Husserl and Weber, Schutz
also sought to overcome the problems he perceived in them
(Thompson 1984: Chapter 1, Wagner 1983). Locating in Weber
a lack of sustained philosophical depth and an absence of any
discussion of intersubjectivity which Schutz saw as crucial, he
tried to provide 'Weber's approach to the phenomena of the social world [...] with a philosophical underpinning' by clarifying
the phenomenological presuppositions of *Vertsehen* sociology
(Natanson 1970: 104). To this end, he was to amend his earlier
egological concerns and move towards a sociological examination of the life-world. Building on Heidegger's conception
of understanding as fundamental to human existence, Schutz
revised the notion of *Vertsehen* to mean not just a specialist tool,
but a precognitive aspect of the life-world: '*Vertsehen* is [...] primarily not a method used by the social scientist, but the particular experiential form in which common-sense thinking takes
cognizance of the social cultural world' (Schutz 1973: 56).

As mentioned earlier, Schutz's attitude to the life-world does
not share Husserl's 'bracketing', but is closer to Heidegger's
conception of it as a priori and fundamental whose investigation falls under the purview of the social scientist. To Schutz,
the *Lebenswelt* is predominantly a social, intersubjective,
shared world–an argument which was not fully developed
by Husserl even in his later work. Schutz's development of

this concept in his writings makes them the place in which, according to Wolff (1975), 'phenomenology and sociology meet' (1975: 17). Also, like Heidegger, Schutz conceived of the life-world (which he referred to variously as the 'natural attitude', the 'commonsense world' or the 'world of daily life') as a self-evident reality into which an individual is born and lives with others–an intersubjective, pre-reflexive, complete world which 'already includes, when our investigation starts, all the reasons for which understanding becomes necessary, and all the resources one may need in order to meet this necessity' (Bauman 1978: 175). This world, characterized by a common sense of reality and a taken-for-granted aspect, facilitates communication between persons.

To Schutz, the term 'taken-for-granted' means

> ...to accept until further notice our knowledge of certain states of affairs as unquestioningly plausible. Of course, at any time that which seemed to be hitherto unquestionable might be put into question. Common-sense thinking simply takes for granted, until counterevidence appears, not only the world of physical objects but also the sociocultural world into which we are born and in which we grow up. This world of everyday life is indeed the unquestioned but always questionable matrix within which all our enquiries start and end. (Schutz 1973: 316)

It follows that, in this taken-for-granted socio-cultural world, understanding plays a key part. Two significant issues arise from this: first, that 'understanding is not a philosophers' feat, as in Husserl. It is a human fate, as in Heidegger' (Bauman 1978: 176). Schutz's idea of *Vertsehen* is not just a methodological tool for the social scientists, but also an aspect of everyday life, a necessity and a task carried out by humans in their day to day interaction. It is, thus,

> ...a particular experiential form in which common-sense thinking takes cognizance of the sociocultural world. It has nothing to do with introspection; it is a result of processes of learning or acculturation in the same way as the common-sense experience of the so-called natural world. (Schutz 1973: 56)

The other issue which needs to be taken note of is the inter-subjectivity intrinsic to the conception of the *Lebenswelt* as a socio-cultural world. Implicit in this is the claim that the *Lebenswelt* is a shared world, in which we function under the assumption that it is the same for others, and interact with them accordingly. As Natanson puts it, 'The intersubjective world is the epistemic context for human action, the significative horizon in terms of which individuals, events, and even things are understood' (Natanson 1970: 104).

Dallmayr and McCarthy express dissatisfaction with Schutz's attempts to provide respective weight to subjective intention and action on the one hand and the social context on the other, in his elucidation of the philosophical grounding of the life-world. To them, Schutz's attempts do not resolve the question of whether 'the social world "originates" from the subjective intentions of individual actors [...] or is it an environment conditioning or constraining such intentions' (Dallamyr and McCarthy 1977: 221). This criticism misses the point. It is more reasonable to see Schutz's philosophy as attempting to demonstrate the dialectic between the subjective and the social, between individual intentions and socialization. This aspect of Schutz's work is elaborated and extended in Berger and Luckmann's *The Social Construction of Reality* (1966) in which society, on the one hand, is shown to exist in the individual consciousness as the subjective reality, before being objectified and reified into the objective external reality, while on the other hand, individuals become members of a society through a process of socialization by which they internalize social reality. What is significant in the present context is the suggestion that an individual's life-world is constituted by his/her own personal experiences, as well as by social meanings 'handed down' to him/her through social interaction. In Schutzian terms, the former results from the 'biographically determined situation' which provides the individual with a 'stock of knowledge'; whereas the latter is a socialized 'commonsense of knowledge of everyday life' which 'is from the outset [...] genetically socialized, because the greater part of our knowledge, as to its content and particular forms of typification under which it is organized, is socially derived, and this in socially approved terms' (Schutz 1973: 61). In 'Equality and the Meaning Structure of the Social World', he again stresses the social nature of the life-world:

> Man is born into a world that existed before his birth; and this world is from the outset not merely a physical, but also a socio-cultural one. The latter is a preconstituted and preorganized world whose particular structure is therefore different for each culture and society. (Schutz 1964: 229–230)

These socio-cultural structures are made up of various elements whose meaning and significance is taken-for-granted by those living within them. These 'folkways of the in-group [...] are taken for granted because they have stood the test so far, and, being socially approved, are held as requiring neither an explanation nor a justification' (Schutz 1964: 230).

The other, experiential element in the individual life-world must be stressed, since the conception of the *Lebenswelt* as a social world highlights the common sense of reality and privileges the intersubjective world as the context of action and understanding. Commentaries on Schutz commonly overlook the biographical–and therefore, to a certain extent, subjective and personal–aspect of the natural attitude. Natanson for instance, rightly underlines the historical features (reminiscent of Heidegger's conception of the Being as temporal) of the social world which 'does not spring magically into being with my birth or yours; it is historically grounded and bears the marks and signs of the activity of our ancestors, most remarkable of all the typifying medium of language' (Natanson 1970: 103). Similarly, Gurswitch (1970) argues that the life-world is 'interpreted, apperceived, and apprehended in a specific way; in a word, it is a cultural world, more precisely the cultural world of a certain socio-historical group, that of our society at the present moment in history' (1970: 50). While these writers are concerned with the social nature of the *Lebenswelt*, their omission of a proper discussion of the individual's biography makes its social context appear deterministic. Although the common sense of intersubjective or social reality provides the framework for all social action and communication, in Schutz's conception each person's everyday life has a unique quality, derived from his/her 'biographical situation', that is, the

> ...physical and socio-cultural environment as defined by him, within which he has his position, not merely his position in terms of physical space and outer time or his status and role within the social system but also his moral and ideological position. To say that this definition of the situation is biographically determined means to say that it has its history; it is the sedimentation of all of man's previous experiences, organized in the habitual possessions of his stock of knowledge, at hand, and as such his unique possession, given to him and him alone. (Schutz 1973: 9)

This is a crucial part of Schutz's social philosophy. It is through their different biographical situations that individuals absorb even the most stereotypical socially derived common interpretation. As Wagner (1970) points out, it is important to recognize that Schutz balanced a potentially deterministic and coercive conception of the 'givenness' of the life-world by emphasizing 'the subjective meanings of a person's membership in his community' (1970: 17). The biographical situation is therefore not deterministic, but generative.

Individuals interpret the world through a 'system of typifications and relevances' which are common to all the members of a community or group, providing them with a 'common relative natural conception of the world.' Schutz distinguishes between 'existential groups with which I share a common social heritage', the members of which are 'within a preconstituted system of typifications, relevances, roles, positions, statutes' handed down to them as 'a social heritage', and 'so-called voluntary groups joined or formed by me' whose 'system is not experienced by the individual member as ready-made; it has to be built up by the members and is therefore always involved in a process of dynamic evolution' (Schutz

1964: 252). Agreeing with Simmel's conceptualization of the individual, standing at the intersection of several social circles, some of which could be 'voluntary' groups, Schutz emphasizes the relative freedom of the member of such voluntary groups 'that he may choose for himself which part of his personality he wants to participate in group memberships; that he may define his situation within the role of which he is the incumbent' (Schutz 1964: 254). Two crucial issues arise from this argument: first, as Wagner observes, this strongly indicates, on a general level, that 'Schutz mediated between the primary sphere of immediate human experience and the derived spheres of preestablished cultural interpretation' (Wagner 1970: 25); and second, on a more particular level, the notion of the individual personality inhabiting several social matrices simultaneously precludes its easy deterministic marking and the prediction of its behaviour along 'classic' sociological variables.

It is in this context that Schutz's insight on 'multiple realities' must be understood. Building on William James's treatment of the various 'sub-universes' or 'orders of reality' in which a person lives, Schutz brought the argument into a sociological frame, replacing James's terms with his own *finite provinces* of meaning upon each of which we may bestow the accent of reality. We speak of provinces of meaning and not sub-universes because it is the meaning of our experiences and not the ontological structure of the objects which constitutes reality' (Schutz 1973: 230). These meanings are, to the experiencing individual, unquestionably real, but each province is incompatible with the others since, according to Schutz, it is characterized by its own peculiar cognitive style; transformation from one province to another is affected through a Kierkegaardian 'leap' or 'shock'. The world of dreams, of play, of science, of religion, are all given as examples of such provinces, but to Schutz, the 'paramount reality' on which is anchored a person's orientation to the world, is the reality of everyday life: 'the world of working in daily life is the archetype of our experience of reality. All other provinces of meaning may be

considered as its modifications' (Schutz 1973: 233). Parallel-
ing this conception of an individual's life-world as containing
multiple realities is the notion that culture, as intersubjective
meanings, is also a varied entity. As Carey observes: 'Culture
[...] is never singular and equivocal. It is, like nature itself,
multiple, various, and varietal. It is this for each of us. Therefore, we must begin, following Schutz, from the assumption of
multiple realities' (Carey 1989: 65).

Schutz's thesis could be extended to suggest that an individual's interpretation of his/her life-world is defined by his/her
existence and experience within the ever-widening circles in
whose intersections he/she resides–from the familial to the
cultural, including occupation/work, education, gender, religion, and so on. Each of these spheres of relevance contributes to the shaping of the social reality of the individual, both
as the given and experiential stock of knowledge, thereby
contributing to his/her subjective identity. It follows that, all
these 'worlds' constitute the ultimate grounding of the system of relevances that guides the life of the individual. To try
to define a person solely according to his/her class, for example, or religion, however strong a part these might play
in the shaping of their life-world, is to squeeze them into a
reductionist straitjacket which neglects their other provinces
of existence. A person's life-world, his/her personal history
or historicity arises out of a uniquely sedimented subjectivity, formed, not only by the prefigured, 'existential' world into
which he/she was born, but also by his/her personal experiences, and therefore does not necessarily correlate with such
strict compartments.

This is not to overemphasize the personal and the subjective at the cost of neglecting the social. The life-world is
predominantly a social world. While individuals define their
worlds according to their own experiences, they are nevertheless rooted in an intersubjective reality, suspended in a web
of significance. In a sense, each of the 'domains of relevance'
which make up a person's world is an intersubjective community with various gradations–from the universal to the

cultural through to the familial, each being defined and bound by a common world-view.

One question remains: how do the multifarious private experiences and interpretations in any collective community combine to form a common sense knowledge? Schutz emphasizes upon the members of a community using the same standard expressions and formulations when expressing the shared view of the preorganized world of daily life, thus arriving at, and maintaining, a collective self-identity and self-interpretation—'the folkways of the in-group'. The experience and creation of various forms of communication are a significant part of this common life-world, and must find their meaning within this world. Within the terms of the phenomenological hermeneutics, communication becomes 'the medium of human existence as intersubjectivity, that is, as belonging together with others in a community' (Grossberg and Christians 1981: 73). With this, we return to Carey's idea of ritual view communication, in which it 'is a symbolic process whereby reality is produced, maintained, repaired, and transformed' (Carey 1989: 23).

In this chapter, by using the Schutzian re-interpretation of the concept of the life-world, together with his notion of multiple realities, we have seen how it is possible to escape the deterministic constraints of conventional sociological variables. The individual's socio-cultural context is still, within Schutz's phenomenological sociology, profoundly social. However, with the reconstruction of the life-world as containing elements from the experiential as well as the existential, the biographical as well as the historical aspects of a person's life, the social context becomes richly varied. The concept of multiple realities offers a further improvement on this refinement of classical norms by positing the individual not within watertight compartments, but at the intersection of several circles of relevance. Understanding and interpretation, as all other human behaviour, are still socially derived, but their investigation requires a more complex elucidation of contexts than those offered by conventional variables.

Thus far, in Chapters 3 and 4, I have attempted to isolate and examine two of the concepts identified in Chapter 2– 'understanding' and 'context'–in an effort to comprehend how social situatedness influences interpretation, while at the same time avoiding deterministic formulations. The next chapter presents an exploration of the documentary 'genre', in order to add the question of mediated communication to the issue of the sociology of interpretive practices.

5

Documentary Meanings and Public Knowledge

Reality has always been interpreted through the reports given by images; and philosophers since Plato have tried to loosen our dependence on images by evoking the standard of an image-free way of apprehending the real [...] The images that have virtually unlimited authority in modern society are mainly photographic images; and the scope of that authority comes from the properties peculiar to images taken by cameras.

Susan Sontag, 'On Photography'

The third term identified in Chapter 2, as in need of unpacking and examination, is 'genre'. In the context of this study, the genre, which is of specific interest, is the documentary. This chapter examines the specific modalities of the documentary representation which marks it as different from its fictional counterpart, and which supports its claims to authenticity and truth. In particular, it appraises the documentary claim in terms of whether it is intrinsic to the text itself, or a cultural convention. Within the broader project of this book, the implications of this argument are twofold: first, they involve first, the 'horizon of expectation' which the viewer brings to the documentary text, and which depends on the belief, doubt or outright denial of documentary's truth claims. Second, documentary's perceived difference from the fictional genres, its appeal to the viewer as non-fiction and the corollary invitation to consider its relations with the non-media world as one of reflection rather than a fictional reconstruction, together constitute its apparent role in informing the public and thereby contributing to the public sphere.

The recent increase in the popularity of the genre, as evidenced in the distribution of the latest documentaries in the cinemas, and the critical reflection they have attracted, attest to this dimension of the documentary as the purveyor of 'truth', whose interventions in the mediated public sphere is of a different order from that of feature films. Non-fiction films, such as *An Inconvenient Truth, Sicko, Fahrenheit 9/11, The 11th Hour* and *The War on Democracy*[1] have had cinema releases recently, as a consequence of which, the perception of documentaries as potential revenue generators has profoundly modified the genre's potential to attract funding. Similarly, cinema releases of documentaries have changed its availability for audiences, thereby transforming its status from a largely television genre, attracting minority audiences, to being films in their own right and with a wider appeal that has increased its social position as a serious genre contributing to public discussions of significant issues.

In terms of audience responses, however, the ambivalence of documentaries as texts persists in constructing diverse positions. As we shall see in this chapter, the textual features of documentaries themselves reveal a close connection with those of fiction, so much so that Renov (2004) describes fiction and non-fiction as 'representational domains that are enmeshed in each other' (2004: 22). If on the level of narrative, the documentary displays affinities with its fictional counterpart, and vice versa, since feature films have increasingly started utilizing documentary or news footage style images as a stylistic device, the difference between them seems to rest largely in

---

[1]Produced respectively by Al Gore (2006), Michael Moore (2007) and (2004), Leonardo DiCaprio (2007) and John Pilger (2007).

audience anticipations. The perception of the documentary's claim to truth is, therefore, a crucial dimension of the interpretive exercise, as audience responses are, as we shall see in our discussion of the data, influenced by their acceptance or rejection of the genre's claims regarding its relationship with the external world.

Documentary as non-fiction

The status of the documentary as non-fiction, as with the other members of the family, such as news and current affairs, elevates it above narrative fiction in the hierarchy of truth in cinematic representation (Winston 1978/79: 3, see also Winston 2000). Grierson's introduction of the term 'documentary' as the adjectival form of 'document' was perhaps intended to signify a new role for the cinema to factually and authentically record reality (Ellis 1989: 4). Both the term and the meaning have stuck, although, as we shall see later in the chapter, it raises philosophical, ethical and aesthetic questions concerning the nature of the documentary discourse and the authenticity of cinematic representation. As Barnouw (1983: 315) argues, the documentary film-maker is assumed to merely select and record images in order to reveal the 'truth', rather than, as does the fictional artist, invent them. This is, of course, a loaded assumption and needs to be unpacked to reveal the precariousness of the status of the documentary as the purveyor of truth, performing the socially acknowledged role of providing information and knowledge. However, the documentary certainly appears to gain its legitimacy from its truth claims; the cinematic equivalent to the essay, the travelogue or piece of reportage, it implicitly directs the viewer to accept its credibility either as an objective account of 'what is going on', or in some cases as the deliberate, reflexive account of the film-maker. The poetics of the documentary is largely one of direct address, and its unfolding either follows or deliberately overturns established conventions of the genre. Realistic or naturalistic, these conventions attempt to smooth over the obvious, inevitable constructedness of the film, and to present its content as 'transparently' as possible. 'Documentaries have regularly sought to present audiences with accounts in which the viewed is to be taken as effectively indistinguishable from the real' (Corner and Richardson 1986: 141). The authority of the documentary, therefore, derives from this transparency; while expository devices make it recognizable as documentary –its credibility is dependent on its successful mimesis.

In this chapter, I shall discuss briefly the nature of the documentary practice and its textual characteristics. I initiate the discussion with an elaboration on what I consider the ambivalence of the documentary: its invocation of authenticity and credibility of its discourse coexists with the inevitability of its narrativity. This paradox informs the diegetic and the mimetic elements of the documentary text, which is, I shall argue, following Nichols (1981, 1991), in its expository form profoundly rhetorical in the Aristotelian sense. The chapter concludes with a brief account of the documentary's 'positioning' of the viewer, and the implications of the characteristics of the genre to the process of viewing and meaning construction.

Despite the relative paucity of theoretical work in the field of documentary film and television–a state of affairs alluded to by Nichols (1981, 1991) and Renov (1993), and originating, as Nichols points out (1981: 172), from its marginalization by Metz, resulting in the inadequacy of definition–one of the main characteristics which has been identified as specific to non-fictional cinematic representation is its truth claims. Documentaries claim to reveal the truth about a particular aspect of the socio-historical world, and they do so dispassionately and objectively. While the objective nature of this depiction has been challenged, restated and denied by theorists and film-makers, and has simultaneously acted as a catalyst to the creative ways in which the film-maker has sought to either suppress his or her own subjectivity, or to deliberately draw the audience's attention to it, the status of documentary as qualitatively different from fiction film in its attempt to reproduce the 'real' has been generally recognized. As Silverstone rightly suggests,

'Television documentary claims a conformity with reality; the label documentary is itself a guarantee of authority and truth' (1983: 146).

In its exposition, the documentary normally employs a narrative not altogether different from the classic narrative structure of a fiction film. Both forms of moving image obey the grammar and semantics of cinematic language; the documentary generating its meaning primarily through conventions of naturalism and realism (Silverstone 1986; Collins 1986). Some styles of documentary film-making, as indeed some styles of fiction film, self-consciously disavow naturalistic conventions, employing, instead, Brechtian breaks of narrative and self reflexivity, as in *Chronicle of a Summer, The Man with the Movie Camera* and *The Thin Blue Line*,[2] in which the film-makers deliberately draw the viewer's attention to the processes of realist representation and its unproblematic access to the world in order to critique it. But the 'believability' in the authenticity of the film is still paramount, and truth claims are only strengthened through these methods. At the level of narrativity and representation, therefore, the classic documentary is not dissimilar to its fictional counterpart. It is difficult to disagree with Rosen's (1993) conclusion that narrativity links both non-fiction and fiction to historical discourse. They speak the same language using the similar syntactic forms.

The discourse of the documentary, therefore, straddles two domains: in its ontological claims it privileges the 'truth', while its aesthetic is strongly narrative in character. Documentaries are in a sense 'true stories', and their poetics resonate with the ambiguities contained in that oxymoron. The true, the real, the factual constitute the subject matter of the documentary. In Tretyakov's words, 'pure documentary is the editing of facts simply in terms of their actuality and social significance' (Williams 1980: 117). The concept of 'pure' documentary 'disappears' for

---

[2] *Chronicle of a Summer*, directed by J.Rouch and E.Moran (1961); *The Man with the Movie Camera*, directed by Z.Vertov (1929); *The Thin Blue Line*, directed by E.Morris (1991).

him when a recorded fact is used to 'construct' a narrative—
the factual loses its authenticity. Montage is ruled out,
and with it, Vertov's work ceases to be pure documentary.
Tretyakov's view embodies the documentary paradox: even
granted that the capturing by the camera of the social action
(a 'fact') retains an element of authenticity, any manipulation of the image by the film-maker, which disrupts the flow
of the single, uninterrupted shot, disturbs the 'purity' of the
image based on the Bazinian aesthetic of photography as an
embalming of time. And yet, editing and montage are necessary in the interest of narrativity. Documentaries are seldom
one-shot units. The norm is a sequence of shots edited together following established conventions of narrative film and
television, designed to present a story. Narrativity is certainly
'an expository option for the documentary film' (Renov 1993:
2), so much so that the documentary shares many discursive
characteristics with the fiction film. As Renov suggests, 'non-
fiction contains any number of "fictive" elements, moments at
which a presumably objective representation of the world encounters the necessity of creative invention' (1993). In a more
recent book, Renov (2004) builds on these insights to argue
that the documentary necessarily, and not merely as a coin-
cidence, shares the tropic or figurative aspect of all discursive
forms. Moreover, the documentary's unavoidable utilization
of fictive characteristics is reciprocated in fictional forms:

> ...while some fiction, and much advertising imagery, does indeed ex-
> ploit documentary's 'lure of authenticity' through a cunning appropria-
> tion of particular tactics or stylistic traits (use of 'witnesses'; the low-
> tech look, shaky camera; grainy, out-of-focus images), nonfiction itself
> displays a number of 'fictive elements'–instances of style, structure, and
> expositional strategy that draw on preexistent (fictional) constructs or
> schemata to establish meanings and effects for audiences. (Renov 2004:
> 22)

Renov suggests that poetic language in narration, music to
heighten moods and characters as ideal-types are aspects of
fictive elements in the documentary.

The blurring of 'truth' and fiction becomes more pronounced in the case of news footage. As I argued in a recent

essay (Harindranath 2004) on the reporting of the Jessica Lynch's 'rescue' by American soldiers from a hospital in the Iraqi town of Nasiriyah during the early part of the Iraq war, what the story exemplified is the potential threat to the credibility of television news,

> ...brought on by a distinctly and politically biased representation of an event whose textual characteristics share more with the Hollywood narrative than with 'objective' news. By merging the narrative of conventional news with that of mainstream Hollywood, the Lynch story, as it was initially depicted, borrowed from mainstream film the tropes of 'good' and 'evil', 'heroes' and 'villains', in a simplistic Manichean dichotomy. (Harindranath 2004: 34)

Particularly significant in this context is the staging of the allegedly 'live' coverage of the night-time 'rescue' of Lynch, captured on night-vision camera and edited into a five minute film by the Pentagon for release to the networks. During this, the military camera person captured a 'live' event which was largely staged for viewers at home. As one of the doctors in the Nasiriyah hospital tellingly commented later, 'It was like a Hollywood film. They cried "Go, go, go", with guns and blanks and the sound of explosions. They made a show—an action movie like Sylvester Stallone or Jackie Chan, with jumping and shouting, breaking open doors' while the hand-held cameras rolled.[3] The *Washington Post* ran a different version of the story a few days later, which questioned the veracity of the television footage, but what is noteworthy here was the blurring of the veridical and the fictional.

The blurring of boundaries between fictional and non-fictional representation is most evident in the documentaries of Flaherty, whose attempts to 'stage' profilmic events, albeit with social actors, is still considered controversial with regard to the authenticity and truth claims of his work. His attempts at

---

[3]A detailed report By John Kampfner on the making of the Jessica Lynch story is available on-line at www.media.guardian.co.uk/broadcast/ comment. The print version appeared in *The Guardian* on 15 May, 2003.

historical reconstruction 'pose special problems since that which was is re-presented as that which is' (Nichols 1981). Documentary dramas, reconstructing historical events using professional actors, underline the ambiguity even further. How far can *Thatcher, the Final Days*,[4] based on a script put together from reports culled after the real event, be said to be a 'true' portrayal of the events in 10, Downing Street during that fateful period? The documentary aspect of such drama derives from close approximation, in their reconstruction, to historical events; while the dramatic aspect, including the performance of the actors, serves to remind us of the discursive (fundamentally narrative) elements shared by all moving image representations. Renov's cautioning against ignoring the fictive, and therefore the creative, elements of non-fiction film is rooted in his argument that 'documentary shares the status of all discursive forms with regards to its tropic or figurative character in that it employs many of the methods and devices and methods of its fictional counterpart' (1993: 3), and points to the 'creative invention' and intervention on the part of the film-maker. Quite apart from the utilization of camera angles and movements, lighting, non-diegetic music, continuity editing and so on, which form the core of narrative structures common to both fiction and non-fiction films, these forms share a similarity of a more fundamental level: 'both are artefacts; both are contrivances [...] both, wittingly or not, embody a viewpoint. [Even] the fact that one eschews and the other employs professional actors becomes in the end an economic detail' (A. Schlesinger Jr quoted in Winston 1978: 4). The documentary text, in its structural as well as its narrative style, shares several characteristics with its fictional counterpart, and thus the boundary between non-fiction and fiction as texts is tenuous indeed. It is, therefore, tempting to treat the documentary and its derivatives as fiction like other cinematic discourses. Despite their best intentions, those seeking the holy grail of documentary purity, through techniques of direct cinema and cinema verite, have

---

[4]Directed by T. Sullivan (1991).

also had to contend with questions involving the actors' (social or professional) performance, the presence of the camera and its use and editing. Fictive elements, conventions from more overtly narrative genres challenge the documentary's position as non-fiction.

In order to unscramble the confusion regarding the status of non-fiction, one is consequently required to look at features other than the strictly textual. For Renov, the unmeshing of fictional and non-fictional forms happens at the level of the sign: 'it is the different historical status of the referent that distinguishes documentary from its fictional counterpart, not the formal relations among signified, signifier, and referent' (Renov 1993). By offering access to the 'real' world, or professing to do so, the documentary reaches outside itself in its claim to authenticity, unlike the fiction film, whose credibility lies within its textual, created world and the outside reality is closed off through calls for willing suspension of disbelief. Fiction derives its logic from its internal consistencies of plot, character and narrative, whereas documentary's existence is dependent upon the accuracy of its representation of the historical world. As V.F. Perkins suggests, the distinction is between authenticity and credibility:

> ...it is important that we avoid confusing credibility with authenticity. The question of authenticity simply does not arise when we enter a fictional world. There is no actuality against which we can check images derived from *One Million Years BC* or *2001*.[5] But the image must be credibly derived from the created world in order to maintain its reality. (Williams 1980)

Due to the 'historical nature of its referent', however, the documentary can and does claim the status of an authentic representation of the external world. The 'truth' of this depiction draws on the viewers' awareness of and familiarity with the world referred to in the film. The measure of its authenticity

---

[5] *One million Years BC,* directed by D.Chaffey (1967); *2001,* directed by S.Kubrick (1968).

lies the approximation to historical reality, and the credibility in the documentary and other non-fiction forms derives its force not just from the 'created world' of the text, but also, and more significantly, from its association with the world it represents. Despite its inevitable fictional elements, the documentary stands apart from the fictional representation through its avowed appropriation and reflection of the real world, and consequently its social relevance.[6]

Documentary's link with the external world raises a number of allied questions concerning the role of the film-maker, the format of representation and viewer expectancy:

> The issues of the filmmaker's control over what she or he films and of the ethics of filming social actors whose lives, though represented in the film, extend well beyond it; the issues of the text's structure, and the question of the viewers' activity and expectations - these three angles from which definitions of documentary begin (filmmaker, text, viewer) also suggest important ways in which documentary is a fiction unlike any other [...] Documentary offers access to a shared historical construct. Instead of a world, we are offered access to the world. (Nichols 1991: 109)

Renov (1993) identifies the first of the documentary's 'constitutive modalities–its conditions of existence' as the desire to 'reveal/record/preserve'–a function fuelled by the 'mimetic drive common to all cinema', derived from the antecedent properties of photographic representation. To him, behind the status of the documentary is the exploitation of the cinema's power to reveal, which only rarely acknowledges its representational function. It exploits the photograph's near transparent iconic nature by which it is often accorded a one-to-one relationship with the object it represents. The process through which the real is transfigured is seldom declared. This collapse of sign and historical referent in photographic representation is certainly fundamental to the 'truth claim which persists

---

[6]Donald Alexander's assertion that documentary fulfils 'a crying social need' to have 'a coherent picture of how humanity lives and works today' (Alexander 1945: 3) is based implicitly on the documentary's perceived social relevance and didactic qualities.

within documentary discourse as a defining definition ("what you see and hear is of the world").'

Veridicality in documentary representation

Sontag's (1982) characteristically eclectic discussion of the nature of photographic images and their place in the creation of knowledge in contemporary society invokes arguments which reflect our belief in the capacity of the moving image to capture and depict 'reality' objectively. In her view photography is particularly effective in 'usurping' the real world because, while painting, however accurate the depiction may be, is the artist's interpretation of reality, the chemical/mechanical processes of photographic image production escape the subjective hand:

> ...a photograph is not only an image (as a painting is an image), an interpretation of the real; it is also a trace, something directly stenciled off the real, like a footprint or a death mask [...] [A] photograph is never less than the registration of an emanation (light waves reflected by objects)–a material vestige of its subject in a way no painting can be.'
> (Sontag 1982: 350)

In her deliberate invocation of Bazin's view of the ontology of the photographic image, Sontag underlines the contentious aspect of such images, which, by extension can be seen to underlie debates concerning the authenticity of documentaries: do they depict 'reality the way it is', or do they involve artifice and the artful representation of that reality, which is transformed by the inevitable process of selection by the filmmaker and by the narrative conventions of the genre? How far do chemical/electronic processes of image appropriation and retention mask the process of mediation, undermining the referential, iconic nature of the photographic sign?

Bazin's own pronouncement on the ontological status of the photograph goes beyond its ability to capture reality to a much stronger claim which treats it as identical to the physical object itself:

> The photographic image is the object itself, the object freed from the conditions of time and space that govern it. No matter how fuzzy, distorted, or discoloured, no matter how lacking in documentary value the image may be, it shares, by virtue of the very process of its becoming, the being of the model of which it is the reproduction; it *is* the model. (quoted in Renov 1993: 22–23)

Bazin's rhetorical, affective declaration of the status of the image apropos the real–which negates the distance between the sign and its referent, collapsing one into the other–points towards the culturally motivated, learnt attitude to the photographic image. As Sontag puts it, 'The powers of photography have in effect de-Platonised our understanding of reality' (1982: 367). The copy corresponds with the original. The profusion of images and our reliance upon them have undermined the gap between the shadow and the real–in effect the shadow is the real. The culture of cinematic production and consumption is dependent upon, among other things, this coalescence of the iconic sign and its historical referent.

However, as Tagg (1988) points out, the iconic nature of the photographic image is in itself no guarantee of its truthfulness. The 'causative link between the pre-photographic event and the sign,' he argues, is the result of a process which combines technical, cultural and historical factors (Introduction *passim*). The chemically induced two-dimensional representation on the paper does not, by itself, produce meaning, nor is it a trace of reality, a momentary slice of time. The photographic process is

> ...the production of a new and specific reality, the photograph, which becomes meaningful in certain transactions and has real effects, but which cannot refer or be referred to a prephotographic reality as to a truth. The photograph is not a magical 'emanation' but a material apparatus set to work in specific contexts, by specific forces, for more or less defined purposes. It requires, therefore, not an alchemy, but a history. (Tagg 1988: 3)

The meaning of a photograph is thus not an existential fact, but arises from complex semiotic processes. The physical existence of the photograph is independently not a guarantor of truth and meaning. Signification and authenticity involve socially, culturally, historically embedded discursive processes.

The truth claims of the documentary are, therefore, precariously balanced, in a fundamental way, on the ontological ambivalence of the photograph. As Vaughan (1986) observes,

> Film is neither raw world nor a symbolic description of the world. It is a representation of the world which gains the status of a simulacrum from the trust which our culture accords the photograph. This 'trust' derives from our recognition of the photograph as a trace, an index, of some prior entity. But the iconic property does not in itself entail anything we would acknowledge as adequate representation, as resemblance. (Vaughan 1986: 170)

This 'trust' is misplaced, Vaughan argues, since the grounds on which the photograph is considered neutral are extremely shaky: 'even if the camera is graphically innocent, our eye is not'. The moving image, with all its different shot sizes and camera movements, underlines further this lack of neutrality. Again, our acceptance or rejection of the images as actuality is clearly tied to our 'cultural, ideological, and individual contributions.'

The authenticity of the documentary discourse is consequently called into question. In her impassioned critique of the acceptance of the documentary as speaking the truth, Minh-ha (1993) remonstrates that 'There is no such thing as a documentary [...] This assertion needs incessantly to be restated despite the very visible existence of the documentary tradition' (1993: 90). Challenging the aesthetic of objectivity that props up the documentary's *raison d'etre* as a purveyor of real life situations and lived histories—'facts' and 'truth'—Minh-ha claims that:

> Truth, even when 'caught on the run', does not yield itself either in names or in (filmic) frames; and meaning should be prevented from coming to closure at what is said and what is shown. Truth and meaning: the two are likely to be equated with one another. Yet, what is put forth as truth is often nothing more than *a* meaning. (Minh-ha 1993: 92)

The concern for Minh-ha is political, constructed in the post-colonial discourse, but it stems from the ambiguity inherent in documentary poetics: the representation of the real world. In its essentially referential nature, the documentary, as any other form of representation, can, at the most claim, only to present a perspective. As Minh-ha points out, the 'interval' between the profilmic event and the meaning needs to be addressed.

The claims made on behalf of the photographic image, and the debates surrounding them, reach an apogee with documentary television and film. The orthodoxies of the genre bring into play what Wilson (1993), calls the 'veridical effect', which he prefers to terms such as naturalism and realism, because of 'their ambiguous philosophical and literary past and present' (1993: 112). While Wilson's argument is tied to production practices and visual cues in television, his basic thesis can be formulated in terms of the truth claims of the documentary: 'Denying their status as selective appropriation of meaning, veridical images resist a reading as other than truthful accounts of the world by a viewer whose horizons of expectations has been easily confirmed' (1993: 108), thereby, masking the human and social agency and enabling a 'visual registering of image content sutured into place in a near seamless and transparent flow.' In its self-conscious manifestation as a form of 'non-fiction', the documentary genre presents itself as diametrically opposed to its fictional counterparts in its claims to present unaltered aspects of the real world. Underlying this claim is the belief in the capacity of the camera to capture reality–pristine and without distortion or interpretation by the artist. Vertov's assertion that the documentary seeks to apprehend and display meaningful combinations of 'fragments of actuality', and Grierson's frequently cited definition of the documentary as 'the creative treatment of actuality' (quoted in Barnouw 1983: 313) illustrate the claims of the documentary discourse, built around the concept of the photograph as neutral and objective. As Tagg comments, the term 'documentary came to denote a discursive formation which was wider than photography alone, but which appropriated photographic technology to a central and privileged place within its rhetoric of immediacy and truth' (1988: 8).

Significantly it is the very 'rhetoric of immediacy and truth' that sets apart the documentary and its derivatives like the newsreel and political broadcasts from the fiction film and television. As pointed out earlier, the status of the documentary as the objective representation of reality is problematic. Notions of objectivity, truth, reality and representation cannot be accepted at face value and need to be explored in greater detail. The documentary's ontological anchorage in the real—from which emanates its truth claims—requires closer scrutiny. However, our present concern is slightly removed from such philosophical speculation, and is more towards the investigation of the truth claims of the documentary discourse and its dialectical relationship with the viewer.

While, as we have seen, the documentary shares many discursive characteristics with the fictional representation, it is still recognizably different in style and presentation. That both are constructions can be of little doubt. For instance, it is difficult, as Renov points out, to distinguish between 'the documentary performance-for-the-camera of a musician, actor, or politician (*Don't Look Back, Jane, Primary*) from that of a fictional counterpart (*The Doors, On Golden Pond, The Candidate*)' (Renov 1993).[7] Renov stresses this point in order to remind us that, the view that documentary is 'the "film of fact", "non-fiction" the realm of information and exposition rather than diegetic employment or imagination', could underplay its aesthetic and creative aspects.

The truth claims of the documentary and other non-fiction film and television, riding on various rhetorical devices, derive from this logic of information.

---

[7] *Don't Look Back,* directed by D.A.Pennabaker (1966); *Jane,* directed by D.A.Pennabaker and R.Leacock (1962); *Primary,* directed by D.A. Pennabaker and R.Leacock (1960); *Doors,* directed by O.Stone (1991); *On Golden Pond,* directed by M.Rydell (1991); *The Candidate,* directed by M.Ritchie (1972).

> If we consider the imaginary realm of fiction as having a metaphoric
> relation to history and lived experience - as a kind of carefully shaped,
> translucent cloud that displays contours and shapes, patterns and prac-
> tices that closely resemble the ones we encounter in our own lives,
> we might think of documentary as a mode where the fictive cloud has
> settled back to earth. (Nichols 1991: 5)

Nichols (1991) makes another useful distinction between the
narratives of fiction and non-fiction as story-telling and argument respectively. While documentaries are as much narrative constructions as fiction films, they differ in their claim to
represent the historical world rather than to imitate it.

> In sum, documentary gives us photographic and aural representations
> or likeness of the world [...] [It] shares the properties of a text with
> other fictions—matter and energy are not at its immediate disposal—
> but it addresses the world in which we live rather than worlds in
> which we may imagine living. This may be partly a matter of con-
> ventions and expectations, but it makes a fundamental difference.
> (Nichols 1991: 111–12)

Although, the documentary text, in its constructedness, shares
qualities with fiction, documentaries are stories about the historical world told with evidence and argument, unlike the fictional representation, whose referent is an imaginary world.
This distinction has special significance in terms of both the
construction of the text as well as viewer expectancy and reception of it.

The rhetoric of documentary

Silverstone's (1983, 1986) convincing argument about the
presence of the mythic and the mimetic elements in television science documentary points towards the dual nature
of the documentary discourse that we have been discussing
so far. In its 'mythic' aspect, the documentary (not just science documentaries) follows generic conventions of narrative while presenting arguments and evidence about the historical world. Although Silverstone (1983: 138–139), in his

concern for the science documentary, identifies the cutting-edge nature of the content of these films as elevating them to the level of the 'heroic' and therefore the mythical, it is not too difficult to locate the 'heroic' in documentaries that deal with themes other than science. While science documentaries undoubtedly perform the function of 'the transformation of another reality unfamiliar perhaps, often threatening - into one that is both familiar and reassuring' (Silverstone 1983: 138); others elevate to the status of the heroic the everyday struggles of Everyman, in the process transforming their lives from the familiar to the strange.[8] While *Man of Aran*[9] is an obvious example in which the everyday is raised to the mythic, in a manner which recalls Hemingway, this is especially true of documentaries which depict lives of (or 'a day in the life of') cultural icons, present day 'heroes' (*Don't Look Back*) and of others in which the intrepid film-maker's quest, seeking the ultimate interview with the subject (as in *The Leader, the Driver, and His Wife*), or tracking down an elusive subject (as in *Roger and Me*) itself becomes the plot.[10]

The mimetic nature of the documentary[11]–what Nichols (1991) calls the 'iconic bind' of the documentary–is in a constant dialectic with the conventions of genre and narrative. As Silverstone (1986) demonstrates, the mythic and mimetic elements of the documentary discourse interweave argument and story, reason and emotion and contain (especially in science documentaries) the rhetoric of persuasion, as well as expressions of the film-maker's creativity. Such a conception of the documentary incorporates both the 'truth claims' as well

---

[8] I use this inversion deliberately with the intention to echo the common classification of science as making the strange familiar and philosophy as making the familiar strange, in order to distil from the taken-for-granted world timeless, immutable truths.

[9] Directed by R.Flaherty (1934).

[10] *The Leader, the Driver, and His Wife,* directed by N.Broomfield (1990); *Roger and Me,* directed by M.Moore (1989).

[11] 'Documentary is, almost by definition, concerned to depict reality. Documentary in this is therefore mimetic.' (Silverstone 1983: 139)

as the ineluctable fictive elements in non-fiction. As suggested earlier, although Silverstone's concern is with science, his arguments can easily be extrapolated to cover documentary discourse in general.

Wilson (1993) similarly argues for a case for the documentary as primarily mimetic.[12] His identification of drama as 'diegetic' and the documentary as 'mimetic', a distinction with which he seeks to oppose narrative and non-narrative, is predicated on the assumption that '[d]rama and documentary television assume different relationships between the text and the non-textual. Drama is first and foremost the production of a diegetic space and time constructed around narrative. Documentary, however, foregrounds a space and time employed in mimesis, a copying of the pretextual' (Wilson 1993). The selection of representational images in drama is therefore driven by narrative logic: 'in dramatic narratives the construction of the discursive precedes and determines the selective appropriation of the non-discursive' (Wilson 1993). Drama is construction, and dramatic discourse creative, imaginary, full of artifice. The documentary, on the other hand, privileges the real; it is description and showing rather than narration, in which images are functional, not to the 'requirements of narrative', but to facilitate the viewer to get acquainted with historical reality. 'Here [in documentary] the non-discursive precedes and determines the discursive' (Wilson 1993). Pretextual reality is paramount, while the actual processes of exposition and narration are geared towards appropriating and conveying this reality.

The severity of Wilson's demarcation of the dramaturgical and documentary spaces, while useful in highlighting some

---

[12]Wilson appears to have misread Silverstone's argument of the mythic and mimetic. Whereas the latter clearly indicates that '[i]n science documentary there is significant place for both the mythic and the mimetic' (Silverstone 1983: 139), identifying the corresponding narrative strategies as 'heroic' and 'natural historic', Wilson reads him as connecting mimetic with science (1993: 118).

of the specific features of the genre, does not take into account the ambivalence of documentary discursivity. As argued in the previous section, the documentary, far from being a seamless 'capturing' of external reality, is usually unfolded as narrative, utilizing various fictive elements. Wilson's observation regarding the documentary's concern with the pre-textual translates into Nichols's point about the documentary providing (or claiming to provide) access to the real world. However, Wilson's denial of the narrative elements in documentary[13] is to fall victim to the fallacy which was underlined by Renov: to consider the documentary as mere 'film of fact' is to be blind not only to its poetics,[14] but also (implicitly) to the ideological content of non-fiction. As Renov points out, 'A view of documentary which assumes too great a sobriety for non-fiction discourse will fail to comprehend the sources of non-fiction's deep-seated appeal' (Renov 1993). More significantly, ingenuous assumptions of the documentary as offering a transparent window on the world is to consider its content as the unmediated depiction of reality. It bears reiterating that the documentary does not deal directly with truth; it is, at best, only a perspective on reality.

The legitimacy of the documentary derives from its status as non-fiction, with its iconic potential linked to the historical rather than imaginary world. It has been argued (Nichols 1981; Renov 1993; Silverstone 1986) that the poetics of the documentary rides on the devices of rhetoric and persuasion. The thesis is stated simply enough: that the documentary 'truth' is not simply revealed; the modalities of the documentary include narration or exposition, implicit in which

---

[13]Wilson grudgingly admits to the possibility that documentary 'can be inflected by the narrative ambitions of entertainment, establishing in the process a diegesis with a varying degree of pretextual existence.' (1993: 121), but he seems to imply that this is a corruption of the documentary endeavour.

[14]Wilson's view echoes the sentiments expressed by Grierson's statement about the irreconcilability of historical representation and beautiful images in documentary: 'the trouble with realism is that it deals not in beauty but in truth.' (quoted in Renov 1993)

is rhetoric–rhetoric as embellishment and as persuasion, as ornament and as power (Silverstone 1986: 89–90). Renov, in his attempt to delineate a 'nascent poetics of the documentary' identifies four fundamental, overlapping modalities 'or rhetorical/aesthetic functions attributable to documentary practice' (1993). For him the 'governing discursive conditions' of documentary, the mode of delivery, crucially involves the instinct to persuade and to convince. This tendency is mostly obvious in films designed to achieve certain social goals, as in the case of 'John Grierson's camera hammering rather than mirroring society' (1993).

Rhetoric as the primary principle in the documentary exposition is drawn out most clearly by Nichols (1981: 172–182, 1991: 134–141). Building on his thesis that 'argument about the world, or representation in the sense of placing evidence before others in order to convey a particular viewpoint, forms the organizational backbone of documentary' (Nichols 1991: 125), and counterpointing the 'documentary logic' in non-fiction to the 'narrative coherence' in fiction, Nichols borrows from the Aristotelian 'proofs' of rhetoric to demonstrate the rhetorical devices of the classic documentary exposition. The most direct way of providing a convincing argument is through evidence, 'factual material recruited to the argument' (Nichols 1991: 134), which Aristotle classifies as 'inartistic' (Nichols 1981: 174). This comes in the form of witness accounts, support from documents and so on, which Nichols implies is most evident in 'indirect address' documentaries (observational cinema),[15] but I would argue, is used intermittently in all forms of documentary and other non-fiction, including news and current affairs. Evidence (or what purports to be evidence) is the life blood of argument and rhetoric, and 'expository cinema' derives its authority principally from

---

[15]In his later work Nichols expands the notion of direct and indirect address to include expository, observational (a term he prefers to cinema verite and direct cinema), interactive and reflexive modes of representation (1991: 32–76).

evidential support in various forms. To Nichols (1981: 174), all three forms of Aristotle's second category of proofs, 'artistic', are evident in documentary:

1. ethical–dependent upon the audience's estimation of the speaker's moral character or credibility as a function of exposition;
2. emotional–dependent upon the speaker's appeal to the audience's emotions to produce a certain disposition;
3. demonstrative–dependent upon the exposition's recourse to real or apparent demonstration. (Nichols 1981)

While Nichols illustrates this by discussing television news as typified in a Walter Cronkite report, it is possible–and in the context of this study necessary–to examine it vis-a-vis the documentary. The discussion borrows from and slightly modifies, and perhaps even corrupts, Silverstone's (1986) classification of the dimensions of television rhetoric: 'look, image, voice, music' (1986: 92).

The classic expository documentary, in terms of its ethical proof, is grounded on the 'Voice of God' commentary. The voice-over/commentary plays a central role in expository documentary: it provides the 'didactic orientation toward an argument. Commentary guides our grasp of the moral, political view of the world offered by the documentary text' (Nichols 1991: 129) and contextualizes, what is seen and heard, in terms of the overall perspective of the film. Less pragmatically, the voice carries authority, both in terms of the possession of knowledge (and therefore implicitly, control over the film), and through the exercise of verbal and paralinguistic features. An uncomplicated, conversational language, which breaks down complex topics into a less threatening body of information, spoken by a 'good' voice, whose qualities are commonly assumed to include not only a pleasing pitch, but also the undefinable characteristic of friendliness, sincerity and authority, complements the content of the commentary. The use of well known anchors or presenters–David Attenborough is a famous example–accentuates the ethical proof. The authority of Attenborough, riding on assumed expertise and knowledge which authenticates the images of even the most unusual animal (and more recently plant) behaviour, is given added fillip by his tone of voice and appearance: avuncular, kind and wise. The presenter's presence foregrounds the generic properties of the documentary as non-fiction; it usurps the narrative from the realms of the diegetic and fictional and presents it as argument and exposition. The logical principle, which unites and arranges the various parts of what Nichols (1981) calls 'direct address' documentary film, derives from the presenter, the voice over, or the commentary. The verbal sound track, therefore, assumes the dominant position, in terms of both exposition as well as the organizing principle. 'Hence the criteria for argument developed elsewhere (in formal logic and rhetoric) can to a large degree be applied as tests of the coherence of narration' (Nichols 1981: 199).

Emotional proof in the documentary, and significantly, in television documentary, emanates from two sources: images and music. Some of the aspects of the final, complete film are determined by the profilmic event and the subject matter; the appearance and content of the film are also dependent, to some extent, on decisions made during the planning stage, prior to filming. The process of gathering the material–visual, verbal and aural (as in location sounds)–is clearly contingent upon these decisions, and this material obviously goes into the final film. However, as Silverstone (1986) observes, 'most of the work of film-making is done in the cutting room' (1986: 97). In any kind of film-making, the editing process plays a significant role, not dissimilar to that of the construction of sentences in verbal discourse: it provides the syntactic and semantic aspects of cinematic representation. The creative potential is enormous, since it is in the editor's hands that a stock of asynchronous rushes are ordered to conform to temporal and spatial requirements of narrative, and acquire rhythm and meaning. In the documentary, this process follows, not only the logic of information and argument, but can, at the connotative level (and often quite overtly), signal 'a move away from the mimetic toward the mythic, and away from arguments towards a story' (Silverstone 1986) and towards rhetoric. Appeal to the viewer's emotional disposition 'is often assigned to compelling images in television news, to music in some documentaries, and to juxtapositions that attach feelings of empathy or repulsion to subjects in a novel way' (Nichols 1991: 135), although, the use of compelling images is by no means restricted to news alone. Documentaries exploit the common ethical and political ground between the speaker and the viewer by utilizing emotionally telling images[16].

Nichols (1981, 1991) indicates that the documentary's employment of demonstrative proof often poses a threat to its claims of authenticity and truth. The demonstrative proof is the site of ideology, where the pragmatics of rhetoric transgresses the boundaries of argument in the move towards persuasion. Evidence forms the backbone of this proof, and in the documentary this comes in the form of witness accounts, expert opinions, and so on. This is also the space where the documentary leaves itself open to contention, since evidence ('real or apparent demonstration'), which serves to support the argument, must be distinguished from proofs of objective truth: 'our acceptance of demonstrations of truth will depend upon the demonstrator's rhetorical skill and our own assumptions rather than procedures of a necessary and sufficient logic' (Nichols 1981: 179). In the pragmatic drive towards persuasion, authenticity is put at risk. Lack of correlation between the viewer's assumptions or political predispositions, and those of the producer results in the film being accused of bias.

As in Renov's taxonomy of the modalities of the documentary, it must be stressed here that this demarcation of the three Aristotelian 'proofs', in terms of the documentary discourse and the various aspects of that discourse that contribute to them, must be seen as an attempt to ascertain the rhetorical

---

[16] This is illustrated quite powerfully in at least two of the films included in this study, *Chain of Tears* and *Whose Children*. The latter also demonstrates the use of specific music on the sound track designed to highlight, through irony, specific images with which it is juxtaposed.

impulse underlying the documentary, and not as functional straitjackets. The discursive elements mentioned here, as contributing to specific proofs, are often conducive to the realization of more than one proof. Interviews with the witnesses, 'social actors' or 'characters' for instance, could potentially contribute to all three proofs

> ...we align ourselves for and against characters according to their apparent credibility. By giving us access to 'ordinary people', the narrator's own status raises: their testimony invariably bears out the narrator's thesis; the viability of our access to knowledge through the locus of He-Who-Knows is reconfirmed. (Nichols 1981: 201–02)

As Renov puts it, 'any poetics of value, despite the explanatory power it might mobilize through an elaboration of conceptually discrete modalities, must be willing to acknowledge transgressiveness as the very condition of textual potency' (1993: 25; emphasis in the original).

The documentary audience

One of the fundamental aspects of the interaction between the documentary texts and the viewer, following Nichols (1981) is 'the desire to know': expository cinema 'usually makes a tacit proposal to the viewer as part of its contract negotiations: the invocation of, and promise to gratify, a desire to know' (1981: 205). This desire has two features: it requires 'to be fulfilled in terms of the real conditions of existence, the pro-filmic event or "real world" apart from the mediation of the system of textual codes' (Nichols 1981: 206). The documentary's primarily realist mode of discourse, riding on the iconic bind that collapses photographic sign and referent, makes this possible. The 'Veridicality' of the cinematic, especially televisual image, from which the documentary derives its truth claims, is eminently suitable for the fulfilling of such a task.

The second feature of this desire, according to Nichols,

> ...involves the characteristics of direct address itself [...] This mode explicitly invokes the viewer as subject. Its appeal to reason presumes a

center for its own discourse, the locus of He-Who-Knows, which reciprocally calls the viewer into being as a comparable center or locus, distinguished by the lack of the knowledge that is promised him or her. (Nichols 1981)

This accommodates the documentary's logic of information and its basic didactic role, operating on the devices of rhetoric. Nichols is careful enough to warn us that the apparent transparency of the invocation and the fulfilment of the desire to know veil a political aspect. Even without exaggerating the tyranny of the text, or succumbing to deterministic notions, it is possible to see the hegemonic potential of such an interaction between the viewer and the text.

One basic question remains. Given the relationship of the viewer and the documentary, and accepting that the assumptions and expectations it invokes are different from that between viewer and fictional cinema, on what basis does the viewer replace his/her suspension of disbelief, which normally characterizes reception of fiction, with an evocation of belief? Nichols (1991) argues that this transformation of the viewer response depends upon the recognition of textual cues and documentary conventions commonly associated with realism, which facilitate the collapse of the distance between sign and referent, and contributes to the 'literalism' of the documentary discourse:

> [M]ost of the time the viewer recognizes a documentary when assumptions or hypotheses applied to the text confirm this set of expectations rather than others. The viewer then sets out to process the film with an understanding that the metaphorical distance from historical reality established from the outset by fiction ('Once upon a time ...') has been closed ('And that's the way it is ...'). The text presents a metonymic representation of the world as we know it [...] rather than a metaphoric rendering. (Nichols 1991: 28)

The employment of procedural skills involved in the viewer's engagement with the documentary text and the subsequent processing of information, Nichols suggests, is a learned activity dependent upon a recipe knowledge deriving from previous experiences with such texts. In hermeneutic terms, this means that previous encounters with texts from the genre construct a knowledge base of differences–recognizable between fiction and non-fiction–a process similar to that described by Jauss (1982) with reference to literary experience, where a work 'awakens memories of that which was already read, brings the reader to a specific emotional attitude, and with its beginning arouses expectations for the "middle and end", which can then be maintained intact or altered' (1982: 23). In other words, the experience of the genre produces 'horizons of expectations' which are then conformed to or refuted by the text.

This latent knowledge is exploited by fiction films such as *JFK*, and *Bob Roberts,*[17] and reinforced or modified by other documentary films. Interestingly, Nichols links this (eventually) habitual, non-conscious activity, which enables us, as viewers, to assume a different correlation between sign and referent (which prompts us to infer the images as originating from the historical world) from that in fiction, to our engagement with external 'reality'.

> These procedures [...] are also intimately tied to matters of ideology. They govern many of our assumptions about the nature of the world what is in it, what appropriate action consists of, and what alternatives can be legitimately entertained. Procedural skills of viewing, like habits and the Freudian unconscious generally, orient us toward the world, or a text, in specific ways that are open to change but also quite capable of coping with setbacks and refutations. (Nichols 1991: 24)

The crucial aspect of the documentary interpretation is, obviously, our assumption that the text relates directly with the outside world. Technically, this means that the projected sequence of images, what occurred in front of the camera (the profilmic event), and the historical referent are taken to be congruent with one another 'Consequently, we use "procedural schemata" to follow an argument and not a story. The

---

[17]*JFK*, directed by O. Stone (1991); *Bob Roberts,* directed by T. Robbins (1992).

documentary viewer employs "procedures of rhetorical engagement" rather than "procedures of fictional engagement" that guide our viewing of the classic narrative film' (Nichols 1991: 25, 26). Nichols goes on to suggest that the viewer's engagement with the documentary film also involves assigning motivations: 'as a formal term motivation refers to the way the presence of an object is justified in relation to the text' (1991). The documentary film includes realist, functional, intertextual and formal motivations which provide the viewer with cues with which to engage with the argument.

Wilson's (1993) concept of the veridicality of images is particularly applicable to the documentary: 'images read as veridical [...] sustain the truth of a subject's (character's or presenter's) discursively established interpretations, upholding them as verbally expressed insights into the evidently real' (1993: 114). Quoting Collins (1986), Wilson claims that 'in documentary the presence of the images, "the visible evidence they offer of an event, authenticates the carrier of the meaning–the commentary"' (Wilson 1993).

We have seen how the modalities of the documentary representation, together with its generic properties, elevate its position in the hierarchy of truth in cinematic, and by extension, televisual representation. The resulting increase in the assumed correlation between image and reality calls for a specific 'horizon of expectations' in viewer interpretation of the documentary, which takes this veridicality into account. In the context of this study, what is especially significant is that, these expectations involve the acceptance or rejection of the documentary's claims to authenticity. As we shall see from the data, the acknowledgement of the genre's authority as the locus of information about the 'real' world and the interpretation it entails is markedly different from that of a stance that doubts its authority.

6

Methodological Reflections on 'Cross-cultural' Audience Research

Bruce: I don't know what sciences you have in mind but in my field, sociology, there is an ongoing debate about the 'correct method'. On the one side we are told that there cannot be any knowledge without statistics. Others say that you have to 'get the feel' for the area you are examining, so you study individual cases in detail and write about them almost like a novelist.

Paul Feyerabend, *Three Dialogues on Knowledge*

In a characteristically polemical essay, Rorty (1982) examines what he calls 'value-free' and 'hermeneutic' social sciences, and finds both opposing methodologies as well as their presuppositions wanting. According to Rorty, positivistic theories and methodologies, with their insistence on 'objectivity', were construed as a corrective against the excesses of German idealism, which, following Kantian transcendentalism, had discarded scientific rationalism in favour of exploring 'the notion of making worlds by creating vocabularies, a notion echoed in our century by maverick philosophers of science like Cassirer and Goodman' (Rorty 1982: 192). The ideal of founding a scientific vocabulary which explained nature 'in its own language' without human intervention was, according to Rorty, a self-delusion; what it amounted to was merely that 'a given vocabulary works better than another for a given purpose.' For instance, in Galileo's case, 'his terminology was the only "secret" he had–he didn't pick that terminology because it was "clear" or "natural", or "simple", or in line with the categories of pure understanding. He just lucked out' (Rorty 1982: 193)–a moral of 'using the right jargon' left unlearned by Galileo's seventeenth century successors. Rorty finds that the hermeneutic, interpretive enterprise on the other hand, in seeking to balance the positivistic desire to discover predictive laws or generalizations using objective methods, 'goes too far when it waxes philosophical and begins to draw a principled distinction between man and nature, announcing that the ontological difference dictates a methodological difference' (1982: 199). This distinction between physical nature and human society seems to me to be, on the contrary, perfectly reasonable; what is at the crux of the debate concerning methods is the conception of society: on one side of the divide are those, to whom society is no different from physical nature and, therefore, is amenable to 'objective' analysis, while to those on the other side the fields of meaning, human collectivities call for different methodological tools. My theoretical commitments, as elaborated especially in Chapters 3 and 4, indicate my stance with regard to this debate.

Briefly, I endorse Schutz's oft-cited distinction between the two fields:

> The world of nature, as explored by the natural scientist, does not 'mean' anything to molecules, atoms, and electrons. But the observational field of the social scientist–social reality–has a specific meaning and relevance structure for the human beings living, acting, and thinking within it. [...] The thought objects constructed by the social scientist, in order to grasp this social reality, have to be founded upon the thought objects constructed by the common-sense thinking of men, living their daily lives within the social world. (Schutz 1973: 59)

The social scientist's constructs are therefore, second degree, 'constructs of constructs made by the actors on the social scene' (Schutz 1973). Rabinow and Sullivan (1979) echo this sentiment in their argument for the need of an 'interpretive turn' in the social sciences which discards the expectations of natural sciences and 'refocuses attention on the concrete varieties of cultural meaning, in their particularity and complex texture' (1979: 4). The fact that the object of investigation, the tools, as well as the investigator him/herself are very much part of the same 'pervasive context that is the human world' (Rabinow and Sullivan 1979: 5), implies the reappraisal of the separation of the 'knower and the known'–or to use Natanson's (1963: 19) terms, the 'observer and the observed'– suggested by Cartesian duality. The distinction between the 'scientific study of objects and holistic study of subjects', in which 'human beings are more than objects. The connection between the knower and the known is also revealed in the distinction drawn between the 'scientific study of objects and holistic study of subjects' in which 'human beings are more than objects', and in which 'by studying them as objects, one ignores that level of reality unique to human subjects' (Lowe, 1982: 164). This recognition, however, does not imply an exaltation of the nineteenth century 'subjectivism' and the allied notion of empathy–'the interpretive denies and overcomes the almost de rigueur opposition of subjectivity and objectivity' (Rabinow and Sullivan 1979: 5). Nor does it suggest a support to Taylor's (1971) extreme idea that since we are caught in a web of significance which makes an outside point from which to collect data an impossibility, the social scientist can only offer interpretations which, in turn, can only appeal to insight and not to any verification procedure. Even granted that the constructs of social scientists are interpretations of interpretations, procedures of accountability and authentication are surely required to support them, even in the form of a 'transformed version of textual criticism' (Rabinow and Sullivan 1979: 8), recommended by Ricoeur (1991).

Intrinsic in this stance is an advocacy of qualitative methodology. Rorty rightly observes that the quarrel between 'objective' social science and hermeneutics is more with regard to the 'competing goals of "explanation" and "understanding"'

(1982:196) than about the correct 'method'. While objective science, in its quest for an explanation of social structures and 'facts', uses quantitative, statistical techniques, interpretive inquiry with its emphasis on understanding culture, the process of meaning production, and so on suggests a qualitative methodology. In the context of audience research, especially in relation to the degrees of involvement with and interpretation of media content, statistical methods are grossly inadequate, as Ang (1991) argues, citing as an example the quantitative, decontextualized 'profiling' of audiences by market researchers, and making the case for more qualitative, ethnographic research that takes into account the contexts of media use. Reception analysis is concerned with the process of meaning construction. In the present study this entails the examination of audience's interpretive conventions and their relation to cultural contexts. The methodology most apposite, therefore, is a qualitative one.

Defining the project

The case study presented in the following chapters involves the comparison of the interpretation of documentaries by audiences in India and Britain. In this chapter, I present the reasons that informed my selection of film-makers and films, and more significantly, of sample audiences in India and Britain; and recount briefly the difficulties I encountered during the course of my fieldwork, which influenced both the data as well as my analysis of them.

My interest in audience research was originally kindled by a desire to discover differences (if any) in audience interpretations of the educational films produced by my department in India, and telecast by *Doordarshan*. Feedback from the audience about these films was confined to the odd letter of approbation or censure, audience research being designed chiefly to find out the number of persons watching educational broadcasts on any particular day. Evaluation of the films made was chiefly through peer assessments—comments by fellow film-makers on how they would have produced a particular film. Qualitative research was rare, the occasional study, evaluating a film's 'effectiveness', being restricted to 'before' and 'after' questions concerning its content. There was, therefore, an utter lack of awareness of the nature of television comprehension in general, and of the possibility of differences in interpretation by audience members.[1]

Initially, my proposal included an analysis of the symbolic features of the televisual text as well as its cognitive effects on viewers, and an assessment of their pedagogic implications. The ultimate aim of the study was to enable producers of educational television to 'construct' their films in an optimum manner, in other words, to make more 'effective' programmes. This proposal reflected both my concerns as a producer as well as my incipient knowledge of academic research in educational media, gained from works such as that of Sless (1981). Working with the assumptions and the research agenda of these studies, I initially proposed to examine the 'effectiveness' of educational television programmes and their rate of success in achieving their pedagogic goals. Conceived this way, the project would have certainly involved a more positivistic, quantitative method of collecting data, since the object of the proposed study was to recommend production strategies which would eliminate equivocal or problematic aspects of textual construction. This stance reflects Hall's critique of the tendency of some television producers, 'who find their message "failing to get across"' to be 'frequently concerned to straighten out the kinks in the communication chain, thus facilitating the "effectiveness" of their communication', an 'administrative goal' reproduced by policy-oriented analyses

---

[1]These comments should not be taken as a rebuke of the makers of Indian educational films only. My conversations with producers at the Open University BBC centre revealed a similar lack of familiarity (but not of interest) with the arguments concerning television comprehension. I find this indicative of the unproductive gulf in communication between academic research and media practitioners.

studying issues such as audience recall (Hall 1980: 135). Following Rorty, such a conception involves questions of prediction and control–elements of 'value-free social science' (Rorty 1982)–which would require a different vocabulary from the one presented in this book.

Film-makers, films and audiences

With my initial proposal in mind, I approached the BBC Production Centre at the Open University, where using 'contacts' and with the help of friends I met three producers who enthusiastically agreed to be interviewed. Two of these producers provided me with copies of their films and even their production notes by way of enabling me to prepare adequately for the interviews. At this time I was still wrestling with the theoretical arguments concerning meaning in televisual texts and intended audiences. The exploratory discussions, which I had at the BBC Open University Production Centre, suggested a strong interest on the part of the producers towards finding out exactly how their programmes were received and interpreted by the 'target' audience. The possibility of different interpretations of the same programme was grudgingly admitted, although my conversations with an editor at the Centre elicited his firm conviction that educational television and documentaries, given the 'closed' nature of their texts, precluded diverse interpretations.[2]

The possibility of conducting a comparative study across audience cultures was suggested initially at my meeting with a senior producer at the BBC Centre who was, at that time, engaged in a project making training videos for agricultural

---

[2]The futility of my attempts at convincing the editor of the possibility of any text being open to different interpretations is a further indication of the gulf between academics and professionals, and the different 'languages' which characterize their occupational spaces. The more theoretical my side of the debate became, the more aware I grew of the different 'worlds', phenomenologically speaking, that he and I inhabited.

extension workers in Kenya. His detailed and reflexive account, in his production notes, of his first impressions of working in an alien culture, together with his reflections on culturally informed differences in perception and communication, added further weight to my incipient idea that I could examine interpretatory divergences along cultural divides. From the producer's point of view, do perceptions of cultural differences, and therefore of audience profile, lead to modifications in production strategies? From the perspective of the audience on the other hand, do these cultural differences manifest different interpretations? If so, how?

Almost simultaneously with this growing idea, a closer acquaintance with the literature of audience research, especially reception analysis, prompted me to reflect on my original research questions, and subsequently to redraw them. Some of the concerns which induced this redrawing have been discussed in Chapter 1 and 2, but it bears reiterating here that this project was primarily born out of a perceived theoretical inadequacy in the literature with regard to the way in which social embeddedness influenced interpretive practices. It would be clear from my arguments in Chapters 3 and 4 that I regard a phenomenological hermeneutics and sociology of knowledge to be crucial in answering some of these queries; that any act of interpretation, which includes the acts of understanding that occur 'normally' within the life-world, is an inevitable result of the social distribution of knowledge in that particular sphere of activity. Such a notion has enormous consequences for the researcher as well as the actual process of research. 'Value-freedom' and 'objectivity' in research–the pillars of the positivistic enterprise–are immediate casualties, and the entire activity of research acquires an intensely reflexive personality. Again, any involvement in the philosophical debates underpinning the utilization of a particular method in preference to another is beyond the rubric of this project, but it should be noted that the account of the research process which follows includes issues which came to the forefront during the process itself.

The Television Trust for the Environment (TVE)[3] was instrumental in my decision regarding the final choice of project, the culmination of a process which began at least partly as a result of my serendipitous discovery that TVE wanted research done in India regarding the distribution, consumption and reception of the programmes, produced as part of their Moving Pictures project. I volunteered to conduct their research in exchange for using their videos and their contacts with film-makers. With their international contacts and funding of television projects across the world, TVE seemed ideally placed for my intended study. My links with TVE provided access to persons and places of which I would have otherwise been unaware, although it must be said that more than a third of the time I spent in India (three months) was taken up by the work I had to complete for them.

To begin with, my aim was to interview four film-makers—two Western and two Indian—about the films they had produced under the auspices of and at least partly funded by TVE, which were intended for a world-wide audience. Did their awareness of the audience, as constituted internationally, affect their planning, research, filming and post-production? Since most of the films were documentaries, I was interested in finding out how, if at all, a particular perception of the 'target' audience altered the arguments and rhetorical strategies in their films. Did they take the audience into consideration while taking production decisions? In what way did such considerations impinge upon decisions regarding narrative strategies, voice-over, editing, and so on? My aim was to explore the authorial intentions

[3]The Television Trust for the Environment was established in 1984 under the auspices of the United Nations Environment Programme to promote environmental awareness with special emphasis on the needs of developing countries. Among its various activities, TVE provides funds and arranges co-production deals for film-makers from around the world to make films and television programmes on environmental issues, and distributes these films free of charge to non-governmental agencies and educational establishments in developing countries.

behind the various aspects of the films, with the idea of making a comparison between the two sets of film-makers, Indian and British, on two fronts: first, a consideration of any differences in the textual construction which hinted at cultural embeddedness, and second, the film-makers' conception of viewers from other cultures and the consequent alterations to the text, if any. I decided to follow this method of analysis of the process of encoding, preferring it to the conventional way of examining the text itself in order to unearth the author. This carries vestiges of the proposal which I had initially started with, since it presents me the opportunity to compare the intended meaning of the producers with the interpretations of the films by audiences from both cultures. My interviews with the film-makers, therefore, included questions about their general production strategies and habits as well as those concerning the specific films I had included in the study.

The two Western film-makers I had identified were readily accessible and were willing to be interviewed. Robbie Stamp, the British producer,[4] agreed to meet me at his office in Central Television, initially only for a maximum of half an hour, although once the interview was under way, he answered my questions regarding his film, *Can Polar Bears Tread Water,* earnestly for nearly 75 minutes. I interviewed Toni Strasburg, the independent producer from South Africa, in her office in London about her film, *Chain of Tears.* Both interviews were recorded without any mishap or interference.

I was, however, not so fortunate with the Indian film-makers. One of them, Manjira Dutta, was away on a shoot during the period of my stay in India, and could not be reached. Consequently I had to discard her films from the study, and include instead two films by Meera Dewan, *In the Dust of Development* and *Whose Children,* whom I interviewed at her residence/office in Delhi. The interview itself was successful

---

[4] I use the terms 'film-maker' and 'producer' interchangeably, following the accepted parlance in television.

since Dewan was extremely forthcoming in her account of her production practices,[5] but the recording of it contained traffic and other noises which sometimes rendered her words unintelligible.

I decided to conduct the Indian part of my audience research at the Central Institute of English and Foreign Languages, Hyderabad, for several reasons. Primarily, as the place where I had studied and worked for several years, it afforded me the opportunity to approach possible respondents and convince them to volunteer to take part in the research. Second and more significantly, the Institute comprised, in its academic, student, as well as non-academic communities, of persons from all over the country, providing me with, if not a typical cross-section, at least a passable microcosm of the diversity which makes up India and its culture(s). Ideally, I would have liked to make my selection of participants from a cross section of the population in each state. However, given the constraints I was working under, this was an impossible task. Lastly, using the Institute as the base for my study provided me with the access to both video recorders as well as to studio facilities for recording the interviews, which saved me a considerable amount of time and effort, since video recorders were, by no means, a common feature in India, especially among the lower classes.

Having chosen the Institute in Hyderabad as the site for my study, I proceeded to select from it a representative sample of an Indian audience. Given the nature of the case study and the questions for which it sought answers, my task was to generate the data which would contribute towards creating a picture of the interpretive practices which were characteristically Indian. With this in mind, I decided to show the films to, and interview, respondents from three sections of the Institute's community:

---

[5]The difference between academic and professional discourses was illustrated in this instance by Dewan's initial lack of comprehension of what I meant by 'production strategies'.

academics, students and non-academics. From among these three sections, I selected twenty respondents (see Table 6.1) from different parts of the country, so as to make the sample as representative as possible of its cultural diversity. Selecting respondents from the three communities within the Institute was designed to create a sample of the Indian audience which broadly exemplified the various economic and social sections of the society. Among the non-academics, I deliberately chose respondents with little or no university education, and at the lower end of the economic scale—technicians and typists who provided another significant variable, that of education and cultural capital which, as will be seen in later chapters, proved crucial to the study.

It is worth reiterating at this point that the intention was to compare interpretations of documentaries by audiences from one national context (Indian) with those of another (British), and not between the various sections within the same national culture. This intention was based on the assumption that: first, different cultural contexts generated equally different interpretive practices, and second, that the national cultures of India and Britain were sufficiently diverse as to engender noticeably different interpretations by their audiences. For the British part of the project, therefore, I attempted to replicate, as closely as possible, the Indian sample. There were, however, few minor differences between the two groups: while I adhered to the three broad categories of academic, student and non-academic, my British respondents included two teachers in the 'academic' grouping; and the British non-academics comprised laboratory assistants and porters. Moreover, as Table 6.1 indicates, the number of respondents in each category also varied slightly.

On the whole, I interviewed 20 respondents in India and 20 in Britain. Each participant was asked to view and later discuss two films, one Indian and the other British. Ten viewers from each culture watched a set of two films: *Can Polar Bears Tread Water* and *In the Dust of Development;* while the other 10 viewers from each culture watched *Chain of Tears* and *Whose*

Table 6.1

Respondents and categories

	Academics	Students		Non-graduates	Total
		Post-graduates	Under-graduates		
Indian	6	6	4	4	20
British	4	6	6	4	20

Source: Study done by the author.

Children. The idea behind getting the respondents to view two documentaries made by film-makers from different cultures was to examine the notion of understanding in relation to cultural proximity. Thematically, all four films dealt with subjects of universal import; on that level, therefore, the notion of cultural 'strangeness' does not arise. The films differed greatly in their representation and type of exploration of these subjects, as well as, in the distinctly personal style of film-making. The Indian films comprised manifestly 'Indian' elements including subjects, witnesses and music; among the British films, *Polar Bears* adopted an unusual style of presentation which highlighted its overtly didactic intentions, whereas *Chain of Tears* unfolded in a clearly more 'traditional' manner (more details in Chapter 7). In getting the participants to view two films, my aim was to explore culturally inspired audience responses to the documentary form in general and to specific stylistic practices, both familiar and unfamiliar. I wanted to examine the ways in which not only cultural but also idiosyncratic differences in documentary film-making affected understanding.

The situations in which these films were viewed and the respondents interviewed, again varied slightly in the Indian and British contexts. As mentioned earlier, basing my research at the Institute in Hyderabad enabled me to take advantage of its viewing and recording facilities. All the Indian respondents watched the films in a sound proof room specially designed for viewing videos and 16 mm films, and were therefore relatively undisturbed during the entire process. I conducted most of the interviews in the same room, and the others in a recording studio. Generally speaking, most respondents appeared to quickly overcome any discomfort with regard to their responses being recorded, although a few found the atmosphere in the recording studio intimidating and consequently took a longer period of time to relax. In hindsight, group discussions could have helped surmount this particular difficulty.

The British respondents, on the other hand, were, on the whole, less threatened by the presence of a microphone and recorder. However, the situations in which they viewed the films were not ideal. Without access to facilities similar to those I had used in India, I was at times compelled to use my own or the respondents' residences, where their viewing was occasionally disturbed. Interviewing in such surroundings sometimes meant competing with extraneous noises, which even if they went unnoticed during the actual interview through selective hearing, were audibly present in the recordings.

The research process

Unstructured or semi-structured interviewing, as a preferred qualitative method, is particularly pertinent in the context of reception research, enabling the researcher to examine audience codes (Jensen 1987, 1991; Hermes 1995). Jensen (1987) makes a useful distinction between quantitative data, which is 'external', and qualitative 'internal' data: whereas 'quantitative analysis tends to emphasize an external perspective on the categories of understanding', qualitative analysis 'attaches primary importance to those categories that can be derived internally from the respondent's own framework' (1987: 31). Quite apart from the theoretical arguments presented in the previous chapters, which orient the methodology unequivocally towards qualitative data gathering and analysis, the exploration of the process of meaning construction, which this study intends, as contrary to the products of meaning (another distinction identified by Jensen (1987: 32) requires a qualitative methodology. As Dahlgren (1985a) observes, meaning itself is a difficult concept to fix: 'it is "decentred" and resides in many intersecting force-fields. Meaning is equivocal and hard to pin down' (1985a: 11)–consequently a study of meaning production is not without problems, whatever the method employed. While acknowledging this, I would argue that the recognition that meaning is produced through the text–audience interplay and is the result of specific interpretive procedures adopted by the viewers, shifts the emphasis away from the meaning itself, to these interpretive conventions. What is of interest here is the audiences' sense-making activity, contra 'the assumption, which text-centred studies have tended to encourage, that meaning somehow exists as inherent properties of textual signification and are thus available there for identification and plotting' (Richardson and Corner 1986: 486). The protean quality of meaning, identified by Dahlgren (1985), therefore, need not erect an insurmountable obstacle in the analysis of audiences' signifying practices.

This shift in emphasis from the conception of the text as the primary site of meaning to the notion of meaning as residing in the text–audience interface raises two methodological issues. First, it questions the analysis of the text in search of its 'preferred' meaning, against which viewers' interpretations are then matched, as in Morley (1980). The identification of this 'standard' meaning is a spurious exercise, especially in the present context, where the focus is on the exploration of viewers' understanding of a particular set of films, and to link it to cultural categories. The comparison attempted in this study therefore, is not between audience interpretations and an 'objective' meaning of the text, but rather between the interpretations produced by audiences from two different cultures. The hegemonic control of media messages suggested in the quest for 'preferred' meaning is not the primary interest here. Wren-Lewis's (1983) critique of the practice of measuring audience accounts by comparing them with meanings drawn out of the text by the researcher is apposite, although in agreement with Richardson and Corner (1986), I find his relativism unacceptable for my purposes. Examining the audience reception without considering the text certainly carries the danger of becoming an exercise in pointless relativism; while on the other hand, an 'objective' analysis of the text is neither possible from the perspective of this study nor desirable. As a way out of this dilemma, I have chosen to provide a description of the four films without attempting to analyze them.

Liebes and Katz's drawing of the ideal situation with regard to the empirical data is pertinent to the present study: ideally, it should have

> ...empirical data on how people interact with their television sets under normal conditions: how they arrange themselves before it; how they decode what they see and hear; how they help each other to do so; how they talk about it; whether they refer to the medium or to specific programs; whether they have categories of classifying programs and criticizing them, and if so, what they are; whether and how they weave the experience of viewing into their social and political roles. (Liebes and Katz 1990: 20)

In other words, audience research ideally ought to include a complex ethnography of media use, interpretation of media content and a sociology of media and everyday family life. As Lindlof and Meyer (1987) observe, these are issues which are particularly amenable to being explored through an interpretive framework. 'Typically, qualitative research [...] also considers the social contexts of media attendance as key conditions on the development of interpretive frames' (Lindlof and Meyer 1987: 13).

There have recently been studies examining all or some of these features of the quotidian, domestic experience of the media, using the ideas of de Certau and Schutz (Silverstone 1989; Morley and Silverstone 1991; Hermes 1995). But while these studies aim to provide complex descriptive accounts of the domestic context of media use, the present project is interested in comparing interpretations made by (hopefully) representative participants from two quite widely different cultures, with the intention of exploring the notion of cultural contexts and their impact on the variance of interpretations. As a result, two features of the data, identified by Richardson and Corner (1986: 487), become crucial: 'the need to get as near as possible to the actual (in a sense, "lowest level") business of audience meaning-making from what is shown, said, or printed', and 'the need to give sustained attention to the features and details of respondents' talk as they develop their interpretative accounts within the overall setting of interview/discussion.' These requirements, concerning the manner of gathering data, as well as the nature of the data gathered, clearly indicate the type of methodology best suited for it: questionnaires and surveys would hardly generate data with the prescribed complexity, so, what is called for is a longer, more involved interaction with the respondents in the form of post-screening interviews or group discussions.

The preference between interviews and group discussions are more often than not based on the twin concerns of practical considerations and the kind of data expected. As Richardson and Corner observe, the relative strengths and disadvantages of the two settings are a matter of deliberation for any researcher interested in generating qualitative data. Whilst the 'problems of speaker identification [while transcribing], the variables of domination, inhibition and consensus introduced by group dynamics [...] and also the quite severe limitations on the opportunities for using "follow up" questioning to elicit supplementary or clarificatory comment' are normally associated with group discussions, the 'advantage of facilitating a form of talk which at times will probably be openly argumentative, questioning, and supportive,' and thereby indicating variations in audience interpretations, make them more effective than one-to-one interviews (Richardson and Corner 1986: 488).

For this study, however, I chose to interview the respondents on a one-to-one basis immediately after the screening. The interviews lasted roughly between 45 and 75 minutes each, totalling nearly 460 pages of transcripts. I chose the interview method not only because of the difficulties with the data generated from group work mentioned above, but more crucially, since my research questions, with their focus on the process of sense-making, demanded a close scrutiny of respondents' understandings and the intricacies of the decoding strategy. This method, of course, was not without problems. The interview situation is hardly a natural setting; however much the researcher attempts to lighten the atmosphere of inquisition, the researcher being in charge of the interaction, entails that respondents' accounts are almost always (except in the case of exceptionally strong personalities) dictated and confined by the questions. For the situation where 'it is possible for the conventions of conversational exchange to modify the dominant ones of question and answer' (Richardson and Corner 1986: 144) to arise, both parties involved in the exchange should cease to be conscious of the circumstances, which is not an easy task. Quite simply, the 'researcher obtrusiveness', to which Lindlof and Meyer (1987) refer to, is an unavoidable condition of existence for a social researcher. A particular merit of qualitative research hinges on its ability to acknowledge this 'presence' of the researcher and its effect on the investigation–the phenomenon of reflexivity which is rarely present in most quantitative studies, although the researcher is as 'obtrusive' in them. To Lindlof and Meyer, 'inherent in the reflexivity principle is the exquisite notion that, while the researcher must be careful not to unduly impinge on the characteristic social patterns (once they are known), selective intrusions–via interviews, changes in the sampling of situations, etc., can be highly revealing' (1987).

Recognition of the artificiality of the situation, however, did not prevent me either from occasionally taking a deliberately opposing view to the one espoused by the respondents, or from asking what might be considered 'leading' questions. These tactics seemed to me to be perfectly legitimate means by which to not only convert a predominantly question-and-answer session into a discussion, but also to trigger a more involved, stronger response. I was also comforted by the idea that, as in Richardson and Corner, the effects of any 'over-prompting' could be identified and compensated for during the analysis of the transcripts.

Before commencing each interview, I informed the respondent of what I wanted them to discuss. I tried to make it clear that my questions were not designed to test their memory, nor were they a test of their intelligence. In all the audience interviews I followed a similar pattern: I began by asking the respondents about their general viewing habits—number of hours of television watched each day, kind of programmes watched and whether they habitually watched documentaries. This part of the interview was directed more towards helping the respondents relax and get accustomed to the situation rather than to elicit answers of direct relevance to the study. I then turned the interview to a discussion of the respondent's conception of documentaries in general, especially their reactions to the truth claims of the documentary. The objective was to match their responses to the particular films against their pronouncements regarding the documentary genre. For instance, if those who expressed scepticism with reference to the documentary's capacity to be an objective 'window on the world' later reacted to the films in a 'transparent' way, their stance was regarded as inconsistent. While discussing the films they had viewed I began with global questions referring the respondent to the films as a whole before discussing particular aspects or specific sections of the films. These were generally features to which the respondents themselves had alluded during the course of their responses to the 'global' questions. Surprisingly, a number of features from the films were identified and discussed in this manner by nearly all the participants. To put it another way, several of these features thus picked out from any of the four films were common to nearly all the responses to that film.

Structuring the interviews in this manner enabled me to identify various points of variance in audience decodings at various levels of interpretation: following Liebes and Katz

(1990), I could differentiate between 'referential' and 'critical' framing of the responses to the film(s) in its entirety; as well as locate, following Richardson and Corner (1986), 'transparent', 'mediated' or 'manipulative' readings of specific sequences. A more detailed account of these analytical categories is given in Chapter 8, but it should be noted here that few of the audience accounts contained a uniformly sustained framing, thus rendering any attempt at a general classification of entire respondent accounts impossible. As I show in Chapter 8, an unexpected outcome of the study was that the few respondents whose frames did retain an element of uniformity were from a similar background in India.

Challenges of reception research

The notion of reflexivity also involves self assessment as researcher. In other words, the constant recognition of the situation of the researcher in relation to the event or person(s) being studied–acknowledging the position of the 'knower'. In the present context, the self assessment these acts of deliberation generated, include evaluations which I was conscious of during the process itself, and others that occurred to me in hindsight. The issues which were thrown up for consideration and reflection as the result of the research activity could be classified into two broad categories: the first category, which includes anxieties with regard to the ultimate concern of the project, the examination of interpretive practices of audience members–and its relation to the method employed–interviewing; the second category, which includes issues created as a result of the difficulties encountered in the actual process of data collection, which I classify as pragmatic concerns, and which (the category if not the particular problems), I suspect are not uncommon in studies carried out by solitary researchers encumbered by lack of funds and the pressure of time, which generate their own peculiar complications not normally experienced in more established research projects.

Generally speaking, these problems revolved around the 'truth' of the respondents' accounts. Most glaringly, the interviews were designed to elicit answers pertaining to the process of a respondent's interpretation of documentary films; processes which are employed 'naturally' as it were. Arguments concerning the truth claims of the documentary, for instance, are rarely part of the process of interpretation in 'natural' settings. As one respondent pointed out, such questions generally arise only when the content of the film counters personal experience or closely held beliefs. In a sense, and to use the language of phenomenology, the interviews induced respondents to 'bracket' their 'natural attitude' and reflect on and verbalize opinions held as common sense. Two points of contention ensue from this observation: first, this activity involves a particular skill—that of presenting a cogent argument as opposed to giving an opinion which two of the groups I had selected both in India and in Britain, the academics and to a large extent the post-graduate students, possessed in abundance, relative to the other groups—the non-graduates and most undergraduates. The differences in the discourses, employed by these two groups, are not dissimilar to the distinction between what Geertz (1983) terms 'experience-near' and 'experience-distant,' referring to everyday and specialist language respectively:

> An experience-near concept is, roughly, one that someone—a patient, a subject, in our case an informant—might himself naturally and effortlessly use to define what he or his fellows see, feel, think, imagine, and so on, and which he would readily understand when similarly applied by others. An experience-distant concept is one that specialists of one sort or another [...] employ to forward their scientific, philosophical, or practical aims. (Geertz 1983: 57)

This distinction was manifested in the present context in the apparently 'theoretical' discourse proffered by academics and the less abstract 'opinions' of the non-graduates.

Getting the respondents to reflect on questions such as the authenticity of the documentary discourse raises another, and perhaps in this context, a more significant concern. Having aligned themselves to a particular position vis-a-vis the documentary genre and its representation of the 'real', would the respondents then have felt compelled to react to the films they had seen from a similar position? I was conscious of this question during the course of my analysis of the data. While most respondents acknowledged the construction of the text and were cognizant of the subjective positioning of the producer, and therefore, the presence of a particular perspective in the films, their responses were not uniformly mediated or critical. A more detailed account of this is given in Chapter 8, but it could be noted here that the respondents' accounts do not indicate an undue influence of their deliberations regarding the documentary genre during the course of the interview.

Issues of a more pragmatic nature were brought to the fore, especially during my interviews with Indian audiences. Again, broadly speaking, they were of two kinds: difficulties relating to language, and the others pertaining to a certain well-entrenched social hierarchy which is an established feature in most professions in India. Language plays a central role in qualitative research. As Jensen (1991a: 31–33) points out, language is used both productively and receptively in qualitative methodologies. As Table 6.2 demonstrates, language functions as the principal tool in data gathering as well as an object of analysis, depending on the particular method used:

Table 6.2

The roles of language in qualitative methodologies

Method	Language	
	Tool for data gathering	Object of analysis
Interviewing	+	+
Participant Observation	+	–
Textual Criticism	–	+

Source: Jensen 1991: 32

Thus, in qualitative interviewing, language performs a dual role: 'Communicating through language, the interviewer and respondent(s) negotiate an understanding of the subject matter in question, which subsequently, in the form of tapes and transcripts, becomes the object of linguistic analysis and textual interpretation' (Jenson 1991: 32–33). In the present context, qualitative interviewing was used as a method to generate discussions regarding the viewers' reception and interpretation of films; these discussions were taped and later transcribed. The transcriptions were analyzed using categories discussed in detail in Chapter 7, with the aim of making a comparison of the interpretive practices between cultures. Language, therefore, was significant both in terms of the interview itself (data gathering) and as the object of analysis.

In the Indian context, language poses problems even in everyday communication. State boundaries run along linguistic boundaries, especially in the South, and therefore communication among persons from different states normally entails abandoning the vernacular in favour of Hindi or English, the two 'official' languages of India.[6] The enormous linguistic diversity in India[7] thus adds to the complications faced by the researcher who wishes to study the lives of persons across these divides. Knowledge of and familiarity with Hindi and/or English is by no means uniform across the various sectors of the population, which belies, even at the level of language, the notion of Indians as belonging to a monolithic culture. Since English is taught in most schools and is the medium of instruction in almost all universities, lack of

---

[6]People from Tamil Nadu, my home state, suffer an additional burden, since linguistic chauvinism has successfully kept Hindi out of schools. Consequently, English is the only lingua franca while communicating with persons from even neighbouring states.

[7]According to Oommen (1992), four language families are currently in use in the whole of India, of which, only the 15 languages belonging to two families, the Indo-Aryan and the Dravidian, have been accorded official recognition.

'proper' education indicates a corresponding lack of familiarity with English.[8]

My audience research in India, as mentioned earlier, was conducted in Hyderabad where the vernacular is Telugu, although a dialect of Hindi is also spoken in most areas of the city. Unfortunately, my knowledge of either of these languages was not proficient enough for me to be able to conduct interviews in them. Therefore, I was compelled to stay with English ('the universal translator') throughout the course of all the interviews.

Within the community of academics and research/post graduate students, this did not pose a particular difficulty. Even ordinary conversations within this community are normally conducted in English, given that the Institute comprised persons from different parts of the country and therefore had different 'mother-tongues'. With the non-graduates and a few of the undergraduate students, however, it was a different matter. English certainly was not their strong point, and on occasions during the interviews, there were indications that these respondents were unable to express themselves with adequate clarity. Combined with the element of articulacy discussed earlier as the norm within the academic community and notably absent in less verbal professions and sub-cultures, the obvious lack of uniformity in the use of English presented me with an additional complication. In operational terms, this meant that a group of my Indian respondents were unable to articulate their thoughts as easily as they perhaps would have been able to in their vernacular. This is crucial in that the project hinged on the respondents' accounts of their reactions to the films, and an inability to express themselves would have

---

[8]This is admittedly a grossly oversimplified statement, since standards in education in schools vary immensely even within cities, and the difference is more pronounced if rural schools are compared with ones in urban areas. The total absence of uniformity in standards of education, not least in language instruction, is reflected in the continued presence of a national elite who hold the social, economic, and often indirect political power in the country.

quite simply undermined the project. Recognizing the significance of this problem, I made deliberate attempts during the interviews to encourage these viewers to talk more freely, irrespective of grammatical mistakes, by repeating questions and returning to what I considered were crucial points of the interview. While these attempts redressed the balance to a certain extent and were reasonably successful in eliciting these respondents' reactions to the films, it is evident from the data that there is an obvious discrepancy between the academics' articulatory skills and the more laconic utterances of the non-graduates.

This discrepancy was further compounded by the social hierarchy which required some of the non-graduates to show deference to me as an academic (especially as one studying 'abroad'). While this deference was indicated by their addressing me as 'sir', which could perhaps be overlooked as a peculiar quirkiness of address symptomatic of the social divisions in Indian culture and as such having no particular significance to the data itself—a more disturbing consideration arises to it affecting the content of these respondents' answers. It is difficult to conclude with any certainty whether or not their responses were those which they assumed I wanted to hear. The possibility that some of the respondents could have suspected me, despite my assurances to the contrary, of testing their knowledge and powers of interpretation, cannot be denied.

Interviewing British audiences, while not posing a particularly significant problem with regard to language or articulacy—although there admittedly exists in the data an obvious difference in discourse between the analytical language of the teachers, academics and post graduate students, and the more 'everyday' language used by the non-graduates—created its own set of difficulties. One of the video tapes I had brought back from India containing copies of the two films made by Dewan was slightly damaged, probably through using it in a faulty recorder. This was not a serious impairment—the visuals were reasonably clear and the quality of sound approximated a first generation copy. Subtitles, however, were rendered indistinct at certain points, and this condition worsened with the repeated use of the tape. Fortunately, most of the translations were offered in the form of voice-overs, but the songs used in both films relied on subtitles for their translation. While the music and the visuals provided sufficient clues, the occasional indiscernability of the subtitles in both Indian films clearly prevented a closer understanding of the text.

Allied to this is another dimension referred to by Liebes and Katz (1990: 25–26) in connection with a particular methodological problem created by the process of dubbing and subtitling. The act of translation inevitably includes a certain amount of distortion of the original text, with the additional disadvantage of the viewing experience involving the audience having to read printed words on the screen in the case of subtitling. Liebes and Katz claim that, while it would be reasonable to assume non-native viewers missing nuances of the story, their own study indicates that 'story and dialogue are faithfully transmitted [...] and that inter-group differences cannot be attributed to subtitling' (Liebes and Katz 1990: 26). In the context of the present study, however, the subtitles endeavoured to provide translations of songs with specific cultural resonances, whose 'otherness' the translations only underlined emphatically. It would be ingenuous, therefore, to suggest that the differences in interpretation between Hindi speakers and others were negligible in this case.

Morley and Silverstone rightly point out that 'as qualitative media researchers we face the difficulty of finally telling stories about the stories which our respondents have chosen to tell us. These problems are both irreducible and familiar' (Morley and Silverstone 1991: 156). Intrinsic in this is the notion of interpretation. We, as researchers, create stories from our interpretations or analyses of the respondents' accounts. In the interest of validity and accountability, it is necessary that we follow a systematic method of analysis of the data, and that we justify the categories of analysis, the analytical framework, within the broader context of the research project.

The favoured method of analysis of interview data is, of course, close linguistic or textual analysis (Jensen 1987, 1991a), which means that the justification and validity of the 'findings' come in the form of an examination of the respondents' language. Language as data becomes text, and fittingly, 'the analysis of interviews and other audience discourses draws on techniques and models from linguistics and literary criticism' (Jensen 1991a: 140). The next chapter contains a detailed explanation of the various analytical categories used in the analysis of audience responses, followed by an account of the results of the analysis using excerpts from interviews illustrative of audience interpretations.

7

Non-fiction and Audience Evaluations

As mentioned earlier, the objective of this case study was to examine the differences in interpretive practices between audiences in India and Britain in an effort to illustrate and support the theoretical argument posited in the earlier chapters, especially Chapters 3, 4 and 5. For this exercise, I showed a set of two films (one Indian and the other British) to 20 Indian respondents and 20 British respondents, and subsequently interviewed each respondent about his/her understanding of both films. While I concur with Liebes and Katz's (1990) lament that an ideal set of data, including details of the respondents' everyday media use within family settings, viewing habits with regard to programmes watched and so on, is difficult to get, the analysis of the data which were generated in this study did produce fruitful, if surprising, results. This chapter provides an account of this analysis.

The framework of analysis

The basic ingredients in the framework adopted for the analysis of the respondents' accounts are the categories of 'transparency' and 'mediation', as set out by Corner and Richardson (1986). These categories reflect the 'framings' used by the respondents in their accounts of the films, given during the interviews: 'their perception of various programme items as a *mediation* and/or as a *transparent* representation of people, settings and circumstances', which an ethnography of reception ought to take into account, since such frames are integral to the interpretations affected by the viewers (Corner and Richardson 1986: 488). Interpretations using the 'transparent' framing respond to the veridicality of the television image by being open to its 'window on the world' quality, and evaluating the various filmic representations as if they were events in real life. In other words, the profilmic events are read as 'authentic', with the camera observing and recording them, and not as generic constructions. 'Mediation' frames on the other hand, resist the rhetorical advances of the film, acknowledging the constructedness of the diverse elements in it, and as a consequence recognizing that, their meanings originate in their existence as representations and not as real life events. An extended utilization of the mediation frame provides for a 'manipulative and/or displaced' reading (Corner and Richardson 1986: 492) which perceives a manipulative intent on the part of the film-maker behind certain representations, and therefore claims to escape manipulation, while conceding, that, a less vigilant viewer could well be influenced by them. A typology, based on these categories, is crucial in the present context, since it allows for the examination of the viewers' accounts of their reaction to the truth claims of the documentary in general and to evaluate their framings of the individual films, whether or not they are open to the veridicality and indexical nature of the television image. Significantly, the interpretation of a documentary film qua documentary involves a fundamental, even if incipient, conception of the genre on the part of the viewer. The 'horizon of expectations' on which the interpretation of the film progresses, acquires its initial impetus from such a conception.

Corner and Richardson observe that,

...for the purposes of an initial classification of the kinds of status, forms of address and intentionality attributed to news and documentary material by viewer/respondents, such a scheme is an alternative to those based more directly on assessing the level of agreement/ disagreement with a programme's propositional content. (Corner and Richardson 1986: 491)

What is proposed here is different from the comparison of audience responses with the 'preferred meaning' of a text. While accepting the usefulness of the classificatory scheme, the present analysis treats the viewers' agreement/disagreement with the films' content not as an alternative to the classification, but as an extension of it. In order to go beyond the initial classification on to a more detailed examination of the respondents' interpretations, this analysis borrows from the framework used in Liebes and Katz's enterprising study, comparing the culturally embedded readings of *Dallas* (Liebes and Katz 1990). Their broad arrangement of the responses into 'referential' and 'critical' groupings are roughly parallel to the categorization mentioned above, though with some significant differences. While the 'referential', similar to the 'transparent' framing, 'connects the programme to real life' (Liebes and Katz 1990: 100), it accords a reading in which characters in the serial are treated 'as if they were real, suspending disbelief so that attention is redirected to the viewers' lives or to the lives of other people, whether intimate acquaintances or of various social categories such as businessmen, women, etc.' (Liebes and Katz 1990: 32). This reworking of the frame in the viewers' own lives is absent in the distinction between 'transparent' and 'mediation' readings, and is not of much use in the present study.

Liebes and Katz's conception of the 'critical', on the other hand, offers a useful tool for the analysis of the respondents' accounts. In this conception, the critical frame incorporates three sub-divisions to accommodate the different types of criticism: syntactic, semantic and pragmatic; corresponding to the 'ability to discuss programmes as constructions, that is, to recognize or define their genres, formulae, conventions, narrative schemes, etc.' (syntactic criticism); the ability to 'perceive a theme or message or even an issue in a fictional narrative' (semantic criticism); and the viewers' 'awareness that they are using analytic criteria–such as schemas, scripts, frames, roles and other notions of viewer processing and involvement in their responses to the programme' (pragmatic criticism) (Liebes and Katz 1990: 135). In accordance with the fact that the present study concerns the interpretations of the non-fiction in which the 'message' or the argument is foregrounded and less equivocal or oblique than in the fictional representation, I have modified the category of 'semantic' criticism to allow for disagreements with or opposition to the dominant argument in the film.

As parts of a typology with which to examine the respondents' statements, the categories outlined are clearly useful. But it must be noted here that any expectation that such an examination would offer clear-cut distinctions between groups of respondents would be unrealistic. The pattern that emerges is more complex. Overlaps and combinations of the various categories are bound to occur, as for instance, a 'transparent–critical' frame, which, while perceiving a film, or sections of a film, as veridical, disagrees with its (their) premise or representation. In other words, a critical reading, especially semantic criticism, need not necessarily coexist only with a mediation framing. A 'transparent–uncritical' frame, on the other hand, indicates a complete acceptance of the documentary premise of truth generally, as well as of the argument proffered by the particular film. 'Mediation' frames are normally accompanied by a combination of syntactically, semantically or pragmatically informed 'critical' reading. Another significant point which must be stressed is that, viewers' accounts seldom sustain a single frame or reading: viewers could switch frames and read critically a section of a film which they had seen, either because of its immediacy or the cultural proximity of its subject matter, thus far, framing transparently and reading uncritically.

The patterns resulting from the analysis of the respondents' accounts are, therefore, not immediately amenable to an exercise of comparison and contrast. There are degrees of difference, as for instance in the interpretations of Indian students–both graduate and under graduate (IGS and IUG respectively)–most of which are overtly critical, and often produce a mediation reading, when compared to the readings of other groups. Similarly, there are occasionally clear indications of the effect of cultural proximity to particular readings, as in the case of some Indian viewers' attitudes to images of street children, which, as one respondent commented, 'In the Indian context, somehow one doesn't find it tragic, one has accepted it as part of the scene' (IGS4). But within the typology used in the analysis, the picture that emerges most clearly is the difference between the frames and the interpretations made by non-graduate Indian viewers (ING) whose responses indicate a relatively uniform employment of a 'transparent–uncritical' frame, making generally veridical interpretations, and the readings of all the other groups, both Indian and British. As we shall see in the rest of this chapter, this difference originates in the conception of the documentary as a genre, and its truth claims.

Ideally, I should present analyses of the comments made by every respondent, but lack of space precludes such intentions, and the presentation that follows contains excerpts of passages selected from the respondents' accounts.[1] Wherever possible, I have attempted to provide examples from each group within both national contexts. These selections are meant to be illustrative of particular meaning constructions, especially those which are pertinent to the project; and their length is the result of a balancing act, in which I have tried to present excerpts which are sufficiently long, without being overwhelmingly so, in order to give an idea of the way I have interpreted the accounts. This problem reflects, in a sense, my central concerns in this chapter with regard to presenting excerpts from respondents' accounts, in that they perform the dual function

---

[1]A reminder of the various respondent groups: IA–Indian academics, IGS–Indian graduate students, IUG–Indian under graduates, ING–Indian non-graduates; BA–British academics, BGS–British graduate students, BUG–British under graduates, BNG–British non-graduates.

of illustrating both the particular viewer's interpretive framing and that of his/her group, as well as demonstrating my own method of analysis. I have tried to cover as many of the respondents as possible, while bearing in mind the primary motive behind the chapter, which is to identify and describe the interpretive framings of the various representatives from India and Britain.

The various subsections of this chapter roughly correspond to the style I adopted during the interviews, where I attempted to begin with general discussions regarding viewing habits and attitudes to documentaries, before moving to global questions about the individual films and from there to discussions of particular sequences which had been mentioned earlier in the interview. In the excerpts that follow most hesitations, except those which I considered relevant, have been removed; 'Int' marks the interviewer and '[...]' indicates an edited passage. I have also attempted to 'clean up' the grammar of some of the Indian responses in order to render them more comprehensible to the native speaker of English, while trying, at the same time, not to change the sense of what was said.

Interpretive frames

As mentioned in the previous section, the respondents' notion of the authenticity of the documentary representation is pertinent in this context since it performs the function of providing the 'horizon of expectation' from which are derived the 'frames' of interpretation, and which precedes the interpretative exercise. The excerpts in this section concern the respondents' conception of the documentary genre and their acceptance or rejection of the truth claims of the documentary. Analysis of each of these passages follows the *en masse* presentation of the excerpts so as to display the differences better.

The 10 excerpts presented here, five Indian and the other five British (representing each group within the cultures at least once), are illustrative of the range of stances evident in relation to this issue. While most respondents indicated a relatively unambiguous stance, others were more ambivalent. Despite this lack of a clear-cut profile of all the respondents or an indication of culturally motivated differences in the conception of the documentary, the picture which emerges, most explicitly even at this stage, is the unequivocal stance of the Indian non-graduates (ING) accepting the documentary authenticity.

EXCERPT 1

Int: Unlike feature films, which are overtly fictional, documentary makers claim that what they show is reality. Do you accept that claim?

IA1: Yes, if they're saying that their aim is to show reality, from my experience of documentaries, yes, they do show reality. But see, I mean, you could also show reality in an imaginative way. At least many of the documentaries that I have seen, yes they are reality, but I wouldn't say much imagination has been used. Or, you know, even the depth at which they deal with certain facts, descriptions, or whatever. So that way it's disappointing. But you're talking just about, OK, they claim to show reality as against fiction, so it's non-fiction, it's what's happening in real life. It's informative.

Int: Do you think documentaries can be objective, as objective as they're made out to be?

IA1: That depends. The question of objectivity, OK on one hand it's something desirable, on the other hand I don't know if you can really be ...you see, the very fact that you're focussing a camera lens on something itself becomes a subjective kind of decision, because you think it's valuable, it's important and so on. So I don't know... OK, how would you define objectivity? Maybe freedom from bias, or freedom from sentimental...in that sense maybe OK, to some extent OK. But if you talk of...the very fact that you're picturizing something, or you think that this is worth portraying, or showing, I think is a subjective choice that you make. So to that extent...Again, I wouldn't call it a negative thing, because I suppose even if you're showing your documentary, the fact that you are filming it again is a reflection that you consider this something worthwhile, or valuable to talk about, to portray, and so it's got to be subjective in some sense. So I wouldn't say objectivity is everything. In fact I wouldn't mind a subjective element creeping in, so long as it doesn't distort the picture.

Excerpt 1 illustrates an ambivalent stance with regard to the documentary's truth claims. While the respondent accepts that, 'from my experience of documentaries, yes, they do show reality', indicating an uncritical, transparent frame, her comment that 'you could also show reality in an imaginative way' suggests a mediation frame which acknowledges an agency behind the construction of the film. Further, her recognition that objectivity, though desirable, is denied by the very act of 'focusing a camera lens on something' is strongly indicative of a mediation frame, and the consequent recognition that documentary, while 'truthful', is undeniably subjective and 'constructed'.

EXCERPT 2

IGS1: Well, the function of a documentary is to enlighten you, whereas a serial is supposed to entertain you, right? But as far as I am concerned what a documentary should do is, since this is basically television, instead of throwing a lot of facts at you, it should try and involve you visually. That is, whatever it has to say, it has to be done through the pictures. Because, for instance the plight of the *Adivasis*–we've read about it–but there was not a single shot to tell you their plight was really bad, except that one shot where I think these people were sifting in that filth. That's the only shot I remember. That was a really good shot.

Int: Yes, could we discuss the films afterwards. Let's first finish talking about documentaries in general. A difference between documentaries and, say, serials, is that documentaries claim to deal with reality, whereas serials are overtly fictional. Do you agree?

IGS1: Not all serials are fiction. Some are based on real life stories. But yes, the documentary is supposed to present reality. That's why I said it's supposed to inform and not entertain. But it can inform without trying to be really pedantic, and that's the problem with most Indian documentaries. They try to bludgeon something into your head; they don't try to convince you in a very nice manner. All they do is bang, bang, bang: 'So the next time you see an *Adivasi* be nice to him.'

The documentary's informative function is referred to in Excerpts 2 and 8. In Excerpt 2, the documentary is clearly 'supposed to present reality', although the concept of 'reality' is ambiguous, since he claims that 'not all serials are fiction. Some are based on true stories.' More than the content itself, the concern here is with the treatment of subject matter in documentaries: 'what a documentary should do is [...] instead of throwing a lot of facts at you it should try and involve you visually.' This evidently indicates a mediation, but a largely uncritical frame.

Excerpt 3

Int: Why do you like documentaries?

ING1: Because what is happening in the world [and] in our country [is shown]. It's a natural film actually. Exactly what is happening they will show us. That's why I like it.

Int: You say that they show exactly what is happening. Do you think documentaries are truthful?

ING1: Yes, I agree with that sir. Documentaries are...almost 99 per cent is truth, I believe.

Int: Why 99 per cent and not 100 per cent?

ING1: Because the script writers for their goodwill they may add some more.

Int: What do you mean, goodwill?

ING1: Goodwill means some of the shots they want to see, they will show them because audience should be [able to] concentrate on that film sir...That means which is not relevant to the programme they will show us to attract the audiences.

EXCERPT 4

Int: What do you think of the claim that documentaries show reality, as opposed to feature films or serials which are fictional?

ING2: That is correct, because as far as I am concerned, they portray what is exactly happening. So I accept that claim. No doubt about it. We have seen it. We are seeing it, and we trust that [our] feelings are correct.

Int: Sometimes there arc [television] programmes which are about things that are happening now, very topical and immediate. Do you think they portray reality?

ING2: Yes, those which are permitted to be screened, we have to trust it, and we have to take it into consideration [...] because the government has permitted it to be shown, so we have to trust it, yes.

Int: Do you think documentaries can be purely objective?

ING2: More than 60 per cent are objective. Maybe...there may be something in the middle they would have inserted, that's all. But you can take it more than 60 per cent. But what we have to say is, what is the aim of the film? That's what we have to say [...] Even if something, a minor percentage of it is not correct, [it] doesn't matter. But what is the aim, the attitude behind screening the film, that matters much, always.

EXCERPT 5

Int: Do you agree with the idea that documentary films portray reality the way it is?

IUG1: Yes, I agree. It is a good idea. Because, you know, that's the best way to know the people's reactions. People have to get what actually goes on. If you put a little bit of artificial element in it, and then try, may be you are taking away things, you know, not giving them [the audience] the real thing. Not allowing them to see or perceive the right kind of thing that's going on actually, the real thing.

  Int: Do you think it's possible to show reality the way it is?

IUG1: Sometimes it may not be possible, depending on the type of documentary you want to make [...] Like suppose, you want to take a real life situation, like child labour. Sometimes it won't be possible for you to really get across to that actual situation while it's going on, and then shoot a film. That is difficult.

A largely uncritical acceptance of the documentary's claims to truth and objectivity is registered in Excerpts 3, 4, and 5. While Excerpts 3 and 4 acknowledge the occasional presence, in the films, of fictional or personal element ('Documentaries are... almost 99% is truth, I believe'), these are considered minor in relation to the predominantly truthful depiction of events, and the motive behind the depiction. 'What we have to say is, what is the aim of the film? That's what we have to say. [...] Even if something, a minor percentage of it is not correct, [it] doesn't matter.' Interestingly, while the faith in documentary representation expressed in Excerpt 3 appears to be based on its generic properties, the belief that 'they portray what is really happening', in Excerpt 4 derives from outside approval of the content: 'those which are permitted to be screened, we have to trust it, and we have to take it into consideration [...] because the government has permitted it to be shown, so we have to trust it, yes.' The only constraint expressed in Excerpt 5 with regard to capturing 'reality as it is' involves the actual filming process: 'Sometimes it won't be possible for you to really get across to that situation while it's going on, and then shoot a film. That is difficult.' A slight indication of a mediation frame is present in all three excerpts, but the acceptance of the truth claims of the documentary overrides such considerations.

Excerpt 6

Int: Do you think documentaries can objectively portray reality?

BA1: No, because nobody can separate themselves from their values, and their values are bound to underlie...[I] mean, their choice of topic is bound to show personal interest, or what sort of beliefs they hold. You can't get away from that. It will be either acknowledged or...I mean the most you could hope for is a...somebody putting...attempting to put both points of view. But mostly documentaries have a message, and I assume it is the view of the people who made it. And of course you often get them tied up with pressure groups as well, and they are using it to convert rather than to inform. So they are not as objective as they make out.

Int: Can't a film-maker take up a particular topic and present it disinterestedly?

BA1: No, because she wouldn't make the documentary if she could be disinterested about it. It wouldn't have been made at all.

Excerpt 7

Int: While feature films are overtly fictional, documentary films are supposed to depict reality as it is. Would you accept that claim?

BA2: I wouldn't contest their claim that reality is offered in documentaries. After all, a documentary, unlike a serial, is focussed on aspects of reality, the everyday scene. And it is compartmentalized: political, economic, cultural. So I wouldn't say...raise a banner of revolt against their claim that they do offer facets of reality.

Int: Could this portrayal be objective, do you think?

BA2: Only to a certain extent. I am one of those who feel that there is a principle of exclusion which constitutes the basis of documentary making. It is quite hard to encompass the entire range of the implications of a particular phenomenon, particular theme. So the segment of the range which is chosen depends upon the viewpoint that has to be presented, that is...which is pre-determined by the director. So the choice of the implications and the range of the exposure offered by a documentary are pre-shaped by the vision of the director...if you want to call it, the message. So I wouldn't say that when a particular topic is handled in a documentary, the viewer is offered the entire panorama of implications available for a particular theme. Only a certain range is covered, and the range is determined by the vision governing the production.

Int: Would you say therefore...that the documentary can depict just one perspective or only a few perspectives, of a particular issue?

BA2: I wouldn't say that a documentary is confined to one perspective of a problem. It can offer several perspectives. But any shrewd viewer of a documentary comes away with a feeling that the entire range of implications of a theme hasn't been encompassed by the film. And alongside this feeling there is also the conclusion that the total exhaustion of the range is impossible because the director has a certain message to put across and the entire range wouldn't be convenient to support his point of view.

In contrast to the previous three excerpts, Excerpts 6, 7 and 10 are deeply sceptical of the genre's claims. While Excerpt 6 offers a philosophical repudiation of the truth claims, based on the view that everyone, including the film-maker, is anchored to their values, and that 'their choice of topic is bound to show personal interest, or what sort of beliefs they hold, you can't get away from that', the respondent in Excerpt 7 accepts that documentaries 'do offer facets of reality' but recognizes that the principle of exclusion which constitutes the basis of documentary film-making' precludes the representation of the entire truth. Both these respondents register strong mediation frames, attributing specific intentions and motives to the film-maker.

EXCERPT 8

Int: Do you think documentaries show life as it is?

BGS1: I don't think you can ever capture life as it is. There's always a perspective, a point of view. So I don't think anyone's really capturing life, because life is too complicated to be captured like that.

Int: How objective do you think documentaries are on the whole? Would you say that documentaries can be objective?

BGS1: I don't know. I don't think I can say anything about the objectivity of documentary. But I think they have [a] very important social function to perform. They can bring out things which were for a long time, and for whatever reason, ignored. Or they can open out [a topic] for discussion. And that I think is important. But objectivity, I don't know. I think film-making is always [a] subjective activity. There's always...it's always, I mean it can only be subjective.

Excerpt 8, unlike Excerpt 2, recognizes agency and perspective, casting doubt on the genre's truth claims, since, 'there is always a perspective, a point of view.[...] I think film-making is always [a] subjective activity.' To this respondent, the documentary's 'social function' is to bring relevant subjects to public notice. Such a firm registration of production values and functions points toward a critical mediation frame.

EXCERPT 9

Int: It's been claimed that compared to fictional films which are...well, overtly fictional, documentaries are more truthful. Would you agree?

BNG1: Yeah, I would. Because fictional...they have to draw in an audience, so they exaggerate; whereas documentaries [are] probably more worried about what they present.

Int: But would you say that documentaries present the truth, reality?

BNG1: [?]. Yes, I would. On the whole.

Int: Would you say that they present an objective point of view?

BNG1: Yeah, on the whole they do, yeah. I think you just take in information they're giving without, sometimes without questioning it, you know. Yeah, you do believe it's objective.

Int: Who does? Do you believe that?

BNG1: Everyone else...[?] but yeah, I do. I would say that I would...accept what they are saying normally, unless I had some prior knowledge of what they're talking about, I would challenge it, but yeah, you've got no way of believing or not, rather than...If it is shown to be a documentary then you would imagine that that's the truth.

A similar sentiment to Excerpts 3, 4 and 5 is present in Excerpt 9, in which the respondent acknowledges the 'truthfulness' of the documentary representation ('If it shown to be a documentary then you imagine that that's the truth'). However, he allows for disagreement with the content, such challenges arising from prior knowledge of the subject. The uncritical acceptance of the documentary claims is not only generically motivated, but is also indicative of an openness to the rhetorical persuasions contained in the film's arguments. The inevitable presence of a bias in favour of the 'director's opinion' is also acknowledged in Excerpt 9, although it is the idea of neutrality and truth that is contested rather than the documentary representation itself. However, the respondent's stance is sufficiently critical of the claims.

EXCERPT 10

Int: Would you agree with the claim that unlike fictional films, documentaries present a true reflection of reality?

BUG1: I would agree with the idea that that's what people say, but that's not necessarily how it is.

Int: Why not?

BUG1: Well...whatever a documentary is going to be about, it's always going to be biased towards the director's opinion, whereby there's a slant. It'll always be biased. And that's true of films as well.

Int: You mean it goes for both feature film and documentary.

BUG1: Yeah. You know, it's just an idea, you know. Like racism and sexism, you know. The idea is going to come across very subtly, but whether it's right or wrong is what is debatable.

Responses to specific films

On the whole, it would be fair to say that these positions that the respondents adopted with regard to documentary representations matched their initial reactions to the films they watched as part of this study. The viewers with a sceptical attitude to the truth claims of the documentary remained unconvinced by the arguments presented in the films they watched. Perceptions of bias deriving from a critical reading of the films ranged from an apparent observation of deliberate partiality in the films' argument corresponding to the perceived political position of the film-maker (a mediation–critical reading, in the sense that it recognized the film as a deliberate construct which was then deemed partial), to transparent–critical readings which posited the films as portraying reality, but only one perspective of it, and therefore lacking in objectivity. However, a clear pattern does not emerge from these framings since most respondents from both the cultures switched between transparent and mediation frames.

Once again, the group which employed any consistency in their reading was the Indian non-graduates, all of whom used a transparent frame, perceiving no overt bias in the films or even seeing them as only partial representations of reality.

This section contains nine excerpts—five from the Indian respondents and four from the British representing the various groups from both national contexts, illustrating audience responses which advanced the discussion from the conception of the documentary genre in general to the specific films. In particular, it includes responses regarding their reaction to the overall argument presented in the film and their perception of any bias in the presentation. Excerpts 14 and 15 can be seen to convey a largely 'transparent' reading which coincides with the respondents' faith in the truth of documentary representation. While this faith may originate from different beliefs, the resulting response to non-fiction films appears to be similar. All the other excerpts from representatives of groups from both the cultures portray varying degrees of scepticism about the documentaries' claims, based on varying degrees of 'transparent' or 'mediation' critical reading. Again, the analyses of the excerpts follow their *en masse* presentation.

EXCERPT 11

IA1: I think the overall point of view is quite subjective. But from the way...you know, OK what happened there were episodes or actual case studies of children having suffered from apartheid, or bandits attacking them, and bombs and mines, and things like that. But then, each child was talking about his experience, or the commentator spoke about the child's experience...when the children spoke about their experience, you know individual episodes like that, I was quite surprised at the objectivity with which they spoke of them, the children themselves, I thought that it lent them...all of them, all the children... it lent them a kind of dignity. So there I found that...it seemed quite objective, and I wondered how, having gone through such a traumatic kind of experience which would have devastated them...I mean, you could see the effects on them, and yet when they related it on the screen, they seemed to have done it with a certain kind of distance. But the total picture, I would say was subjective, but not in the negative sense, but in a desirable sense, because the aim is to...awareness raising kind of thing, and to say how it's children who suffer the most, and the innocent, in cases of war. Mainly it was about war and the horrors of war. Then I think you do need to be subjective to that extent if that's the message you want to get across. So I thought it was subjective.

Int: Subjective in what way? What makes you say it was subjective?

IA1: Again, as I was saying, the choice of, you know, incidents the children went through, the experiences the children had, then the various authorities talking about the children–the doctors, then this lady who was the rehabilitation person, and then the government official. It's the total picture, the way it's all combined, and the way they keep going from the general commentary back to the children and their personal experience. Maybe it's the way...it's the getting back again and again to the children and talking about their very personal traumatic experiences, and making them relate what happened to them. Yes, to that extent I think it was subjective. Getting the audience in to see at close quarters...the first hand kind of experience.

Excerpt 11, which treats the film *Chain of Tears* as 'quite subjective', expresses a certain level of ambiguity or inconsistency with regard to framings: the respondent's reaction to and estimate of the children's accounts of their experiences–'it lent them a kind of dignity [...] they seem to have done it with a certain distance' –inferred from the straight-to-the-camera interviews of the children, is framed at a 'transparent' level. The attribution of certain personal qualities to the children is based on a transparent reading of what was shown, on information derived visually, which, when matched to the audio, she feels conveys certain meanings about the children. On the other hand, 'it's the total picture, the way it's all combined and their personal experience' indicates a significant cognizance of the textual and rhetorical strategies of cinema as exemplified in that particular film, and although the respondent's interpretation utilizes mostly transparent framings, her perception of alleged bias or 'subjectivity', while positive, emanates from a more 'mediated' reading. The meaning of 'subjectivity' that emerges from this excerpt is curious: what the respondent implies is not the usually held idea where it signifies the film-maker's own idea or interpretation of an event, but the notion that the text was handled in such a way as to draw the audience into a 'first hand kind of experience'. In other words, the 'subjectivity' suggested here is that of the viewer inscribed in the text. However, the respondent indicates an awareness of the manipulation of the filmic components, which clouds the otherwise near transparency of reading.

EXCERPT 12

IGS2: I think it [*Polar Bears*] failed. I think it failed in its objectivity, because it mistook reality for objectivity. Like...
in the programme [*Polar Bears*] there was a sentence saying, 'show us'. By chasing that kind of philosophy or showing the effects of environmental degradation, they forgot to analyze the true causes of environmental degradation, which I do consider such an analysis, I do consider part of reality. And...furthermore, by some sort of constraints, I don't know whether they were production constraints, or they were constraints put by people who funded the programme, they came out with the kind of statements which, though they may be real, I mean, people may be harbouring these kinds of thoughts, but were equally repulsive. Especially when the programme contained veiled threats to Third World that if environmental degradation is not stopped military means would be employed by the First World against the Third World to stop it.

Int: Could you give me a specific instance of that happening?

IGS2: Yeah, I can give you two instances. One was, a person whose name began with Bill, the person wearing a sweater, towards the end of the programme, he said that military means will have to be used against countries like Brazil, though it directly did not say that, but the documentary maker related it with Brazil. He was giving figures about Brazil, and he kind of you know, said that [the] Brazilian government claims that it is our land and we'll decide what to do about it...an aeroplane, a military aeroplane, flying aggressively from one end of the screen to another. That was enough of a threat. And if that's not enough, the person who is supposed to be the father of [the] Montreal...

Int: Mustafa Tolba?

IGS2: Yeah, Mustafa Tolba, he said that now wars will be waged for environmental reasons. Though he was talking with reference to Egypt and Ethiopia, still this can be taken in its context and [a] generalization can be made from this to war of First World against Third World.

The comments in Excerpt 12 are aggressive allegations of bias and distortion on the part of the film-maker. Again, the interpretation suggests a combination of transparent and mediation frames. By registering a certain amount of scepticism on the intentions of the film-maker working under 'some sort of constraints. I don't know whether they were particular constraints, or they were constraints put by people who funded the programme', the respondent shows an awareness of the forces that limit the objective and 'truthful' presentation of the 'real' world. It is clear from the comments that the respondent considers the film to be politically suspect in its apparently partial representation of facts to suit the West and to blame the South. However, he does not carry the reading forward to its logical limit, replacing instead the mediated frame he had initiated with a near transparent one, in which he responds to witnesses as if they were directly perceived. Ironically, this respondent's severe intellectual disagreements with the film ride on interpretations which run counter to the intentions of the film-maker that were overtly expressed during my interview with him.

EXCERPT 13

IUG1: This was, I think, sort of...I felt that they took the film after they heard about the attacks, not while it was actually going on.

Int: You mean, when the war was actually going on?

IUG1: I mean when all these children were actually...when all the ill treatment was actually happening. It was not filmed at that time, but afterwards.

Int: Do you think the film suffers as a result of that?

IUG1: No, I don't. This film [*Chain of Tears*] in a way doesn't.

Excerpt 13, which reiterates the belief expressed with regard to documentaries in general that the portrayal of reality is dependent upon the subject area, identifies the film's [*Chain of Tears*] subject of war as impossible to film as it 'was actually happening'. The profilmic event which would have lent the film credibility and immediacy is therefore problematic, and the film is reduced to reporting the effects of war through interviews instead of capturing it 'while it was actually going on.' Profilmic events as reality are construed as 'live', and their representation as 'live coverage'. Any subsequent attempt to film the results would as a consequence be removed from reality.

EXCERPT 14

Int: Would you consider the *Chain of Tears* to be truthful depiction of what actually happened?

ING2: Yes. Because we read and sometimes we see on TV, and this is a special programme on children of South Africa, so naturally you have to take it as true. Even if you take some part of it as not true, but this is happening there, which should not happen. That's all.

Int: Could you remember anything from this film which you thought could not be true?

ING2: I could not find anything like that. No.

EXCERPT 15

Int: Do you think the film [*Polar Bears*] is a truthful depiction of environmental degradation?

ING1: This is...yes sir, it is 100 per cent truth because what [is] happening and what will be happening...expectations are there in that. There is no other addings [...] It will show us the reality and what [is] happening they are showing us. It is a reality sir.

Excerpts 14 and 15 correspond closely with the respondents' attitudes to documentaries in general. In excerpt 14, the film attains its credibility status from the perceived characteristics of the medium: 'Because we read, and sometimes see on TV, and this is a special programme on children of South Africa, so naturally we have to take it'. The framing here is as pellucid as in Excerpt 15, which expresses a complete transparency of reading in its emphatic declaration of authenticity–'it's 100% truth'–originating from the idea that the documentary is preeminently truthful.

EXCERPT 16

BA1: I thought with the first one, *Chain of Tears*, there were great many interviews of children that it was trying to get over the reality of the situation for the child. So it was treating the children as important, children's experiences and children's views as important. Whereas in the second one [*Whose Children*] it had a different social construction of childhood because the children were not allowed to be children. They were talked about, but very few were interviewed. And I wondered if that reflected the cultural views of....I mean, this is stereotyping, isn't it? Or, shall I say, a cultural background where children are valued and seen as individuals, or a cultural background where they are seen as producing cash in order for the family to survive because of poverty. There were two different views there.

Int: Do you mean that was because of the cultural background of the producers?

BA1: No, I saw in the way it was presented. It might have been to do with the cultural background of the producers. Or was it a way...I mean, African culture is too broad a term, but the cultures of those areas where children seem to be seen as individuals, whereas in the Indian film they were really seen for their earning potential, and that was all, which isn't actually the impression I get from working with Indian and Asian students at school.

The level of abstract reasoning in Excerpt 16 is comparable to that of Excerpt 12. Both respondents extrapolate from the audio-visual clues to make an assessment of the film-maker's intentions (as in the earlier excerpt) and cultural constraints. The respondent's comments in Excerpt 16, grounded on a recognition of the mediatedness of the genre, revolves around the comparison of the presentation of children in both the films: whereas *Chain of Tears* 'was trying to get over the reality of the situation for the child', *Whose Children* 'had a different social construction of childhood because the children were not allowed to be children.' The perceived cultural embeddedness of the different constructions of childhood implies a notion of the film-makers as operating as social agents, and constrained by their social/cultural position. Another notable factor in this excerpt is a level of self reflexivity–'I mean this is stereotyping, isn't it?' rarely present in the responses.

EXCERPT 17

BGS1: About the first film [*Chain of Tears*]...I think it took a very moralistic or ethical view on the whole issue of the effects of war on children. I think the whole film

...there was no analysis of the other, power structures or, other things involved, or matters which really precipitate this sort of suffering. I got a feeling that it was just...that it had a fetishistic fascination for the suffering. I mean, of course it was meant in a certain way which...it sympathized with the children who were suffering, but the analysis of the social or political issues was inadequate.

EXCERPT 18

BUG2: Well, you could say that they are morally biased. You know, they painted a very clear picture of what was moral and what was immoral. [...] the treatment of the children was very cruel and very unjust. But, in those two instances [*Chain of Tears* and *Whose Children*], you know, vast majority of people would agree. You know, that treatment of children, there's no way you can justify on any level. Whereas something more contentious, more debatable, like abortion, you can have a moral opinion, whereas most people in the case of child torture say that it's not acceptable.

Int: So would you say that these two documentaries were more balanced than say a documentary on abortion which states one view only?

BUG2: Yes. In the second video, *Whose Children*, no government official was interviewed to maybe explain why money isn't being put into children's education or something like that. While it wouldn't change my opinion by the end of the documentary, it wasn't there, you know, to give them an opportunity to try and justify the situation. And also, in the first documentary, they didn't interview any of those bandits, really [...] They didn't give their side of the story.

The films were often understood as presenting only a part of the argument, or as otherwise limited in their presentation. Excerpt 17 contains another mediated framing which develops the idea of the film as exhibiting a bias towards the creation of an emotional response rather than a discussion of the various social and political issues concerning the war. The film's 'fetishistic fascination for the suffering' is to the respondent an indication of the subjective concerns of the film-maker, which amounts to the presence of a bias.

A similar position is indicated in Excerpt 18, in which the respondent refers to a 'moral bias' in the films with which 'a vast majority of people would agree', implying that the very subject matter of the films, the ill-treatment of children, inhibits attempts to take an opposing perspective on the issue. The perception of bias and lack of balance arises from pragmatic considerations—'while it wouldn't change my opinion by the end of the documentary', the films evidently did not have any opposing voice.

EXCERPT 19

BNG1: It was very sad and very cruel the way the children had been maimed. The film [*Chain of Tears*] covered that aspect well. Sometimes it was gruesome, but that's war. And the way it was shown, it was quite powerful, you know, the wounds and things. But I didn't like the suggestion...the film suggested that the people in Africa...the Africans can't take care of their own children, which is a terrible thing to say. They have always been shown as somehow less civilized than us, [and] suggesting [that] they let their children suffer supports that view, doesn't it? That's terrible. It's the same thing with the other one [*Whose Children*]. I mean, it's alright to sit here and criticize other governments for letting [their] children work, but they have to eat, don't they?

A critique of the construction of characters, based on a perceived cultural stereotyping, is suggested in Excerpt 19. The 'transparent' response to the 'gruesome' images of war is replaced by a sufficiently mediated interpretation of the films' 'terrible' characterization of children in African and Asian cultures. This reading compares favourably to Excerpt 16 and its critical response to the construction of childhood in the same films. Both interpretations, in varying degrees, move beyond the confines of the immediate texts to infer a 'typical' textual construct.

A comparison of interpretations of the films

For the actual comparison of audience receptions of the films themselves I examined their interpretive framings on two levels: primarily, 'global' interpretations of the films in which their framings were most clearly discernible, as well as the interpretations of particular sequences which had been referred to by most of the respondents earlier in their interviews, and which included images of a less indexically binding, more symbolic nature. Audience understanding of these sequences provided an opportunity to examine the interpretation of culturally embedded images used in a metaphorical sense.

The picture which emerges most distinctly at the end of my analysis of respondent accounts of their overall understanding of the films confirms the initial classification which arose on comparing the respondents' conceptions of documentary texts in general and their reactions to the documentary's truth claims. While nearly all the viewers from both cultures, in categories other than the Indian non-graduates, generated varying degrees of critical readings of the films from transparent or mediated frames, the Indian non-graduates were almost uniformly uncritical, accepting the films' premises. The critical readings of the other respondents were by no means identical: there were variations in the degree of transparency and mediation frames used; differences were perceptible in the utilization of syntactic, semantic or pragmatic criticism. However, with few viewers using a sustained frame, points of comparisons between them were not apparent. Most of these viewers, as mentioned earlier, switched between transparent and mediation frames in their responses. In other words, their responses changed, without following any perceptible pattern, between accepting the films as truthful depictions of profilmic events, and recognizing them as constructions of an agent, the film-maker. Correspondingly, the nature of criticism also changed: a transparent–critical frame generated criticism which was mostly semantic, pointing out inconsistencies in the argument of a film while accepting its overall depiction as truthful; whereas a mediation–critical frame gave rise to syntactic criticism, where the respondent was cognizant of the film as a construction and the responses questioned depictions as mediated representations, or more rarely, pragmatic criticism, which allowed for the constructedness of the film while reflexively examining the viewer's own interpretive process. Pragmatic criticism at times led to a manipulative reading, which perceived the film-maker's apparent intentions and consequently escaped manipulation.

The excerpts that follow illustrate and hopefully clarify some of these different interpretive frames. I have included examples from three 'groups': the Indian academics and students, the British respondents, and the group which emerged as significantly different from these two: the Indian non-graduates. Since the excerpts are long, the analysis follows each passage. Excerpt 20 is an example of the critical framing employed, in varying degrees, by nearly all the Indian academics and students.

Excerpt 20

IA2: [*Polar Bears*] If I hadn't watched the documentary, I would have still got a vague idea of the content from the title. I would've...might have thought that it had something to do with wild life and polar bears, but certainly the angle of ecology and conservation and other things hinted there. I thought the title was catchy enough, and the montage that went with the title, with shots of the polar bear merging with animated shots. I found that very good and attention catching, and along with the title became meaningful [...] I think it's a bit too long. I think...they had divided it into chapters, seven chapters, and I thought up to chapter three it was something new. But from then on people tended to repeat themselves, and the content repeated itself. In different words, of course, and through different people, but the points were more or less the same [...] If I said the first three chapters had something new for me, then I change the word 'new', because the content there wasn't new for me. I've read quite a bit about the greenhouse effect, and the greenhouse gases, and the warming of the global temperature, and things like that. So the content wasn't new at all, but the presentation certainly was, especially because the producer has used all the technological capabilities at his command to merge real life shots with animated and computer shots in a very fluid way, which held my attention...only to tell us that the forests...acres and acres of forests are destroyed every day in Brazil, we don't need someone from New York telling you that if you can see that happening. But as I said, if he comes and tells you that because of this carbon dioxide is rising into the air, etc., if you want a scientific explanation to what's happening because you don't want to alarm people, to frighten them by saying water level is rising and the Maldives is going be submerged in another 10 or 15 years, so beware, and all that. In order not to make it sound like a Biblical prophecy, you perhaps need a scientist explaining in very scientific terms why Maldives will be submerged in whatever, 15 or 20 years' time, that lends credibility. But otherwise I don't think you should have this procession of scientists [...] [*Dust of Development*]. First of all let me talk about the title itself. I don't remember the title of this *Dust of Development*, I mean, I am not sure if that's what it's called. That's because it's such a typical Indian title. I'm not trying to degrade Indian things. I'm a very patriotic person, but we have this, what one of my professors called a penchant for the florid. Whatever it is, a radio programme, or a television programme, or a newspaper article, we choose the most florid style that's available to us, at least for the title. And this was one of those florid things, *In the Dust of Development*. I don't know what it means. What is the dust of development? [...] If I sit and analyze it, it could mean something. Because of development these people had to suffer, and the dust raised by development has affected the lives of these tribals. So they are in the...as if it's the tail of a comet, taking the brunt of this technological development, industrial development. But it doesn't have a straightforward relationship with the content. [...] What I felt was good about this film was it's brevity.

Brevity in comparison with the other film. It had only one point, and it stuck to that point. It didn't try to expand on that by bringing in experts on sociology and sociological research. There was one point, and it made an honest representation of it. [...] Here you know...length in a sense determines your format and the structure of your programme, because these people [*Polar Bears*] had 50 to 60 minutes to play around with. And the format, the structure tended to be a bit diffuse. Whereas the other people [*Dust*], probably because they didn't have money or resources, they had to compact their stuff into may be 20 or 25 minutes. They didn't have the...they couldn't afford to be diffuse. [...] It [the interviews] didn't look contrived to me. But that was because, as I said, the questions were edited out. The questions were terrible, and if I meet these people I'd like to ask them to find a better interviewer. Another thing, now that I've mentioned translation, another thing that struck me as a terrible thing to do was to use that Hindi song, film song. It's a beautiful song, a very meaningful song. But... and for a non-Indian audience it might be appropriate enough. But for an Indian audience which associates this song with a film, and with a film actor, and a filmy situation, it was totally inappropriate. [...] The intention of the producer was probably to drive home the point of the plight of the tribals, and philosophize it, perhaps.

If that was the intention, then that was an unwarranted thing to do. I don't think we need any philosophy on this subject. We need only hard facts and hard decisions. The song unfortunately did that, or rather the repetition of the song did that. Philosophize the subject, take it into an ethereal, whatever, plane. [...] [Because I am an Indian viewer and I've seen those over and over again, scenes like this.

Perhaps that's what went against the specific film sticking to the mind. But otherwise, I don't think there's anything memorable, visually. Those people talked to you, straight from their hearts, and it's their words which ring in your ears, rather than their faces, or the setting. So visually there wasn't much that stayed in my mind, but the content of the sound track, yes.

This excerpt demonstrates a predominantly critical framing in the global understanding of the two films. The interpretation of the title of the first film and the resulting expectations as to the film's content–'certainly the angle of ecology and conservation are hinted here'–are indicative of a certain familiarity with the genre as well as of intertextual recognition. This is also reflected in the reaction to the title of the second film as 'typically Indian', a generalization which is extended further, and taken as an instance of the Indian 'penchant for the florid'. Interestingly, the respondent's interpretation of the title *In the Dust of Development* is a straightforward literal reading: 'the dust raised by development has affected the lives of these tribals', rather than a more metaphorical sense which might be said to be closer to the film's content. Nevertheless, these responses to the films' titles are symptomatic of both a familiarity with the genre as well as a critical framing.

This critical framing is strongly syntactic, with most of the responses concerning the various generic and formulaic elements of the films. The suggestion, therefore, is that the respondent is acutely aware of the constructedness of the text, and the principles of combination of the visual and aural aspects, as for instance in 'the content wasn't new at all, but the presentation certainly was, especially because the producer has used all the technological capabilities at his command to merge real life shots with animated and computer shots in a very fluid way'. Even the discourse is indicative of an acquaintance with the conventions of the genre and the production strategies normally employed.

The notion of documentary credibility, discussed in terms of the use or overuse of expert interviews, demonstrates a syntactic critical reading based on the truth claims of the genre, and the modalities of the documentary text designed to promote these claims. This stance again corresponds to the respondent's conception of the documentary and scepticism of its ability to capture and present 'reality' objectively. Curiously, however, the critical distance adopted by the respondent is threatened by his reaction to the witness accounts in *Dust* as 'talking straight from the heart'. But whether this is indicative of a difference in interpretation caused by cultural proximity is doubtful, since he employs a significantly 'manipulative displaced' frame in his analysis of the use of the song in the film: 'for a non-Indian audience it might be appropriate enough. But for an Indian audience which associates this song with a film, and with a film actor, and a filmy situation, it was totally inappropriate.'

Although mainly syntactic, this respondent's critical reading of the films also contains some semantic and pragmatic elements. By inferring the producer's intention to 'philosophize' the plight of the tribals in *Dust*, which he perceives as the (misplaced) motive behind the use of the song, this viewer ascribes intents to the producer which go beyond the merely conventional and touches upon the manipulative. This is derived from the qualities that are assumed of the song, its 'filminess', which is held to be immediately apparent to an Indian viewer. The pragmatic elements in the reading are indicated by a reflexive statement alluding to the every day familiarity with some of the representations in *Dust*: 'Because I'm an Indian viewer and I've seen those scenes over and over again, scenes like this.

Perhaps that's what went against the specific film sticking to the mind.'

While this reading of the two films is not typical of the Indian teachers and university students, it is certainly illustrative of the critical distance which is present in almost all the responses. Admittedly few of the responses contain the level of sustained syntactic criticism indicated in this excerpt. However, the interpretations of all four films are on the whole made within 'critical' or 'mediation' frames. This framing is evident in interpretations of both Indian and British films, despite frequent comparisons of the perceived merits or problems, thematic and stylistic, of the two films that were watched. Few of the respondents from this group refer to their acquaintance with the subject matter, the visuals, and the strategies of the Indian films and attribute it to cultural proximity, but apart from one or two respondents, the general reaction to the four films were uniformly critical.

Excerpt 21 illustrates the predominantly transparent–uncritical frame adopted by all the Indian non-graduates. There were occasional indications of a critical frame, but these were too few and fleeting to make a significant difference.

EXCERPT 21

ING3: In the first documentary [*Polar Bears*], the more important is to preserve the forests...forests...and [we] should not destroy the...our forests. [...] Yes, it showed the reality. [...] If we destroyed the forests, the environmental changes will occur in the earth, and that will spoil our human lives and climate changes, and floods will come and droughts will arise [...] The film showed us what we are doing in the present situation, whether it is good for nature or we are doing harmful to our own nature, that we will observe in this documentary, sir. It is shown with reality, sir [...] Length of the film also, it is very convenient to view the film. [...] By cutting the forests, and big industries they are not controlling their pollution, and ruin the air, and...Due to heavy motors and...the air will be polluted and the carbon and carbon monoxide and this coal also is damaging the atmosphere. By burning...Almost all industries are using coal for producing electricity and other industries purposes. [...] It [computer graphics] is only showing the difference between...what is the difference...what is the situation is the previous, the...the particular year and after 10 years, and after 20 years what will happen. That is showing graphically. Some people may not understand this computer graphics sir. Only that educated people will understand this [...] Normal viewers can understand by this computer graphics. [The] totally uneducated, they cannot understand.

The second programme [*Dust of Development*] mostly that documentary showed that life of the *Adivasi* in the state of Bihar. Ah, Bihar and Orissa [...] Even though they are having lands, they are unable to feed the food properly sir. Because contractors...the landlords occupying their lands, and the jobs are going to other people. They understand that's why they are not getting job and proper food. In the first documentary only about the climatic changes and save the environmental changes. In the second documentary, about the *Adivasi* how they are getting...getting...problems for getting food in this regions. In second film also directly showing these people are cutting the forests, and these people in trouble it is showing us. [...] Here *Adivasi*, in this film *Adivasi* is using wood and everything, there people are using petrol and coal and making carbon monoxide. [...] Those people are saying in my land we are since long time, but other factories have started run here, those people are not giving us chance. But the child is asking something for meal, but we are not able to give. How to live, the lady is saying. [...] The thing is, *Adivasis* are not getting employment, actually. Who is already settled here, those people are not getting. That's why they are not happy. If these people are also getting the employment they won't care other things. Their land,

and from outside the people are coming and enjoying this land, they are saying like that sir [...] 50 per cent that persons should be...the *Adivasis* should get employment. 50 per cent we can't say because skill should be there for the factories. And that technical knowledge should be there, that's why must give 50 per cent to the *Adivasis* and 50 per cent to qualified persons. [...]

Here is actually, interviews who is in the picture. That people only, with *Adivasi* only we are getting interviews. There the first film, what happened, who is researching on...or concerned officer is saying. It may be correct or not, we can't say that. But here, who people...in this people *Adivasis* already suffering or already in role of the picture, those are saying the trouble. That will be truth I think sir. [...] Pity their situation, I have pity on that, not on the interview sir.

But thing is immediately what problem they are getting, they are expressing sir...First film also interviews I can't say [are] wrong. But at least it has been planned interview I can say. [...] Because already these people are studied, which is good which is correct, which is... they decided. Even not interviewer person, before interviewer person also, already they are studied, that's why I can say that is a planned interview. [...] In this case, all of sudden we are going them and we are asking their trouble, they are saying their trouble, that is why...that is the difference between that people and this people.

Excerpt 21 exemplifies the mainly transparent frame–'it is showing us reality'–adopted by the Indians in non-academic occupations. *Polar Bears* is read as explicitly didactic, in which the message is clear: 'if we destroyed the forests, the environmental changes will occur in the earth, and that will spoil our human lives and climate changes, and floods will come and droughts will arise.' This prognostication of doom arises from a reading of a cause and effect narrative in the film, indicating the general level of comprehension achieved by the viewer, who is therefore, able to correctly identify the film's central thematic concerns. His retelling of the content shows an uncritical acceptance of the documentary's premise, understood through a transparent reading of its visuals and a fairly competent (given the problems with the language) understanding of the arguments presented through the voice-over and expert interviews.

This is not to say, however, that the reading is entirely transparent. The respondent's idea regarding the difficulty for 'totally uneducated people' in understanding the computer graphics in *Polar Bears* points to an acknowledgement of the film's constructedness. Similarly, a hint of a recognition of mediation is suggested in the respondent's comparison of the interviews in the two films, in which he implies that the studied, academic position adopted by the experts in *Polar Bears* lacks the spontaneity–it is 'a planned interview'–of the witness accounts in *Dust*. The immediacy and experientiality of the latter are, to the respondent, indications of their truthfulness. Witness accounts are read more transparently than the statements of experts, and the second film is thereby elevated to the position of truthful depiction of the life of *Adivasis*.

This difference in the perception of the status of interviews in the two films is indicative of an increased level of transparency in the reading of the second film. The respondent's direct reporting of witnesses' speech while commenting on the plight of the tribals contains clear suggestions that he is responding to them as persons rather than as mediated characters: 'those people are saying, "in my land we are since long time, but other factories have started run here, those people are not giving us chance. But the child is asking something for meal, but we are not able to give. How to live?," the lady is saying.' His recommendation that the government reserved 50 per cent of the jobs for the tribals, while going beyond the confines of the text and suggesting a degree of the use elements of knowledge constructed elsewhere, is nevertheless based on a transparent framing of the interpretations of the interviews. He views the witnesses' accounts as 'authentic', and not as the creation of generic conventions.

It would be fair to say that all the four respondents from this group of non-graduate Indians produced transparent interpretations of similar consistency. The occasional reference to the mediating conditions of any of the four films serves to highlight the otherwise uncritical acceptance of the truth claims of the two films that each of the respondents watched. A marked increase in the level of transparency with regard to interpretations of the Indian films is also discernible in all the four responses, suggesting the effect of cultural proximity in understanding not generally present in the other Indian respondents.

The final passage in this sub-section, Excerpt 22 from a British graduate student's response, is an example of the transparent–critical and mediation–critical frames which the British viewers used. While the responses indicated varying degrees of criticism, they were all predominantly critical.

EXCERPT 22

BGS4: Well, they [the makers of *Polar Bears*] tried to be fair, but they...I think they...the instances are taken from all over the world: China, India, Africa, and the West, South America, etc. But when it came to finding the solution, it was rather vague, rather vague, wasn't it? [...] Except for the last chapter, the seventh chapter, I wouldn't have faulted them at all. There it says, well, what shall we do? It asks you a question, and we're not told anything at all, except [to] switch off the light when you leave the room, and things like that. And use the car less...

I think this film was made primarily for a Western audience. [...] For instance towards the end, people were talking about ways we have...ways we could conserve energy, etc., prevent global warming, the greenhouse effect. They were mainly what we in the West could do. There was nothing there on how it would benefit the Third World, and how the Third

World could change their ways without destroying their economy, what is usually called progress. You know, there was nothing at all about that. [...] I mean apart from things like switching the light off, and driving your car less often, they had nothing to say at all. Nothing constructive, just pious statements. What is it, what aspect of our lifestyle has to be changed? What exactly did they mean by consumerism? Where is the problem? For instance most of the industrialized countries build things with built in...built in...obsolescence. They go out of fashion in two years, so then you go on producing more. You are going to have to tackle that. They didn't talk about that at all, which is hypocritical in a sense. [...]

No, I don't claim they are anti-Third World, I'm not saying that at all. All I'm saying is that it's natural that they should think more about the West than about the Third World. After all, it was made in the West, naturally...some bias. But the most important thing is, what is the root cause of the problem. Instead of concentrating on the peripheries, the frills, tackle the root cause of environmental destruction. [...]

For instance, what are the ways through which you can ensure that environmental laws are obeyed? You know, how industries can't evade these laws. A lot has taken place [changed?] in the West, you know, cleaning up all those activities. They could have talked about those, how it affects industries in the long run. I mean, they might spend quite a bit of money restructuring their units, but in the long run what benefits would accrue, etc. They could have talked about it as [an example?]. [...] The other film was about tribal people in India, how their lives were affected by industrialization. [...] Not really a film on the environment, more a human story, a human film, you know what I mean? [...] I liked the way they used that song, to structure the film. It had a single strand running through it, and only one point of view, which went through [with] the presenter, right through. All the interviews support the same idea. It had a fairly simple structure, that way. [...] It was fairly obvious that the presenter doesn't belong to that society, that she's trying to depict [their lives?] as an outsider. But you could tell that she was very sympathetic. [...] There was a lot of repetition in the interviews, as if they weren't sure [that] the other person, the person who was interviewing them, would understand what they were saying, they felt the need to repeat. [...] There were more gestures, to ensure communication, I suppose. [...] The song? Well, it was sentimental; the lyrics were poetic and all that. But so what? [...] It ought to work, but for whom? Who's the audience? Who's it meant for? What is the point, for instance, what is the person trying to say? [...] It worked for me in the sense, I hadn't realized for instance, that these people [tribals] were forced to fish in that muck. What did they get out of it? I was curious. So I hadn't realized their condition was that bad. But what is going to happen to them? What does the presenter want the government to do, the authorities to do? That's not clear at all. So apart from sentimentalizing the whole thing, and making everyone feel sorry for the tribals, what else do they expect from a film like this? Apart from shedding a few tears, what else do you expect?

The critical stance adopted in this excerpt from a British graduate student's response to *Polar Bears* and *Dust* finds both films inadequate in their suggestions to remedy the situation they depict, while accepting their premises. For instance, whereas he is in agreement with the state of the environment as presented in *Polar Bears*–'but for the last chapter, the seventh chapter, I wouldn't have faulted them at all'–the practical advice offered leaves him unconvinced. As a case of semantic criticism, this runs close to a transparent framing since the critical stance adopted is on the basis of an alleged gap between actual ('authentic') circumstances and possible solutions. His criticism of the perceived lack of alternative ideas to improve the environment, and his own suggestions regarding the arguments that the film could have made, are based on knowledge from 'real life' situations, as for example the reference to industries' compliance to environmental laws.

However, there are other instances in which the viewer moves away from a transparent acceptance of the content to inferring the film's mediating conditions. The perception of a 'natural' bias in *Polar Bears* in favour of the West and therefore as a film made primarily for a Western audience illustrates this. While continuing to respond to the actual circumstances as presented in the film, the viewer acknowledges an almost inevitable bias in the film-maker's approach to the subject. This reference to the role of the producer suggests the recognition of the conditions of mediation, if not of the film-maker's manipulative intent.

The responses to *Dust* similarly indicate the operation of different interpretive frames. A mediation–critical (semantic as well as syntactic) frame is used in the discussions of the film's structure and argument, and the song's role in it. This is replaced by a more transparent frame which perceives the repetition of witness accounts not as a compositional quality, but as if the interviews were 'real' events, whereby the repetitions were a deliberate ploy employed 'as if they weren't sure [that] the other person, the person who was interviewing them, would understand what they were saying, they felt the need to repeat.' The respondent's final criticism of the film is similar to his reservations regarding *Polar Bears*: it is couched in the terms of the utility of the film.

Once again, the kind of framing evident in this reading is not typical of the British viewers, but it illustrates the generally critical, mediation frame employed by nearly all the British viewers. There is, yet again, no discernible difference in the interpretation of the two films, although statements like 'I hadn't realized that their condition was that bad' are made more in relation to the Indian films, suggesting a lack of familiarity with the Indian society. Generally speaking, these interpretations, like those of Indian academics and students, show a fairly consistent critical attitude with regard to both films.

In order to examine the respondents' interpretation of particular sequences, I chose two series of images—one each from *Chain of Tears* and *Polar Bears*. As mentioned earlier, these sequences had been alluded to by most viewers in their accounts of the films, and where this did not happen, I deliberately drew their attention to them.

The sequences from *Chain of Tears* were the images of helicopters which, as mentioned in Chapter 6, are present both as part of the montage sequence which begins and closes the film, where they figure most prominently, as well as occasionally in the body of the film. Neither the commentary nor any of the voice-overs drew special attention to these images. I was interested in finding out whether the images were interpreted as symbols signifying something outside the immediate narrative, while simultaneously contributing to the film's atmosphere, or as part of the narrative itself. Generally the frames adopted in their interpretation corresponded to those employed in interpreting the entire film, as can be seen demonstrated in the following six extracts where, once again, the Indian non-academic representative interprets the sequence differently from most others. The analyses follow the extracts.

EXCERPT 23

Int: There are a lot of shots of helicopters in the film. What did they signify to you?

IA4: Some kind of reconnaissance thing. I mean...I don't know, government troops coming in? I mean, helicopter gunships is what I thought of.

Int: What made you think of helicopter gunships?

IA4: I don't know. Think the kids had drawn some also. But even without that...I must have been reading too much of too many war comics or something, I don't know. That's what it reminded me of. Even though they were pretty harmless in the documentary and they weren't doing anything. So obviously they were out on a kind of

mission. But that's what it reminded me of. Something
that the children...Perhaps they were there to create an
impression of, the impression of fear. Terror striking
across unexpectedly, well, not unexpectedly perhaps.
I'm not sure.

The discussion of the symbolic significance of the helicopters
in Excerpt 23 contains a combination of both transparent and
mediation reading. Within the transparent frame, the shots of
helicopters are interpreted as part of the narrative in which
the helicopters perform a straightforward functional role, as
demonstrated by the respondent's inference that they were,
'Some kind of reconnaissance thing. I mean... I don't know,
government troops coming in? [...] obviously they were out
on a kind of mission.' The helicopters are therefore seen as
part of the overall linear narrative, a reading very much influenced by, as the respondent suggests in a moment of reflexive
illumination, a degree of familiarity with other 'war' texts, in
this case, 'war comics'. The feeling that the images of helicopters could be performing a symbolic role, designed 'to create
an impression of, impression of fear. Terror striking across unexpectedly, well, not unexpectedly, perhaps' indicates a mediation frame which recognizes the presence of a production
decision behind the images, and attributes intentions to it.

Excerpt 24

    Int: What do the shots of helicopters signify?
    IGS3: I think they signify the war. It's...all the bewilderment
        of the child not being able to understand what...It's
        war, it's something beyond the understanding of the
        child, something to do with adults. Can't understand
        why it is...So it's bewilderment, it's wonder, it's fear,
        from the child's...
    Int: Child's eye view?
    IGS3: Yeah.
    Int: Otherwise you think...to you it signifies war.
    IGS3: Yeah, it's like some ominous presence.

EXCERPT 25

ING2: The helicopters belong to the military, and the military people are taking care of the camps. That's what I thought. Yes. Because there was no mention about it in the commentary, as far as I heard it.

Int: Do you think these were the same military forces which you think they referred to as bandits?

ING2: You are right, because I once said bandits may be military people. I don't know the reasons for all these things. That is cutting children's fingers, etc. I thought military people were doing that, which means...that may not be correct. But rebels are doing all kinds of things, and military people are safeguarding the children. That's what I have come to the conclusion.

Excerpt 24 illustrates a more sustained employment of a mediation frame. To this respondent, the images of helicopters perform an overtly symbolic role, contributing to the general atmosphere of the film. Their 'ominous presence' is interpreted as connoting the children's uncomprehending 'bewilderment, it's wonder, it's fear'. This reading is remarkably close to the producer's version of her intentions. Among the Indian academic and student viewers the interpretations of these visuals vary from a literal-metaphorical framing (as in Excerpt 23) which assigns both a functional as well as a indexical role to the images within the narrative, to a more consistent metaphorical framing (as illustrated in Excerpt 24).

Compared to this, the interpretation offered in Excerpt 25 attributes a signification to the images which corresponds closely to a transparent reading. Based on information derived visually ('there was no mention about it in the commentary'), the helicopters are assigned a purpose within the narrative, indicating a literal interpretation of the images imputing a 'operational' role rather than a symbolic significance adding to the 'atmosphere' in the film: 'the helicopters belong to the military, and the military people are taking care of the camps. [...] Rebels are doing all kinds of things, arid military people are safeguarding the children.' Here the action is perceived as immediate, the profilmic events occurring 'authentically', as suggested by the use of the present continuous tense. Without any indication of an awareness of generic conventions the reading becomes entirely transparent. This interpretation is again illustrative of the frames most prevalent among non-academic Indian viewers. While not all the respondents from this group register as much confusion between the rebels ('bandits') and government forces as does this viewer, there is a great deal of commonality in the attribution to the images of helicopters a functional capacity within the narrative.

EXCERPT 26

Int: Let me draw your attention to a few particular sequences. There were a lot of shots of helicopters. What did those helicopters mean to you?

BA1: I thought that it was supposed to be evoking the fears that the children had, that those things would appear from nowhere, and therefore they would be a sort of hidden danger. Although most of the stories had nothing to do with helicopters, they had to do with bandits who came out and...I don't know enough about wars in Angola or Mozambique to...Yes, I thought too, I mean, when they were looking at the map at the beginning they were showing Vietnam, Laos, Cambodia, where you tend to have images of helicopters associated with war. But not really the...the children had been injured by people, not helicopters. Yes, I think they were supposed to create the atmosphere of fear. They seemed to create tension. They were part of the entertainment element, if you like.

EXCERPT 27

BUG2: Images of war. And it corresponded with what the children's pictures were at that time, children's pictures of helicopters that were sort of shooting down at them.

Int: Yes, that's right.

BUG2: And I think the picture was shown first, and that sort of associated [with] the battle. And then you saw the real helicopter. Just conjures more images of war. And, you know, we see shots of Vietnam, you know, you'll see helicopters somewhere there.

Int: So the helicopters signified war?

BUG2: Yeah, that's it, yeah.

EXCERPT 28

Int: What did those helicopters signify to you?

BNG3: War.

Int: Did they signify war?

BNG3: Yeah.

Int: What about war, exactly?

BNG3: I think because at the very beginning they were, the helicopters were shown as they were saying, as they were talking about the war. So every time they showed it, that's what I...and there were some military look-ing helicopters there...[?] And so, because they spoke about...because when they showed it first of all, they spoke of war, and every time afterwards they showed them, then you thought about war. Yeah, they were about war, the concept perhaps.

In Excerpt 26, the reading of the images as 'evoking the fear that the children had' results from a conscious delibera-tion of their role in the narrative which suggests a mediation frame: they were 'supposed to create the atmosphere of fear' because 'the stories had nothing to do with helicopters'. In other words, the images are assigned an indexical role since they are perceived to be inconsistent with the film's 'story', and therefore as not performing an operational function. The reference to Vietnam and Cambodia and their link with images of helicopters indicates a fair degree of mediation framing. Excerpt 27 makes a similar intertextual connection between these helicopter images and the potent symbols of war employed in films on Vietnam. Drawing on this link as well as from information derived from other images in the film, 'it corresponded with what the children's pictures were at that time', the respondent concludes that the helicopters are 'images of war'. Other comments such as 'the picture was shown first' suggest an attribution of intention to the film-maker, and provide an indication of the familiarity with the compositional characteristics of the documentary. Clues from the voice-over and interviews are used in Excerpt 28 to connect the helicopter images with the 'concept' of war: 'when they showed it first of all, they spoke of war, and every time afterwards they showed them, then you thought about war'. This excerpt contains a more emphatic attribution of agency ('they showed it first'), and a specific intention behind the film's construction, which suggests a manipulative reading.

The British respondents were generally prone to interpreting the images of helicopters symbolically, as indices contributing to the atmosphere of the film, which indicates mediation framing and a degree of manipulative reading. There are hardly any instances of a transparent reading, or a suggestion that these images could be a function in the progression of the narrative.

The other visual sequence, from *Polar Bears*, which was used as an indicator of interpretation is a shot to shot transition using a dissolve, which shows the image of the earth (seen from space, as it were) turning into a circular bell. This visual transition is accompanied by the sound of an electric bell. In this case, there is little ambivalence as to the symbolic nature of the images, since there is no obvious connection to the narrative. Moreover, the nature of the dissolve itself draws attention to its symbolic nature rather than positing it as a capturing of profilmic reality. In this instance, therefore, the interest was in discovering whether the reading of the bell required culture specific knowledge. The following excerpts indicate the range of differences in the interpretation of what was generally recognized as a symbolic image.

EXCERPT 29

Int: There was the shot of the earth dissolving into a shot of a bell.

IA2: Oh yes, yes. That was one of the things I liked very much.

Int: What did it mean to you?

IA2: It meant that time was ticking away for the planet, because I thought it was something like a metronome. You know, a device which beats time, which shows you time.

Int: Is that how it struck you? Wasn't it a bit too shrill and sudden, for a clock?

IA2: Mmmm, it was like a gong. But then I thought a gong wouldn't have any meaning there. And I thought this thing was beating fairly regularly on the...what looked like a gong, this circular thing, which was in effect the earth. The picture of the earth dissolving into this clock like thing. So I thought it meant that time was running out for us. Yes, that was a shot which I should have remembered and mentioned. There were some other shots like that...especially the dissolves. I liked the dissolves very much, and that's one of the examples of the fluidity I talked about earlier.

EXCERPT 30

IGS2: The earth turning into a gong?

Int: Yes.

IGS2: And it being struck? Ah, no, that was childish. That was awfully childish.

Int: Why do you think it was childish?

IGS2: Well, because, the transition...like...yeah, the problem is the same. When I criticized the computer graphics, that was the same thing. Like, there got to be an easy step by step transition form one sort of picture to another sort of picture, one sort of a frame to another sort of frame. The transition was a bit too crude. Like, the image in itself, if I think of it, would be quite nice, quite apt. But the way they presented it, the way they thought of it, was not proper. And...

Int: What did it signify to you? I mean the image as they presented it?

IGS2: The image as they presented it signified to me the desperation that anti-Christ is coming, that sort of, you know, that desperation that one has to turn devout. I mean, that the end was near.

Int: Is that what the shot signified to you?

IGS2: Yeah, the gong signifies that. In...even in other literature, it's a cliché. I mean, another thing is that it was very clichéd...that the end is near, days are numbered. I mean, that sort of stuff. And that...there is a gap fortunately between what we are doing now and the destruction that is going to come. It isn't like these people suggest, that today we are alive and tomorrow we are dead.

Excerpt 31

Int: Do you remember the shot of the earth dissolving into a shot of a bell?

IUG3: Clichéd.

Int: Why do you think it is clichéd?

IUG3: I've seen too much of it already.

Int: And what does it mean to you?

IUG3: Alarm bells ringing. I mean, it's about time to take notice.

Int: Right. But a cliché?

IUG3: Somehow I've seen too much of it...

Int: You've seen too many...

IUG3: Documentaries which use the same symbol, you know. It wasn't anything new. Probably...! mean, if you are seeing it for the first time, it would be successful.

Int: So to you it was a kind of alarm bell ringing, please take notice, this is something we have to do.

IUG3: Yeah.

Excerpt 32

ING1: Ah, yes sir. That is a warning...warning...to the human persons it is going we are in dangerous times.

Int: Is that what it meant?

ING1: I understood sir, immediately, but now I didn't remember it. When you said to me, I got an idea. The bell is nothing but a warning.

Excerpt 33

BA3: Ah, yes, the bell. It was mix from something else, wasn't it?

Int: A mix from the shot of the earth.

BA3: Oh yes, I remember that.

Int: What did it signify to you?

BA3: Let's see. The earth...I think at that point they were talking about what is global warming, weren't they? And then suddenly you have this bell, and the bell rings. Perhaps it was a kind of warning. Yes, when I saw it I think I was reminded of the fire alarm. So it could be that the earth is hotting up, so you better put out the fires.

Excerpt 34

BGS3: Maybe it was a kind of warning?

Int: Do you remember what kind of bell it was?

BGS3: It was an electric bell...it wasn't struck like a gong or anything. It was an electric bell, a sort of automatic one, like a fire alarm or burglar alarm. So maybe it was a warning of the disaster that technology and development by technology could spell? But I wouldn't have thought about it...I had forgotten about it. It might have come back later, but since you remind me...

While all these respondents interpret the images symbolically, the way the bell itself is perceived differs to a certain extent. Excerpts 33 and 34, both from the accounts of British respondents, see the bell as a fire alarm or burglar alarm, and consequently as representing 'a kind of warning' in the film. The link established here is a straightforward connection between the images in the film and the knowledge derived from every day experience. However, respondent IA2 (Excerpt 29), working with textual clues ('But then I thought a gong wouldn't have any meaning here'), associates the bell with 'a metronome', which leads him to interpret the images, and their transition, as metaphors of time–'I thought it meant that time was running out for us.' This clearly demonstrates the link between the specific interpretation of the bell as a fire or burglar alarm, and cultural proximity.

A similar link between the images and the passing of time is established in Excerpt 30, which is dismissively critical of the metaphor: 'it signified to me the desperation that anti-Christ is coming, that sort of, you know, that desperation that one has to turn devout. I mean, that the end was near.' Within this critical–mediation frame the images take on a sense of doom, a 'cliched' symbol commonly used in the representative arts. Excerpt 31 contains a comparable registration of a critical–mediation frame, which also sees the images as a 'cliched' metaphor. To this respondent, however, the metaphor signifies alarm: 'Alarm bells ringing. I mean, it's about time to take notice.' In contrast to this reading, in Excerpt 32, the images are interpreted simply as 'nothing but a warning'.

The most obvious conclusion which suggests itself at the end of my analysis is that, in the interpretation of these four documentaries there is little discernible difference between the interpretive framings employed by most Indian and British respondents. The differences which do emerge are connected to images which evidently require culture specific knowledge, as in the case of the electric bell mentioned in the above analysis. In other words, there is little variation among these viewers in the interpretation of the films qua documentaries. The utilization of the categories identified at the beginning of the analysis, 'transparent' and 'mediation' frames, are generally present in varying degrees in all these respondents' accounts, as are varying degrees of critical readings. Comparison on the basis of the use of these frames by these respondents is consequently pointless, since the most that can perhaps be ascertained is the extent of critical framing applied as part of the interpretive act. Such an exercise, however, would require an analysis different from the one employed in this case study, applying quantitative categories to count the number of critical statements present in viewers' accounts, as in Liebes and Katz (1990). It would appear from the results discussed here that critical readings are necessarily unsystematic, and therefore difficult to codify in ways other than content analysis, which, by counting statements out of context, would defeat the object of this exercise.

By the same token, is consistency possible only in transparent–uncritical framings? The predominantly uncritical decodings of the Indian non-graduates do indicate their acceptance of the films as true, engendered by their acknowledgement of the truth claims of the documentary genre. The more definitive conclusion that does emerge as the result of this study is that the difference in the interpretive frames between those consistently employed by Indian non-graduates and most others from both cultures is, from the perspective of the initial hypothesis, unexpected.

The challenge now is to understand and explain this result in terms of the theoretical framework discussed in Chapters 3, 4 and 5. From within the context of philosophical hermeneutics, how is this difference between the signifying practices of persons belonging to the same culture and therefore 'tradition' possible? Phenomenologically, is this difference in interpretive activity indicative of the Indian non-graduates occupying a cultural space different from that of the other Indian respondents within the Indian nation-state? Likewise, do the similarities in interpretations between these other Indian respondents and the British viewers signify a similar proximity in 'cultural' space? These are some of the questions tackled in the next chapter.

8

Ethnicity, Multiculturalism and Interpretive Practice

Recently, two kinds of research on global audiences have emphasized the role of ethnicity: those engaging with certain assumptions of the cultural imperialism thesis, and those examining the role of the media in the formation of diasporic identities. This chapter's main argument is that, while these two streams of audience study have contributed significantly to the reformulation of media/cultural imperialism, and to the study of the formation of diasporic communities respectively, their conception of ethnicity is extremely problematic, both on epistemological and political grounds. Using the works of Liebes and Katz (1990) and Gillespie (1995) as exemplars of a particular kind of cross-cultural and diasporic audience research, this chapter will argue that, emphasizing racial or ethnic difference as determining audience behaviour is problematic. Given the consolidation of the politics of the New Right (Giroux 1994), the blending of 'race', ethnicity and culture raises uncomfortable political and conceptual issues. As Gilroy (2000) has observed, the politics of 'race' and ethnicity, always constitutive of debates on multiculturalism, has taken on a new dimension following more recent apprehensions relating to the 'war on terror', particularly in North America,

Europe and Australia. Given this situation, it seems to me that a great deal of sensitivity is required while dealing with the complex dimensions of ethnic identity, belonging and transnational cultures.

Tomlinson's (1991, 1999) approach to different conceptions of cultural imperialism is in many ways indicative of the variety of critiques that have been aimed at the thesis. These have included outright attacks that seek to undermine the presumption of unequal power relations that underlies the thesis, attacks which, for instance, celebrate the apparent 'semiotic democracy' (Fiske 1991) and the diverse kinds of pleasures that audiences gain from their experience of the media. Other critics (such as Ang 2001) attempt to refine what are seen to be the excesses of the thesis, as for example, the emphasis on the homogenization of global culture, in an attempt to sustain the fundamental aspects of the thesis while jettisoning its more extravagant claims. Ang (2001) is justifiably suspicious of the at times simplistic anti-Western sentiment that formed a significant part of some of the arguments about cultural imperialism, claiming that the 'West' has become 'decentred' as both an analytical and geographical category. She is, however, unwilling to forgo the analytics of the contemporary forms of global capital, underlining its incorporation of cultural and racial differences (Ang 2001: 34). By extension, Ang's position relates to the politics of inequality while acknowledging the complexity, brought to the global cultural landscape by efforts at promoting discourses of cultural nationalism. As she argues, the issue of the nationalist discourse is particularly relevant in the case of East Asia, where the economic growth in the early 1990s contributed to a corresponding increase in national and regional self-confidence which turned critiques of cultural imperialism from a largely defensive discourse pointing to a putative 'West' imposing an alien culture on the region, to a call for the initiation of a cultural 'counter-offensive': a move that Ang interprets as indicative of a contradictory impulse constituted by both confidence and anxiety (2001: 41).

Central to the issue of researching audiences across cultures is Ang's observation that

> ...the 'real' significant differences within the region [South East Asia] cannot be easily subsumed within a unifying and unified pan-Asian whole...; it is something that Western satellite broadcasters were quick to learn when they realized that there is no such thing as a pan-Asian television audience. (2001: 41)

The Murdoch-owned Star TV's decision to promote separate services for different languages is a consequence of that realization–an indication, as Ang remarks, of the 'localization' of globalization, that is, the recognition of the cultural diversity within a region and consequently of divergent audience participation and interest.

This is important to our present concerns in broadly two ways: first, the acknowledgement of the precariousness of attempts to locate a cultural whole within a region given the sheer diversity of languages. What is generally regarded as a 'region', however, becomes an interesting issue. Granted that pan-Asianism is problematic, but how are we to regard even pan-Indian or pan-Malaysian or pan-Indonesian, given the sheer diversity of languages, religions and other social divisions that characterize those cultures and indeed have played a significant role in the constitution of those cultures? This question is crucial to the analysis of both the mediation of global culture as well as attempts to promote a variation of cultural nationalism riding on conceptions of a putative national culture. What constitutes a 'national culture' is, as a result, imbued in issues of the power to define it, the role of elites, and ethnic and cultural differences within a nation-state. The legitimacy of various forms of cultural nationalism consequently becomes questionable. The second way in which this acknowledgement of cultural difference within a region is important for us is more closely linked to the debates we are covering in this essay, that is, the diversity of global audiences and the questionable assumptions regarding ethnicity and cultural difference that underlie few well-known international audience studies that seek to interrogate the claims of media or cultural imperialism, or to trace the links between diaspora, cultural change and ethnicity.

Challenging the idea of the global media as a vehicle of particular ideologies, with its attendant assumption regarding international audiences who are, more often than not, read into the analyses of texts as ideologically loaded, there has developed more recently a stream of audience studies which set out to explore the ways in which audiences engage with different texts. Building on advances in audience ethnography and sophisticated analyses of qualitative data, generated through innovative research methods, these studies have begun to offer interesting insights into the audience behaviour, interpretations and preferences with regard to mediated culture. The guiding assumption in these studies is that audiences 'actively' engage with media texts, and that this engagement is informed and influenced by social and cultural factors. I have argued elsewhere that these studies do not offer sufficiently complex explanations of how socio-cultural factors influence audience interpretations (Harindranath 2000), but in the present context, it is worth exploring the achievements and problems in such research.

Ethnic difference and interpretative practice

One study that is often referred to by media scholars as offering the definitive challenge to the cultural imperialism thesis (as espoused for example, in Tomlinson 1991), in particular the uncritical assumptions regarding international audiences, is Liebes and Katz's (1990) examination of the ways in which 'ethnically homogeneous' groups of families engaged with specific episodes of *Dallas*. The main aim of this research was to investigate the ways in which 'the melodrama of a fictional family in Texas is viewed, interpreted and discussed by real families throughout the world' (Liebes and Katz 1993: 4). The primary rationale behind Liebes and Katz's choice of families representing putatively diverse ethnicities was that, such diversity constituted different symbolic resources and values systems which could then be studied in their interaction with the episodes of the soap opera. Here was a text that was demonstrably different in terms of the centrality of its action and its main characters and the centrality of its action being located in Texas, culturally removed as it were, from most of the selected group of audiences. This cultural distance did not, however, affect its popularity among diverse global audiences. In what ways then, would cultural differences affect the ways in which audiences responded to the characters' motivations and actions? On the face of it this seems a reasonable proposition.

The main argument underlying Liebes and Katz's exploration of diverse audience responses to *Dallas* is the potential for critical readings among different audience groups:

> Having long assumed that the texts of popular culture inscribe themselves hegemonically in the defenceless minds of the readers, critical theorists realized that their theory left no room at all for social change. How to explain feminism for example, if culture is totally mobilized to maintain the status quo? In recent years, therefore, critical theorists... have made room for alternate readings, thus acknowledging that the ordinary viewer, not only the theorist, may know how to read oppositionally. (Liebes and Katz 1993: 18)

Coinciding with this conceptual challenge to the power of the text over the reader/viewer came the development of 'new audience research' built on qualitative research methodologies seeking to trace the different meanings and pleasures audiences gained in their encounters with television and film. The attempted correlation between the progressive politics, informing critical theorists and the empirical demonstrations of alternative and 'oppositional' audience responses, however, remains at best tenuous. Part of the problem here lies with the difficulty in demonstrating how alternative readings of the television fiction or the documentary translate into cultural or political practice that challenges the status quo. Another relevant issue here is a vexed one—what constitutes a culture? In their attempt to replicate a putative global audience from different cultural groups, Liebes and Katz chose to work with ethnically diverse groups: Arabs, Russian Jews, Kibbutzniks and Moroccan Jews within Israel, comparing their responses to specific episodes of *Dallas* with each other and with those of an American group. Once again, on the face of it their claim to be replicating the microcosm of a global, culturally diverse audience seems well founded. What is less convincing however, is their suggestion that ethnicity, seen here as being constituted by race, determines audience responses.

Liebes and Katz generated interesting data which suggest clear lines of interpretive difference running along the fault lines of 'ethnic' difference among the various groups. In their assessment of the groups' retellings of an episode of *Dallas* they claim for instance:

> The two more traditional groups–Arabs and Moroccan Jews–prefer linearity...They select the action-oriented subplot for attention, defining the hero's goals and his adventures in trying to achieve them. They tell the story in closed form as if it were an inevitable progression, and the characters they describe are rigidly stereotyped; indeed, they are often referred to by role–family role, of course–rather than by name... The Russians speak of the episode in terms of themes or messages. They ignore the story in favor of exposing the overall principles which they perceive as repeated relentlessly, and which, in their opinion, have a manipulative intent... Americans and Kibbutzniks tell the story psychoanalytically. They are not concerned with the linearity of the narrative but with analysing the problems of characters intrapersonally and interpersonally. Their retellings are open, future-oriented, and take into account the never-ending quality of the soap-opera genre. (Liebes and Katz 1993: 80–81)

The reasons for this difference, according to Liebes and Katz, is to do with the 'traditional' nature of Arab and Moroccan cultures, the inherent critical attitude of Russian Jews, and finally the 'comparative security' of the 'modern' American and kibbutzim groups. In framing their discussion of the different takes on the episode of *Dallas* by different groups along racial lines, Liebes and Katz reproduce a monolithic conception of ethnicity. Their discussion delimits the mutability of ethnicity as opposed to the biographically determined category of 'race', what Fanon referred to as the 'corporeal malediction' of racial markers.

Given the context of their research, Israel, the reference to Arab and Moroccan communities as 'traditional' falls uncomfortably close to what Said (1986) represented as 'the ideology of difference' which positions the Arab community within Israel as homogeneous and culturally backward (see Harindranath 2000 for a more detailed discussion of this point).

In a significant contribution to the assessment of the constitution of racism and to debates on difference and equality, Malik (1996) presents a nuanced and closely argued case for the approach to 'race' as a social category rather than the insistence on it as a kind of cultural difference that characterize current 'culture wars' (Giroux 1994). The insistence on racial difference as constituted by immutable cultural difference is in danger of reproducing, in a different form, the earlier nineteenth century depictions of the biological difference as underlying racial diversity, which were given spurious 'scientific' validity by social Darwinism. The privileging of cultural difference as an immutable, defining and essential category of putative racial difference collapses 'race' into culture. The argument that such cultural ('racial') differences are fixed and static 'reveals a view of culture as a predetermined, natural phenomenon... [The] concept of race arises through the naturalisation of social differences. Regarding cultural diversity in natural terms can only ensure that culture acquires an immutable character, and hence becomes a homologue for race' (Malik 1996: 150).

Despite the best intentions of the researchers in presenting their data and analyses as explorations of the near global popularity of a typically American text such as *Dallas*, and as a challenge to the often assumed belief that mediated texts such as American television programmes are accepted uncritically by international audiences, the conceptual rigidity of their division of their respondents into ethnically self-contained groups has unfortunate and damaging consequences. The tautology inherent in dividing audience groups in this way and then arguing that their responses to television reinforce their ethnicity presents two different elisions: it elides the distinction between ethnicity and 'race' and then presents 'race' in terms of culture. Unlike the concept of 'race', used to denote apparently immutable biological differences, 'ethnicity' as a term is generally considered to refer to mutable, more fluid differences between groups of people in terms of cultural practices and beliefs, thereby, avoiding the problematic aspects of 'race'. In practice however, as Malik argues, the terms are often interchangeable. As he demonstrates, even sociologists like Giddens make the fundamental error of presenting ethnicity along racial lines in statements such as 'most modern societies include numerous different ethnic groups. In Britain, Irish, Asian, West Indian, Italian and Greek immigrants, among others, form ethnically distinct communities within a wider society' (Giddens quoted in Malik 1996: 176), which delineate various immigrant groups along racial or national lines while purporting to consider them in terms of more changeable criteria that constitute ethnicities.

Liebes and Katz's analysis similarly confound the distinction between 'race' and 'ethnicity' as conceptually different categories. Presented as a defining characteristic, the distinction between race and ethnicity collapses in their case when, for instance, Moroccan Jews are considered to have 'traditional' values as opposed to the 'modern' Americans or Kibbutzniks. Furthermore, used this way, ethnicity loses its mutability and becomes an essentialist, particularist concept which defines and delimits the behavioural aspects of racially different communities, but simultaneously avoids the pitfalls of defining difference along 'race' by making the dubious link between ethnicity (used in this instance as conceptually similar to 'race') and culture. The elision between 'race' and cultural difference has been commented on before (Malik 1996). Given that Liebes and Katz's stated objective was to challenge ideas of media imperialism and the alleged homogenization of diverse global cultures, however, this elision takes on a different significance. In claiming that the cultures of Moroccan Jews or Arabs have something immutable, essential and unchanging their research comes close to 'new racism' in which, according to Gilroy

>...culture is conceived along ethnically absolute lines, not as something intrinsically fluid, changing, unstable, and dynamic, but as a fixed property of social groups rather than a relational field in which they encounter one another and live out social, historical relationships. When culture is brought into contact with race it is transformed into a pseudobiological property of communal life. (quoted in Giroux 1994: 36)

As noted earlier, in a later book, Gilroy (2005) underlines the enduring legacies of the politics of cultural difference which have, particularly since 11 September 2001, intersected with issues of national security and 'race', and with the reassessment of immigration and multicultural policies. Given such developments, eliding 'race' and cultural difference becomes even more problematic.

Ethnicity, media consumption and diasporic identities

Liebes and Katz's reification of 'race' as a defining category and the subsequent collapsing of 'race' into culture as synonymous concepts are mirrored in some of the literature on the diasporic groups and the media. In their anxiety to explore the links between the collective identities of such groups and their experience and use of the media, a few of the studies similarly elevate 'race' to normative levels, that is, racial identity becomes a self-fulfilling category. In terms of media audiences, this becomes in essence a problematic formula, suggesting that certain ethnic groups watch particular programmes and films that then contribute to the maintenance of a collective identity in those ethnic groups. Most damagingly, such circular arguments, in their refusal to recognize the relevance of the politics of the location of various groups in a diaspora, amount to a disavowal of the critical issues of histories of migration, and the localized histories marking the changing relationship between such communities and the host culture. It is through such histories that identities are forged, contributing to differences between generations of immigrants, and between new arrivals and older immigrants. The 'social and historical relationships' that Gilroy emphasizes as constituting cultural encounters are neglected in some of the studies on the diaspora and the media.

Gillespie's (1995) study of the 'South Asian' youngsters and their media use is a case in point. Arguing that 'the media and cultural consumption–the production, "reading" and use of representations–play a key role in constructing and defining, contesting and reconstituting national, "ethnic" and other cultural identities' (1995: 11), Gillespie attempts to explore the ways in which the practice of television consumption among young South Asians in the London borough of Southall is indicative of and contribute to cultural change. That is, how they use the media to negotiate an identity that simultaneously addresses the desire to relate with their peers within and outside their 'ethnicity', while dealing with the pressures of parental concerns and values. Her main focus is on an ethnographic account of every day, domestic practices among these youth as audiences of a diverse range of television programmes and formats, and on the role of 'TV talk'–'the embedding of TV experiences in conversational forms and flows [which] becomes a feasible object of study only when fully ethnographic methods are used in audience research' (Gillespie 1995: 23).

As in the case of Liebes and Katz (1990), Gillespie's is an important study, in this instance making a valuable contribution to debates on the ethnography of diaspora cultures and identities, and those on the complexities of audience negotiations with and appropriations of the media. Her laudable aim is to avoid the political and methodological pitfalls of construing diaspora cultures in terms of binary oppositions or in terms of putative 'purity', by conceptualizing 'the term "ethnicity" in the sense of an array of strategic positionings in a field of differences, and [adopting] a dynamic concept of culture, in the hope of challenging in some small way the limiting, paralysing or destructive effects of such binary thinking' (Gillespie 1995: 207). This challenge takes its cue from Hall's (1992) formulation of ethnic identity as discursively and contextually constituted by history, language and culture. The discursive aspect of identity formation makes the 'strategic positionings' referred to by Gillespie possible, particularly in relation to the media which are seen to contribute, as Gillespie demonstrates, a variety of possibilities for audience groups to 'translate', appropriate and 'indigenise' strategic readings which are then used to refine their notions of local cultures and group (ethnic) identities. Seen from this perspective, audience groups 'read' media texts along ethnically influenced ways, while at the same time these readings engender constructions of ethnic identities. For instance, Gillespie argues that the availability of diverse media

...encourages young people to compare, contrast and criticise the cultural and social forms represented to them by their parents, by significant others present in their daily lives, and by significant others on the screen. This is the kind of context in which the construction of new ethnic identities becomes both an inevitable consequence and a necessary task. (Gillespie 1995: 206)

What is being proposed here is the apparent effectiveness of a cosmopolitan encounter with diverse cultures—here in a mediated form—in the redefinition of identities. Apart from the problems of the circularity of the argument that different ethnic groups read media differently which then contributes to a reworking of their identities, the focus on 'race' as a defining category and the neglect of other factors such as class and gender is problematic, particularly in the context of diasporas.

This elevation of 'race' as a determining factor in audiences' reception of and engagement with television texts is problematic in both political and epistemological terms. Politically, the reification of 'race' amounts to a refusal to recognize the significance of patterns of inequality embedded in socio-cultural factors that influence engagement with the media as well as access to cultural resources (Harindranath 1998). Construed as a socially coherent and significant group, whether they be South Asians (which is too broad a category in itself) or Moroccan Jews or African Americans, such communities are then given certain defining characteristics, either overtly, as in the case of Liebes and Katz's reference to Moroccans and Arabs as 'traditional', or less directly but nevertheless in a discursively significant manner, as for instance the South Asian teenagers' response to *Neighbours*, or to television advertisements of consumer goods. The question of whether that defines them as South Asians or as teenagers is not sufficiently explored, and Gillespie's study is discursively positioned in such a way that it seems to suggest the former. Given this disavowal, such superficial acknowledgement of ethnic or racial difference hides more than it reveals. For instance, the gender and class politics intrinsic to any diasporic community is not taken into account, even at times glossed over in the attempt to demonstrate the role of the media in identity formation. While on the surface Gillespie's project differs from that of Liebes and Katz in the important sense that she conceives of diasporic cultural identity as fluid and dynamic, along the lines advocated famously by Hall (1990), her consideration of the South Asians as a monolithic category threatens to undermine her project.

As Brah (1996) and others have argued, diasporic identities are constituted not only by who travels 'where, when, how, and under what circumstances' (Brah 1996: 182), but also that they are 'at once local and global. They are networks of transnational identifications encompassing "imagined" and "encountered" communities' (Brah 1996: 196). Most importantly, diaspora is a relational term, with implications of power relations between and within diasporic communities, as well as between diasporic and host communities. The emphasis on the complexity of the historical circumstances of migration, as refugees, or indentured labourers, or skilled migrants, and so on, as well as the relations between diasporic and host cultures, not least in terms of racist practices, figure significantly in the formation of diasporic identities. Tracing the complex routes and histories of migration that make up the Indian diaspora for instance, Mishra (1996, 2002) makes a distinction between 'old' and 'new' diasporas, marked respectively by migration as indentured labour and by economic migration—the 'diaspora of plantation labour' and the 'diaspora of late capital'. The second moment, mostly post 1960s, 'is very different from the traditional nineteenth and early twentieth century diaspora of classic capital, which was primarily working class and connected to plantation culture (examined in great detail by V. S. Naipaul in his novel *A House for Mr Biswas* (1961)). The diaspora of late capital has now become an important market of popular cinema as well as a site of its production' (Mishra 2002: 236). To promote a putative and unitary Indianness as common to Indian communities in Europe, the Caribbean, Malaysia, Kuwait and Fiji is therefore problematic.

Diaspora as a concept productively deconstructs the reification of 'race' as a signifying category. As Gilroy (2000) has brilliantly argued in the case of the 'Black Atlantic', the complexities that such heterogeneous histories of mobility bring to diaspora formation requires a re-thinking of place, geography, and genealogy in terms of hybrid and non-territorial identities:

> As an alternative to the metaphysics of 'race', nation, and bounded culture coded into the body, diaspora is a concept that problematises the cultural and historical mechanics of belonging. It disrupts the fundamental power of territory to define identity by breaking the simple sequence of explanatory links between place, location, and consciousness. (Gilroy 2000: 124)

This extends Clifford's (1997) formulation, in which diasporic communities retain a creative tension with national spaces and identities, constructing public spheres and forming collective consciousnesses that transcend national boundaries and form alliances with similar others elsewhere.

The disregard of the material histories that define the reality of the migrant experience in different sites in the search for a putative 'transnational' culture threatens to undermine the intellectual legitimacy of racial politics in these different locations. Highlighting the apparent commonalities of experiences of the cultural consumption across a diverse community grouped predominantly by their ethnic or racial aspects belies the complexity of the cultural and social formations of such communities. Such uncritical use of 'race' as a defining characteristic teeters at the edge of a particular kind of racial profiling–suggesting for instance, that Moroccan Jews employ 'traditional' values to the assessment of the actions of characters from *Dallas* is but a step away from portraying the group as backward or at best 'different' from allegedly 'modern' communities. Can the racialization of the apparent 'clash of civilization' be far behind? This is not to suggest of course, that media scholars such as Liebes and Katz deliberately set out to divide multicultural societies along racial lines, but merely to underline the dangers of focussing exclusively on race as a determining behaviour, including television viewing or film watching. Given the strong racial aspects underlying various immigration, policing and legal aspects of contemporary global politics, not to mention the obvious perils of ethnically defined nationalism, it is vital to be especially vigilant against contributing to the politics of difference constituted along such lines.

As mentioned earlier, a lot of these problems stem from epistemological inadequacies: it is a mistake to conceive of 'race' as a determining category in the exploration of the practices of consumption of the media and how these are linked to identify formation. A significant contributor to such conceptualizations is the lack of an adequate theoretical explanation for the link between social groups and media reception, that is, the answer to the question, how do social or cultural factors impinge on the way people respond to film or television? One can equally pose the question the other way round: in what ways do particular kinds of responses to film and television characterize social or cultural factors? For instance, the popularity of mainstream Indian (Hindi) films among different groups of South Asians in Europe, North America and Australia is indicated by the regular screening of such films in city cinemas. But how far does that interest–leave alone the more intricate and complicated issues of different audience responses to them–characterize South Asian ethnicity? Does my lack of interest in popular Hindi cinema make me an exceptional South Asian as well as a snob? What does it signify in terms of my 'ethnic' identity? It seems to me that promoting my responses to mainstream Hindi films as somehow contributing to my 'Indianness' is clearly wrong.

Gillespie (2000) argues that the similarities that she sees between her ethnographic study in London and Mankekar's (1993) examination of diverse audience responses to the televising of the Indian epic *Mahabharatha* is a clear indication of the validity of her findings: '[t]he parallels in the readings of Mankekar's informants and my own are striking' (Gillespie 2000: 176). Such insistence on the shared interpretive frameworks that transcend national boundaries underlines the problems with Gillespie's conception of an alleged Indianness that subsumes and overcomes differences within communities. Without a competent exploration of the political and social factors underlying both similarities and differences in audience responses, such stances become problematic. Contrary to Gillespie's claims, however, Mankekar's exceptional analysis (1999) of the textual privileging of specific patriarchal and nationalistic discourses in the Indian television serialization of the *Ramayana*, and the diversity of responses to it from disparate Indian groups, demonstrates a reassuring degree of sensitivity to the political significance of both the serial as well as audience interpretations and evaluations of principal characters. Far from presenting audience responses as a unified and singular take on the serial, Mankekar's study reveals nuanced multiple positions along the lines of gender, religious, regional and linguistic differences which highlight various points of divergence from assessing the patriarchal underpinning of Sita (the main female character) as an ideal woman, to interrogations of different versions of the epic, as for instance between the serialized version and the one by the Tamil poet, Kamban. The discussions sufficiently demonstrate her view that

'popular' narratives [such as the television serialisation of *Ramayana*] do *not* yield an infinite range of interpretations. At the same time, the heterogeneous responses of viewers (including Hindu viewers) reveal that the 'popular' is not a monolithic category: viewers modes of engagement were shaped by their life experiences, gender, and class (Mankekar 1999: 196).

She presents several instances of this diversity in modes of engagement. For example, in terms of class difference, 'although some upper-class viewers complained that the *Ramayan's* sets...were kitschy and gaudy, many lower-middle-class viewers I worked with described the sets as "glorious" or "magnificent"'. And that

> while upwardly mobile and English educated Uma Chandran complained that she was 'bored' with the 'plastic expressions' of Ram and Sita, Poonam Sharma, who was precariously middle-class, said: 'What was amazing about the *Ramayan* serial was that Ram and Sita looked exactly like I had imagined' (Mankekar 1999: 191–92).

Even in terms of aesthetic assessment, therefore, issues such as class and educational background figure as important influences.

In other words, what emerges as significant in Mankekar's study is the diversity of cultural positioning with regard to the serial, depending on the different cultural resources that various audiences were able and willing to call upon. Given the emergence of Hindu fundamentalism in the late 1980s, which was rapidly consolidated as the validation of a form of cultural nationalism and a political force from the early 1990s, Mankekar's work underlines the relevance of such research which go beyond either merely challenging the media/cultural imperialism thesis, or the gestural aspects of studying diasporic groups conceived on notions of ethnic absolutism.

Two other studies which may be mentioned here as emphasizing the importance of factors other than racial difference are those done by Strelitz [2002] and Harindranath (1998). Seeking to examine the role of consumption in identity formation and the impact of global media on local cultures, Strelitz's analysis of the spread of global culture among students in a university in South Africa undermines the easy correlation between 'race' and media consumption and reception, thereby erasing the clear lines traced by Liebes and Katz (1990) and Gillespie (1995) between race/ethnicity and response to the media, and profoundly complicating the analytics of international audience research. Crucially, what emerges in his research, as reported in his work (Strelitz 2002), is the distinction between the urban, middle class African students, educated in superior schools, comfortable with English, and in many ways similar to their white counterparts, and the 'homeland' viewers, that is, the group of African students from 'rural peasant or working class' backgrounds and inferior schools, who created 'their own television viewing space' (which they refer to as 'homeland') in which they regularly viewed largely local productions (Strelitz 2002: 459). Strelitz identifies several sites of difference ranging from the feeling of estrangement among the 'homeland' students, not only from their white classmates but also from the urban middle-class African students whom they perceive as so markedly different from them in terms of cultural tastes and their preference for English.

> The 'homeland' represents a psychological space within which these students can re-confirm and live out their feelings of difference...The 'homeland', where only Xhosa is spoken, is a space which enables these students to interact with each other confidently, free from the ridicule of the better educated, urban, middle class students. (Strelitz 2002: 466–67)

The difference was further confirmed by their choice of programmes to watch: their preference, argues Strelitz, is informed by their eagerness to make sense of the structural inequalities inherent in South African society.

Strelitz's study not only challenges the convenient use of 'race' as a marker for behaviour, but also supports his insistence on the importance of 'the interplay between media consumption and other social factors—such as social location, social networks and so on—in the construction of social identity' (Strelitz 2002: 473). That education and class are significant contributors to and definers of social location was confirmed in my analysis (Harindranath 1998, 2000) of the differences between Indian and British audiences' interpretations of documentaries.

Linking media spectatorship and interpretive strategies to 'race' alone, whether in the search for the elusive international audience or the diaspora identity is, therefore, clearly inadequate. Not only do other factors such as education and class impinge on the access, preference and response to global media products, but the formation of identity has to take into account other kinds of social and cultural elements that constitute the life-worlds of different communities. Straubhaar's useful concept of 'cultural proximity' is valid here, particularly the suggestion that the impact of global media on local cultures is uneven. But whereas he associates culture with particular geographical zones, both my study and Strelitz's strongly indicate the presence in different locales of audiences who have the willingness and the cultural resources to engage in different ways with global (Western) television programmes and films, so much so that there is evidence of a clear preference for such fare. The uneven distribution of cultural resources and capacities impinge on audience choices, pleasures and responses. Clearly then, it is no longer valid to either consider entire populations in developing regions as a monolithic group of audience, or to make clear-cut distinctions between 'Western' and 'non-Western' audiences on the basis of geographical locality. The emergence of studies such as Strelitz and others (see for example, Tufte 2002) offer clear indications of changes in audience research in terms of accommodating the complex interlocking dynamics of 'race', class, gender and ethnicity.

Dirlik's (1997) distinction between the hegemonic culturalism that characterizes ideological relations between the West and the non-West on the one hand, and the one that operates within the non-West on the other, is crucial here in order to trace the complexities and over-determinations imposed by class and gender issues in both diasporic and 'national' or ethnic cultures. As he argues, 'culturalist hegemony within the context of global relations is a "double-hegemony": it involves, in addition to the relationship between the West and the non-West, the hegemonic relations within non-Western societies. The interplay between these two creates a complexity over the question of hegemony' (Dirlik 1997: 37). The consensual homogeneity of discursive 'ethnicity' removes from attention the material aspects of diasporic and national cultural and social formations that are constitutive of the complexity of the experience of diaspora or ethnicity. That is, considerations of ethnicity as delineating a homogenous whole, either in terms of diaspora or nation, to be found both in the works of those who promote the notion of cultural imperialism as well as in research studies highlighting the multiple interpretations by culturally differentiated audiences, overlook the influence of the inequality intrinsic to the distribution of cultural resources within these putative homogeneous groups. Tsing's distinction between 'cosmopolitans' and 'poor migrants' seems apposite here: 'Both cosmopolitans and poor migrants erase the specificity of their cultural tracks, although for different reasons: poor migrants need to fit in the worlds of others; cosmopolitans want more of the world to be theirs' (Tsing 2000/2002: 469). This recognition of disparities within diasporic groups is significant in two ways: first, it offers a conceptual framework with which to grasp the cultural differences within these alleged monolithic groups identified purely by their 'race' or nationality. Second, it highlights Dirlik's observation on hegemonic relations within non-Western cultures and states which need to be accommodated in audience studies seeking to examine the claims of cultural homogenization through global media, and by those interested in looking at the media and diasporic communities. In terms of the latter, as Gillespie (2000) rightly points out, a 'multi-sited ethnography' goes some way towards addressing the complexities that attend to transnational communities. However, if we follow Rouse's (1991/2002) argument that migrants occupy a transnational rather than a particular national space, we need to move beyond considering audiences in specific locales and their reception of mediated texts, and towards examining the ways in which communities use communication technologies to establish and maintain relations within what Rouse refers to as the transnational migrant circuit. This requires an epistemological and methodological reappraisal of transnational audience research.

9

Making Connections: Media Audiences and Cultural Citizenship

We will not cease from exploration
And the end of all our exploring
Will be to arrive where we started
And know the place for the first time.

T. S. Eliot, *Four Quartets*

In this chapter I attempt to bring together the theoretical arguments presented in the earlier part of the book with the analysis of my data in an effort to understand the results of my case study. I initiate the discussion by first considering the data in the light of the notions of 'understanding' and 'genre', which were unpacked and examined in earlier chapters, before I explore the implications of the study in terms of the socio-cultural 'context', as proposed in Chapter 3. Bearing in mind the Gadamerian notion of understanding as irretrievably linked to historicity, the results of the data analysis, presented in Chapter 7, appear incomprehensible. However, I shall argue in this chapter that, given the Schutzian refinement of conventional sociological variables, it is possible to understand what might initially appear to be aberrant decodings of the films.

Documentaries and interpretive practice

As we saw in Chapter 7, one of the significant outcomes of the case study is that there is little systematic difference in interpretation of the films across national contexts to form a recognizable pattern. As demonstrated in that chapter, the respondents, apart from a particular group, generally utilized framings and interpretive procedures in a manner that was far from uniform or sustained. Many of them moved freely between 'transparent' and 'mediated' frames, and between 'critical' and 'referential' readings.

Identifying statements for easy positioning of responses, therefore, would be a spurious exercise. While it is possible to locate statements with which to mark off a particular respondent's account as either 'critical' or 'transparent', as in Liebes and Katz (1990), such a strategy would eliminate the possibility of taking the responses in their entirety. Moreover, it would belie the complexity of the respondents' accounts, substituting instead an easily categorizable set of frameworks which could provide a totally false impression of the responses.

The motif that emerges from the data is at once simple and unsurprising as well as complex and unexpected. On the simplest level, it is hardly surprising, given the characteristics of the documentary text (as discussed in Chapter 5), especially its rhetorical strategies and its logic of information, that the films posed few significant problems to the respondents' understanding of them, whatever the 'framings' or interpretive strategies that were mobilized. Given the direct form of address of documentaries, a basic level of comprehension among those with at least a passing knowledge of English was more or less guaranteed (see Corner 1995: 152). Nor is it startling, given the documentary's truth claims and its relatively high position in the hierarchy of truth among moving image genres, that many of the readings utilized a 'transparent' framing, even while some were critical of the argument being proffered in the films. The textual cues inherent in the documentary, as we saw in Chapter 5, call for a processing of the text different from that of fiction; intrinsic in this difference is the acceptance that documentary representation (metonymic) is different from the fictional (metaphorical). On the other hand, given the implicit assumptions, on which were based the categories underpinning the gathering of data–selecting respondents from 'Indian' and 'British' cultures, implied an expectation of these categories performing a normative function, generating interpretations significantly different from each other and the results which emerged on analyzing the data were unexpected, making any explanation of this 'discrepancy' more complex than what a monolithic conception of culture would suggest.

The group which emerges as markedly different from all the others in both cultures in its consistent use of 'transparent–uncritical' framings is the one comprising Indian non-graduates, forming an interpretive 'repertoire' (I borrow this term from Jensen (1991a: 42), since it signifies a concept which 'implies that audiences are not formal groups or communities, but contextually defined agents who employ such repertoires to make preliminary sense.') which is, in itself, deeply instructive. Fundamentally, this interpretive community or 'repertoire' undermines the easy, relatively straightforward classification of all Indian viewers as belonging to one 'culture'. Before going into a discussion of the issue of culture as context, however, it would be useful to examine the results of the study in relation to the other two terms which were identified in Chapter 1 and examined in Chapters 3 and 5, 'understanding' and 'genre', in order to specify how and to what extent the group of Indian non-graduates differed from the others in their interpretive practices.

As argued in Chapter 3, the interpretation of the television is linked to the concept of 'the horizon of expectations' in specific ways. Genre recognition is crucial, as is familiarity with the mode of moving image representation in general. An audience's visual and generic expectations combine to give the impression of veridicality to the moving image. In the case of the documentary, however, this veridicality is further compounded by its truth claims and its socially accepted position at the top of the hierarchy of truth in the cinematic representation. The horizon of expectations generated by the documentary genre, therefore, necessarily involves either accepting or rejecting its claims to authenticity and truthful depiction.

That these specific expectations relating to the documentary affect the employment of interpretive frames was demonstrated in Chapter 7, where it was shown that nearly all of those respondents who either accepted the generic claim or were at least ambivalent about it utilized largely transparent frames. There appeared to be a link between those (the Indian non-graduates) who concurred most strongly with the idea that the documentary as non-fiction depicted 'reality' and their interpretation of the films as representations of profilmic reality. While this might seem an obvious outcome of their horizon of expectations, what is interesting is the difference between this interpretive repertoire and the others who were less certain about documentary authenticity, and whose readings indicated a level of 'critical' framing. What distinguishes the Indian non-graduates from the rest of the respondents is their relatively consistent transparent–uncritical reading of all four films.

In other words, the Indian non-graduates, unlike the other respondents, accepted all three proofs contained in the films' rhetoric. In doing so, these viewers acknowledged the authority of the documentary, both in general as well as in the case of the particular films. The distance between the modalities of the filmic representation and historical reality were, as a consequence, collapsed, making the viewers react to the images as if they were real. On a more semantic level, their acknowledgement of textual authority positioned them in the role of 'the desire to know', which, as Nichols (1981) observes, is part of the viewer–documentary contractual arrangement (1981: 205). These respondents' uncritical framing accepted the texts as the locus of 'He Who Knows', correspondingly positioning themselves as willing subjects, accepting the films' arguments as reflections of 'that is the way it is'.

Critical frames used by most respondents (from both cultures) themselves were varied, as we saw in Chapter 7, in their treatment of the images as veridical. While there were only rare instances of a sustained mediation–critical reading which recognized the films as constructions and at times projected an authorial intent behind sequences, most critical responses contained a variety of positions on the transparent–mediation continuum—at some points in their responses, the viewers appeared to treat the films as depicting reality in an unmediated fashion, and their criticism came in the form of questioning the objectivity of the producer; on other occasions, the same viewers employed a type of syntactic criticism which acknowledged the films as mediated.

The degree of semantic criticism was again varied. While with most respondents (from both cultures) who adopted a critical frame this amounted to a questioning of the film's argument as possibly partial (thereby doubting its demonstrative proof), indicating a level of transparent framing inherent in their critical frames; few respondents (especially one Indian post graduate student) demonstrated a more sustained mediation–critical frame which occasionally moved into a manipulation frame, identifying in the films' argument authorial intentions which they considered politically unacceptable. While these readings did not form a sufficiently systematic pattern, their presence is in themselves interesting, since it suggests a horizon of expectation which includes a level of scepticism about documentary representation and its truth claims. In this specific instance, their scepticism was manifested in their rejection of the ethical and demonstrative proofs in the films. Witness accounts were estimated as specially incorporated in the text, while others were specially left out, in order to support the film-maker's particular ideological leanings.

On the whole, the pattern that does remain posits the Indian non-graduates as uncritically accepting the veridicality of the films, acknowledging documentary's logic of information and the didactic intent inscribed in it. Opposed to this position are the other respondents, Indian as well as British, whose readings combined a variety of critical and uncritical, transparent as well as mediation frames.

Re-thinking 'contexts' of interpretation

In relation to the category of 'context', the data and results of
their analysis are instructive in broadly two ways: first, they
underline the crucial flaw in my implicit assumption, while
dividing the respondents into two mutually exclusive camps,
'Indian' and 'British', that these categories would generate significantly different interpretive procedures; and second, the
results from the data which indicate the presence of an interpretive repertoire within the 'Indian' category suggests a
reassessment of my initial classification. In Chapter 3, I argued, following Gadamerian hermeneutics, that understanding occurs only within 'tradition' or 'effective history', which
proscribes any effort at 'objective' understanding. Interpretations are not made in a social vacuum, but on the contrary
are the consequences of the socio-cultural contexts of the
interpreters. In this formulation, interpretation of texts is an
extension of the general understanding which is a fundamental characteristic of human being-in-the-world, ineluctably circumscribed by historicity. The reverse of this argument is, of
course, that different interpretive practices are symptomatic of
different socio-cultural contexts. By this argument, the Indian
non-graduates appear to constitute a 'world' separate from
other groups from both cultures, while at the same time, the
rest of the Indian respondents must coexist with their British
counterparts in the same or at least similar 'world'.

The first of these issues—the unthinking utilization of the
classical notion of culture as corresponding with the geographical space—could legitimately be seen as falling into the
same trap as classical anthropology. In labelling the categories
of audiences as 'Indian' and 'British', I was unconsciously acknowledging the colonial practice of dividing the world into
the West and the Other, a position which is neither politically
desirable nor intellectually fertile. Traditionally, anthropology
opposed the West to the Other, participating 'in a significant
way in the establishment of Western selfhood via its otherness;
modern versus traditional, developed versus undeveloped,
civilized versus primitive' (Lash and Friedman 1992: 27). From

this position were drawn power and authority, the anthropologist or ethnographer supplying details of an alien lifestyle–often inscribed in the 'ethnographic present' tense–law-like and 'objective'–which Rosaldo (1993) parodies brilliantly and with telling effect in 'After Objectivism'–to be better governed by the colonial power, while simultaneously supporting its increasingly precarious bulwark of moral authority by positing the Other as primitive, child-like and premodern, needing the guiding hand of 'progress' of the Western industrial civilization. Rosaldo's quintessential pre-1960s anthropologist, 'the Lone Ethnographer' was 'willy-nilly complicit with the imperialist domination of his epoch. [His] mask of innocence (or, as he put it, his "detached impartiality") barely concealed his ideological role in perpetuating the colonial control of "distant" peoples and places' (Rosaldo 1993: 30).

Needless to say, my original proposal contained no such intention. As already mentioned in previous chapters, the objective of my case study–the comparison of interpretations of documentaries across national contexts–was based on the assumption that the culturally different spaces inhabited by audiences in India and Britain would generate diverse interpretations. Yet, my conception of Indianness and Britishness as monolithic, even while it assumed, like Liebes and Katz, a link between 'race' and responses to the media, amounted to a tacit subscription to the Victorian divide, with its implicit hierarchy in which Occidental culture held the privileged position and in which any 'study' of non-Occidental culture implied an unspoken evaluation of it using Western norms.[1] Morley and

---

[1] My use of the past tense here must not be taken to mean that I believe such norms to be no longer in currency. They are very much in evidence, even in the popular media, where the 'us' and 'them' opposition is invoked from time to time. In academic anthropology, however, the tide seems to be turning. As Rosaldo (1993) observes,

> When people play 'ethnographer and natives', it is ever more difficult to predict who will put on the loincloth and who will pick up the pencil and paper [...] One increasingly finds North American Tewas, South Asian Sinhalese, and Chicanoes are among those who read and write ethnographies. (1993: 45)

Silverstone (1991) refer to the need for reflexivity which recent debates concerning ethnographic research call for, in order to counter what Edward Said has called 'Orientalization': 'the process of imaginative geography which produces a fictionalized Other as the exotic object of knowledge' (Silverstone 1991: 161). The questionable politics, intrinsic in the data collected from an assumed 'value-neutral' position is suspect, since such a position overlooks the important fact that these data are the results of particular discursive practices generating culturally informed knowledge. To pretend otherwise is to be either disingenuous, or naively blind to the politics inherent in the researcher's position. Said's argument linking knowledge to power is pertinent in this context. The seemingly 'neutral' observations of the ethnographer, riding on objectivist conceptions of social science, posits a generalized Orient as a homogeneous entity. 'Under such descriptions, the Orient appears to be both a benchmark against which to measure Western European "progress" and an inert terrain on which to impose imperialist schemes of "development"' (Rosaldo 1993: 42). The notions of progress and development are tied with the project of modernity, whose juggernaut-like inevitability (as Giddens 1990 conceives it) is likewise connected to debates concerning globalization. Such debates fall outside the scope of this book, but it is worth noting that my initial conception of 'Indian' and 'British' as hermetically sealed, independent cultures is questionable on these grounds.

More importantly, and perhaps from a less overtly political posture, the conception of cultures, especially national cultures, as discrete compartments is becoming increasingly rated as invalid. I have explored in greater detail elsewhere the problems accompanying conceptions of 'national culture' (Harindranath 2006). In the context of this study, this is crucial, since in dividing the respondents thus, and expecting each 'culture' to then be represented in the form of different interpretive repertoires, I was guilty of a degree of reductionism that I observed (in Chapter 2) in Morley's (1980) conception of the audience. Geographical space does not necessarily correspond to cultural space, as if such spaces existed within confining, protective boundaries that excluded any 'outside' influence. Moreover, to assume a nation to possess a monolithic culture, the inhabitants of which exhibited a certain measure of uniformity in their behaviour is patently erroneous. Therefore, the apparent 'discrepancies' that the data produced were more or less inevitable, given the simplicity of the framework with which I had initially formulated the comparison between different audience groups. This is akin to Liebes and Katz's classification of 'race' with culture (1993), which I critiqued in an earlier chapter. To conceive of a putative national culture as unitary and consequently a determining factor in individual behaviour presupposes a causal link between conventional structural elements and behaviour that this study has been arguing against. The notion of culture, as elaborated in Chapter 4, embodies an attempt at formulating it as the site shaping individual behaviour (including media use and interpretation), while avoiding the reductionist idea of culture or any other social variable controlling such behaviour.

This raises two significant issues: one, a thematic consideration with regard to cultural differences across geographical space on a broad scale, and the other, concerning the data generated in my case study, particularly the decodings of the Indian non-graduates. The first concern involves a balancing act: denying the presence of different cultures is difficult, and yet conceiving this difference as based on static, timeless and homogeneous cultures is clearly wrong. In some ways, this is linked to the conception of what culture is—culture as a system of values, tradition, or a way of life is at once dynamic and evolving as well as linked with 'traditional' beliefs, that is, the conception that national culture is inherently dynamic. Using such broad brush strokes it is possible to describe the Japanese notion of honour, the Indian belief in fate and destiny, or oppose American bonhomie to British reserve and so on, as characteristic features of these cultures, thereby emphasizing the difference between them on a general level. The forces of modernity and the realities of international trade and politics have produced a thin veneer of uniformity across the twentieth century international life, bringing disparate cultures closer in time and space in an effort to create one cosmopolitan culture. In a sense, these attempts at minimizing pluralism lie at the heart of debates concerning normative international regulations based on an allegedly universal moral discourse, whose origins in the Western (Enlightenment) thought has been a source of disagreement and dissent in cultures and nations of the South.[2]

In this context, philosophical hermeneutics provides a useful platform from which to overcome the apparent incommensurability of cultures, leading to conversation and agreement. Shapcott's (1994) intriguing analysis linking Gadamer's hermeneutics to the study of 'the place of culture in international society' suggests that in order to arrive at universal principles while recognizing differences in perspective inherent in disparate cultures, 'hermeneutics, with its celebratory attitude to difference, may provide the orientation' (Shapcott 1994: 78). Shapcott interprets Gadamer's 'fusion of horizons' as presuming a genuine desire to understand, a desire which overcomes the problem of relativism contained in Gadamer's notion of historicity and tradition.

> It is important to remember that we only know ourselves by contact with the other [...] If cultures, peoples, traditions are not hermetically sealed, if our cultures are, in part, constituted by cultural interaction, then relativism becomes less problematic. Gadamer argues that in such circumstances we must be open to genuine discussion and interpretation to really know each other. (Shapcott 1994: 76)

This recognition and accommodation of difference means that moral claims cannot be assumed to be self evident; they have to be acknowledged as based on certain philosophies, whose legitimacy arises from certain interpretations. What is called

---

[2]The issue of human rights is a particularly contentious example, based, as it is, on the Western notions of individual rights which many countries from the South see as subsumed under collective responsibility.

for, in other words, is the awareness 'that before we can judge and pontificate, we are obliged to engage in critical dialogue' (Shapcott 1994: 82). As argued in Chapter 1, the notion of dialogue across perceived cultural difference is a significant part of current political theory, as demonstrated in Benhabib's (2002) attempts to build on Habermas's notion of communicative competence and deliberative democracy. Allied to this is Benhabib's insistence on the right to cultural expression—riding on collective identity and expression of difference—being grounded on citizenship rights.

The thesis presented in this book and the case study which supports it are, however, concerned with issues on a more micro-sociological level, where the primary sphere of interest lies with the data generated. As we saw earlier, the interpretive strategies employed by the Indian non-graduates stand out as anomalies precisely because the framework used to create audience categories was based on the classic notion of culture. The idea of culture propounded in this book (Chapter 4), however, recasts it within phenomenological sociology, and especially Schutz's reconception of the life-world. To reiterate, culture in this formulation forms the pre-given, 'handed-down' part of an individual's knowledge-at-hand with which he/she engages in daily life. Formulated thus, it does not differ greatly from the normative notion of culture as the determining factor in behaviour. But Schutz's conceptualization of the life-world contains two factors which set it apart from deterministic notions. The first of these is the idea that the individual's stock of knowledge consists of not just passively received elements from his/her existential condition of 'thrown-ness', but also elements of a more experiential sort—an idea which allows the individual to escape the confines of his/her existential world into other 'worlds'. While the individual's 'paramount reality' remains anchored to that of everyday life, his/her social reality also derives from other 'provinces of meaning' or 'multiple realities'—the second factor which distinguishes this formulation of collectivity from uni-dimensional conceptions. Schutz's idea of multiple realities brings to the individual other socializing agents such as religion, education and so on, providing a richer, multi-dimensional notion of the life-world. Instead of a deterministic straitjacket in the form of a unitary sociological variable which the individual is expected to 'inhabit', this posits the individual at the intersection of various possible realms of 'reality', which while still socially contextualized, are not unitary or normative. The argument proposed in Chapter 3 identified understanding not as the methodological reconstitution of the author's intentions, nor having an empathic unity with the author's mind, but as, following Gadamer, inevitably and insurmountably linked to the interpreter's 'horizon' or socio-cultural context. Combining the insights of Schutz and Gadamer, therefore, it follows that understanding and interpretation, while an intrinsic part of everyday life, ensues from the individual's life-world.

Higher education and cultural capital

To return to the data, the responses of the Indian group of respondents are indicative of, first, the role of education in the formation of a particular life-world, and second, the presence of a 'third', hybrid culture whose members retain their Indian identities within some aspects of their life-worlds which simultaneously possess 'modern' or Westernized attributes in others. Let me examine these two issues one by one.

At the end of their study examining the different interpretations of *Dallas* by different ethnic groups, Liebes and Katz's (1986, 1990) conclude that 'the more "modern" groups are less involved in the programme, knowing the mechanisms of distancing and discount, while the more traditional groups are more "involved"' (1986: 169). It is tempting to concur with this conclusion since it offers a seemingly straightforward explanation of the different interpretations. However, while *prima facie* feasible, on reflection, their modern–traditional dichotomy appears simplistic and politically loaded. Primarily, Liebes and Katz's conclusion, that the degrees of involvement in and distanciation from mediated communication correspond to the degrees of modernity, reinforces the perception of the West (on whose terms modernity is conceptualized) as the repository of modernity and 'progress', as well as all its positive connotations. Their finding that the Russian viewers were more critical than the other groups is interesting, but their conclusion which suggests that Russians were somehow innately critical seems tautological, and certainly begs the question. Liebes and Katz's study could perhaps be considered symptomatic of the inadequate theorizing which was referred to in Chapter 2. Arraying the different 'cultures' which their respondents were assumed to represent along a 'multi-dimensional plane' (Liebes and Katz 1986), indicating patterns of involvement and distancing, and by implication, referential and critical readings, appears to call out for a more complex theorizing, not only of the process of diverse decodings, but also of the nature of the 'cultures' which encourage such readings. Without such detail, their rich findings remain unexplained, and open to critiques such as that offered by Corner (1991) which question the critical potential of such studies. -

In the present context for instance, to take the Indian non-graduates' reading of the films simply as an indication of the 'traditional' culture to which they belong, in relation to the 'modern' critical readings of the Indian academics, post graduates and some of the under graduates, as well as the British group of respondents, would be to examine the results only superficially. This group's 'horizon of expectations', deriving from their obvious acceptance of the documentary's truth claims, produced uniformly transparent–uncritical decodings which positions them differently from other Indian groups. Among the variables encountered in the study, this group is also distinguished from the others by the respondents' lack of university higher education. The question arises, therefore, as to whether education could be assumed to create a prominently different 'culture' among Indians, both generally as well as with regard to this particular case study involving interpretation of documentaries.

Education as a major socializing factor has been discussed often enough in sociological, especially phenomenological literature, exemplified in Berger and Luckmann (1966), and Berger et al. (1974). Berger and Luckmann address the issue of education as one of the factors involved in the process of 'secondary socialization' (1966) in the creation and maintenance of social constructions of reality, as well as arguing the case of education (particularly formal education) as creating 'modern' consciousness. The role of education is central to Bourdieu's influential notion of the 'habitus' (elaborated in Bourdieu 1977, 1984). As Reed-Danahay (2005) has argued, 'Bourdieu was a sociologist of education whose work demonstrates that educational systems reproduce social class, and that children of working-class parents, through their inculcated habitus and its associated dispositions, generally fail to succeed in the French educational system' (2005: 23), although Bourdieu himself was an exception to this, moving successfully out of his working-class background to the highest position in the French academe. Thus, in this conception, education emerges, not merely as a question of heuristics, but also as one of the 'secondary carriers' (Berger and Kellner 1974) of the modern consciousness: 'Mass education, while it certainly cannot be considered an important factor in the creation of the modern world historically, is today a modernizing force of very great importance indeed' (1974: 105).[3]

In the 'plurality' of life-worlds, characterizing the modern consciousness, religion has been, to a certain extent, replaced by education and mass communication (a feature of mass media and contemporary life developed by Gerbner, see for instance Morgan 2002) in its role as the provider of meaning in everyday life. This is a complex argument and of only tangential

---

[3]Berger and Kellner (1974) conceive of 'modernity' and industrialization more in historical terms than in terms of 'development', as attested by the section on 'Demodernization' in the book which emphasizes counter culture movements within the West as well as the 'demodernization consciousness' in other cultures.

interest here. However, the notion of education as contributing to the creation of one aspect of the 'multiple realities', or to a 'sub-world', which make up a person's life-world, is crucial. The relative uniformity of formalized education creates a potential for homogeneity (as suggested by the term 'formal') among its subscribers. This homogeneity might appear to paradoxically contain within itself the possibility of dissonance, but even this is subsumed under the general orientation of the 'reality' or 'sub-world' engendered by formalized education. In other words, education provides a preconstituted system of values and typifications with which a person makes sense of and exists in everyday life; formal education helps promote a common conception of at least some elements of the 'world' of its members. It should be noted that a classical, deterministic version of culture would prevent any attempt at examining such 'sub-worlds'. Indeed, it can be argued that such conceptualizations are possible only from the perspective of Schutz's formulation of the 'multiple realities' which make up a person's life-world. While being socially derived, these multiple realities transcend normative categorizations to take into account the sheer variety that makes a life-world unique. In the present context, what is pertinent is the presence of two distinct sub-worlds characterized by formal higher education and the lack of it, existing under the rubric of 'Indian national culture', which, from the perspective of classical notions, would be considered a normative whole.

Whether this system of relevances and typifications, created by formal education, engenders a 'distancing' from the mediated text is arguable. However, while there is no evidence to prove a causal link between education and critical distancing in the reception of media, the data from this case study indicates a possible connection in the Indian context. A possible question to consider here is whether the difference in framings between the Indian non-graduates and the other Indian groups can be attributed to differing degrees of familiarity with the moving image and its mode of representing reality. This seems unlikely, since India produces the highest number of films, and cinema-going has long been a favourite pass time both in rural as well as urban areas. While the arrival of television has, to some extent, dented cinema attendance in some sections of the population, it still could not be said that watching television has perhaps replaced visiting cinemas. The seductive power of and the fascination with the moving image is as yet undimmed.[4] However, from the perspective of the theoretical arguments presented in Chapter 4 regarding the documentary, the interpretation of this genre of the television and the film requires the recognition of its truth claims and the consequent rejection or acceptance of it. In other words, the documentary genre calls for a slightly varied set of expectations from the fiction film. This is where education and/or a relative familiarity with the genre itself could perhaps be significant with regard to different expectations from and interpretations of documentary films.

Higher education in post-colonial India

In the Indian context, the difference created by higher education is particularly germane. The notion of India's 'national' identity, which is under constant threat from the sheer diversity which the political nation-state encompasses, has been questioned elsewhere (Das and Harindranath 1996). The multi-lingual, multi-ethnic, multi-religious nature of the population suggests a multi-cultural state. The current prognosis by researchers such as Kumar (2003) retains concerns regarding the hardening of separate identities: 'In the context of India's pluralism, the new technologies of information and communication can be expected to consolidate linguistic identities, including sub-regional identities. This may constitute a process of localization and regionalization of commitment in the face of the homogenizing influence of the global imperative'

---

[4]The number of film actors and actresses who have successfully entered political careers is indicative of their enduring popularity with the 'masses'.

(Kumar 2000: 12). Among the forces instilling a sense of national integration, education, particularly formal, higher education, should rate as one of the most important. In order to appreciate the force of higher education in India, however, it is necessary to be familiar with some of the features of its history. Two of these features are particularly pertinent to this study. First, the social value accorded to higher education among certain sections of the population, which has been exploited for political gain by the powers that be, especially in terms of appeasing an economically significant, politically active minority. The sudden spurt in enrolment during the five years preceding 1966–1969 (Table 9.1) was a direct response to, as Rudolph and Rudolph (1987) claim, 'demand politics'. Ignoring the advice of the Central government, state governments across the country 'responded to the insistent demands of the urban middle-class and rural notable constituents for more college seats by creating intellectually and physically jerry-built institutions or underfunding existing ones' (Rudolf and Rudolf 1987: 296).

Table 9.1

Enrolment growth rates for primary, secondary and higher education

Year	Primary		Secondary		Higher	
	Enrolment	% increase	Enrolment	% increase	Enrolment	% increase
1950–51	18,677,642	–	4,817,011	–	423,326	–
1955–56	24,511,331	31	6,826,605	42	736,124	74
1960–61	33,631,391	37	10,942,293	60	1.094,991	49
1965–66	48,912,678	45	17,132,945	57	2,095,217	91
1970–71	55,167,533	12	21,773019	46	3.502,357	67
1975–76	63,108,492	14	25,999,227	19	4,615,992	32
1978–79	72,390,000	14	27,090,000	4	4,192,934	-9
					(5,049,957)	(+4)

Source: Rudolph and Rudolph (1987: 298).

This politically expedient state of affairs resulted in 'skewed' funding allocations favouring higher education. One of the consequences of this is the neglect of primary and secondary education, especially in the rural areas, although the constitution guarantees free education up to the secondary level for all. The share of funds assigned to each level of formal education is illuminating:

> Of the funds allocated to education under the fourth [five year] plan (1969–70 to 1973–74), only 30 percent went to the elementary level, which accounted for 68 million enrolled students, while 18 percent and 25 percent went to secondary and higher levels, respectively with enrolments of only 22 and 3.5 million. [...] Fifth-plan allocations followed a similar pattern. (Rudolph and Rudolph 1987: 297)

In this way, the political and social elite continue to exert their disproportionate influence while the majority uneducated, semi-literate population remain in the wilderness. As shown in Table 9.1, the number of students entering higher education is considerably less when compared to the number enrolling for primary and secondary education. In other words, despite growing student numbers higher education remains accessible only to a relative minority. Thus an elite group has become the chief beneficiary of formal higher education and the resulting social and economic gains. 'In a hierarchical society such as India, education has always been accepted as the preserve and prerogative of a small class of people. [...] The ancient Brahminical values were replaced by the modern educated middle-class values which were "transmitted" by the education system' (Pattnayak 1981: 67). Sociologically, this development can be viewed from a variety of perspectives. From within the conception of 'culture' advanced in this book, this signifies the presence of a category of persons possessing the norms and values of the 'sub-world' created by higher education, existing within the population of the state but differing from the majority.

Another important factor to be noted with regard to higher education in India is its colonial legacy. Most of the university education is Western oriented, which is reflected in course design, syllabuses and reading lists, but most importantly by the fact that the medium of instruction in universities is English. The consequence of this has been profound, creating and sustaining a politically influential, Westernized, hybrid culture significantly different from the majority indigenous one. According to Pattnayak (1981), the advent of English has had a negative implication for local cultures:

> English engendered among its speakers an attitude of indifference to the local languages and cultures and thus created a communication gap between the elite and the masses and between innumerable islands of cultural and linguistic minorities. [...] The middle class elite [for whom English represents their culture] who consider themselves the repository of all values and who expect others to emulate their values have failed to recognize difference as having a different perspective and ethos. (Pattnayak 1981: 68)

Thus higher education in India has generated a 'culture' significantly different from others within the country. Not only does the minority, who occupy this cultural space, possesses the values inherent in the educational 'sub-world' that is denied to the majority, but the essentially Western orientation of these values and norms sets this group or category apart from the rest to an even greater degree. Even at the level of education, therefore, India's claim to a cultural unity is weakened. The 'modern consciousness' provided by higher education is markedly Western and therefore inimical to the indigenous 'sub-worlds'. In essence, formal higher education effectively creates 'two nations' in India consisting of two groups of people: those who are 'Westernized', English-speaking and 'modern', and those who are not.

However, it would be wrong to assume that this divide in contemporary Indian life creates an insurmountable dichotomy, or that indigenous life-worlds are completely alien to the educated minority. Certain spheres, 'sub-worlds', or 'realities' of their lives are bound to coincide or criss-cross with each other. Normative claims suggesting mutually exclusive, watertight compartments are as erroneous as the simplistic West–Other divide, and as unproductive, apart from being unacceptable from the point of view of the phenomenological conception of the collective that has been proffered in this book. The two 'worlds' described here, therefore, are neither unchanging nor incontrovertible wholes, and cannot be expected to perform a law-giving function as in a physical property. Again, such conceptions are more the norm in demarcations generated by classical anthropology discussed earlier. A more constructive approach would be to conceive of the Indian with formal higher education as residing in a 'cultural borderland', a notion in which 'the fiction of the uniformly shared culture increasingly seems more tenuous than useful. Although most metropolitan typifications continue to suppress border zones, human cultures are neither necessarily coherent nor always homogenuous' (Rosaldo 1993). Such a conception coincides with the new ethnographic move from 'closed communities' to the idea of 'open borders' (Rosaldo 1993), reconstituting the task of social analysis from that of discovering law-like intractable variables to exploring heterogeneity, change and the way culture changes and is changed by human behaviour.

From this notion it is possible to conceive of the persons inhabiting the 'borderland' between indigenous Indian culture and Western 'modernity' as a cultural hybrid. The concept of hybridity in culture has recently been highlighted in postcolonial cultural theory, as in Bhabha (1994) for whom,

> A contingent, borderline experience opens up in-between colonizer and colonized. This is a space of cultural and interpretive undecidability produced in the 'present' of colonial moment. [...] The margin of hybridity, where cultural differences 'contingently' and conceptually touch, becomes the moment of panic which reveals the borderline experience. It resists binary opposition of racial and cultural groups, sipahis and sahibs, as homogenuous polarized political consciousness. (Bhabha 1994: 206–07)

The political stance evident in this quote is not of concern here; what is pertinent is the invocation of the notion of hybridity as the 'in-between' space between the West and the Other. The existence of Western-oriented higher education, I would argue, lends a handle with which to grasp the otherwise 'undecidable' bridge touching both the cultural monoliths at once. Straddling this divide is the university educated Indian, retaining within his/her life-world the 'realities' of Indian existence as well as Western-oriented norms adopted through the socializing force of higher education.

Two points need to be acknowledged here. First, as the product of that system of higher education, I am caught in the predicament of what Geertz (1973) refers to as 'Mannheim's Paradox' in relation to the unavoidability of ideology: 'the realization (or perhaps it was only an admission) that sociopolitical thought does not grow out of disembodied reflection but "is always bound up with the existing life situation of the thinker"' (Geertz 1973: 194). While desiring to avoid arguing away my own case, or to succumb, like Mannheim, to 'an ethical and epistemological relativisim that he himself found uncomfortable' (Geertz 1973), I cannot, given the theoretical argument I have elaborated in this book, reasonably escape the fact that the way this research problem has been formulated, investigated and presented is itself an indication of my own position within the 'hybrid' culture which I described above. Whether or not this admission detracts from or enhances this study is a moot point.

The other acknowledgement is in relation to the methodology of this study. From a prominently micro-sociological project it is difficult to make generalizations. A relatively small percentage of the respondents in this study can be said to represent an interpretive repertoire of their own, which, according to the data, is more different from that of other Indian respondents than are the differences between the interpretive practices of the latter Indians and the British respondents. While there is no conclusive evidence to suggest that these two Indian 'cultures' generate different interpretive practices, from the perspective of Gadamerian hermeneutics, it appears that the 'tradition' or the sub-world which the Indian groups other than the non-graduates operated from was the one created by education. As I pointed out in Chapter 7, the responses of the Indian non-graduates could have been influenced by their desire to provide me with the responses which they assumed I expected from them. From the data, however, the less educated appear to assume a subject position posited by the documentary (as discussed in Chapter 5), and less likely to challenge the authority of 'He Who Knows'. Is it then possible to argue that a critical attitude is necessarily correlated with education? Answering a question like this requires a study formulated differently from this one.

Concluding Comments

This project originated as a desire to rectify two aspects of media research: first, what I considered a theoretical inadequacy in most audience researches which have investigated the connection between sociological categories and audience interpretations of various kinds of televisual texts. While concurring with their basic assumption that the socio-cultural contexts of the audience members were in some way linked to interpretive practices, I detected a lack of theoretical sophistication in these studies which rendered them unable to explain exactly how contexts affected decodings. The first part of this book is the result of my attempts at answering this problem. The empirical part of my research, designed to compare differences in interpretation by audiences in India and Britain, was originally intended to illustrate and support my conceptual interventions; while the case study does, I believe, lend its support, it does so in a way that had not been anticipated at the point when the project was initially conceived.

The second issue is related to conceptualizations of the role of the media in democracy which, as I argued in Chapter 1, has tended to ignore the audience. Public knowledge and its contribution to democratic functioning have mostly been seen in policy or textual terms, and this book has sought to rectify that lacuna by examining the significant role of education, particularly higher education, in the interpretive practices of audiences. The documentary genre, along with other non-fictional television programmes, with its claims to truth, is recognized as one of the main contributors to the production of public knowledge—the *raison d'etre* of factual television. The findings in this study reveal the profound differences in interpretation of documentaries as riding on the acceptance or rejection of the genre's veridicality. Alejandro's (1993) reconceptualization of citizenship, using Gadamerian hermeneutics, is significant in this regard: 'Citizenship, on this view, would appear as a fusion [of horizons] between past and present; as a web of different vocabularies; and as an interpretive practice against the backdrop of different and conflicting traditions' (Alejandro 1993: 36). Citizenship, in the hermeneutic vocabulary, then becomes 'a space where citizens can decode languages and practices' (Alejandro 1993) including national symbols, myths and traditions.

In order to explore the assumptions underlying research in audience decoding practices, I have identified three distinct but interlinked areas for a more comprehensive theoretical enquiry: 'understanding', 'social context' and 'genre'. A caveat is required at the outset: while I maintain that my attempts have succeeded in drawing attention to and elucidating these terms to a certain degree, I believe that they would benefit from a closer examination. In a sense, each of the chapters in this book that deal with each of these areas has the potential of becoming a book in its own right. I shall briefly rehearse some of the arguments while indicating areas of possible future research.

With reference to 'understanding', I have, using Gadamerian philosophical hermeneutics, tried to argue that the inevitable historicity (and by extension, the social embeddedness) of the individual necessarily prescribes his/her interpretive activity. While *prima facie* this assertion achieves nothing more than confirming what was already assumed in audience research, the presence of two related sub-arguments help clarify these assumptions. First, the Heideggerian notion which Gadamer built on–that the understanding and interpretation of texts is linked to understanding in general which is an essential feature of human existence–refers us directly to the social distribution of knowledge and its connection with the acts of understanding within particular spheres of human experience. The notion of understanding, therefore, has to be looked at with reference to the 'prejudices' which an individual brings to that particular sphere. Second, the concept of the 'horizon of expectations' formed in part by the individual's historicity, and the idea that a text is understood in the process of an ever changing part–whole dialectic, in which expectations are constantly 'thrown forward', anticipating the meaning of the whole, point us to the importance of the familiarity with and expectations from particular televisual genres. These aspects of familiarity and expectation are the elements which drive the interpretation of individual texts, while simultaneously these particular interpretations also have the potential to modify generic expectations. These ideas have been explored at length in relation to the interpretation of television in works such as Wilson (1993). However, they could benefit from more empirical work which could investigate in greater detail their links with specific interpretive practices.

The first of these notions brought out by the employment of Gadamer's hermeneutics, that understanding is ineluctably circumscribed by the 'prejudices' which form the individual's 'horizon', is potentially deterministic. In an effort to counter that, while at the same time exploring the social groundedness, the 'context' of human experience and behaviour, I have employed Schutzian phenomenological sociology, which, through the concept of 'multiple realities', situates the person not in the rigid compartments of positivistic sociology, but in the intersecting spaces of various existential as well as experiential circles which make up his/her life-world. It is worth noting here that one possible way of moving between Gadamer's idea of 'prejudice' and Schutz's phenomenological sociology is through Habermas's conception of life-world as 'a culturally transmitted and linguistically organized stock of interpretive patterns', which 'circumscribes action in the manner of a preunderstood context that, however, is not addressed' (1987: 124, 132). Positioning the individual thus, and accepting the notion of the 'intersubjective' nature of these circles of relevance, make it possible for the investigator to accept individual behaviour as shaped by the social context while avoiding deterministic notions. This, and the formulation of culture, or any form of collectivity as a meaningful, intersubjective world which accords the individual the 'pre-given' aspect of his/her life-world, throws up a number of methodological questions with potential for further research. In the particular context of this study, for instance, the notion of intersubjectivity as created and sustained by a web of meaning suggests a conceptual framework with which to explore the notion of national identity and democratic politics, and the role of the media in maintaining and contributing to it.

The importance of 'genre' in Gadamerian hermeneutics has been already discussed, but specifically pertinent to this study are the generic features of the documentary. In Chapter 5 of this book, I have explored the claims of the documentary, first, in relation to fictional films in terms of textual characteristics, and second, with regard to its claims of authentically portraying 'reality'. After arguing that there is very little to distinguish the documentary from fiction textually–that, in other words, the documentary contains many fictive elements–I concluded that, what separates it from fiction is the 'horizon of expectations' which viewers bring to the text, which is determined by whether they accept or reject the genre's claims to depict historical reality the 'way it is'. The authority of the documentary voice depends on this.

While my case study, based on original research on the comparison of the interpretation of documentaries by audiences in India and Britain, supports my theoretical efforts, it does so in a manner I did not expect. Briefly, my finding is that while most respondents across both the cultures interpreted the films in similar ways, with a varied employment of 'transparent' and 'mediated' frames which generated readings which were at times critical of the films' arguments and representation, the one group which emerged as markedly different was that of the Indian non-graduates. The similarities between the interpretations of the Indian audiences with higher education and those of the British audiences, and equally the differences between the interpretations of these Indians and those of their compatriots without higher education are suggestive. The importance of higher education as a 'sphere' in a person's life-world, with the potential of creating an intersubjective world of its own, suggests the presence of a hybrid culture which bridges the gap between indigenous Indian and Western cultures. At the same time, the results of the study also underline the inadequacy of linking culture solely with geographical and political spaces. Such a conception fell into the trap of distinguishing collectivities along conventional lines, failing to acknowledge the 'multiple realities' that constitute a life-world. Politically as well as intellectually this was not a productive position. The outcome, however, does indicate avenues for further research into the different interpretive practices within India.

Primarily, it calls for a more systematic analysis of the decodings of audiences from various sections of the population. Given the sheer diversity of the Indian nation-state along the religious, cultural, linguistic, as well as social and economic lines, these categories must be taken into account and theorized upon. In that context, the possibility of a range of intersecting circles of relevance constituting a life-world is heightened, and therefore, a theory of collective and individual identity similar to the one presented here would be pertinent.

Intrinsic to this, as suggested in Chapter 8, are debates concerning the global and the local. In the current climate of economic change, where the balance attempted in India's experiments with 'mixed economy' has been rapidly transformed into a market-oriented economy, issues of globalization ought to take centre stage. One of the dichotomies which immediately suggest itself is the notion of the Westernized Indian and the non-Westernized Indian. As indicated in this study, higher education appears to play an important role in establishing and maintaining this division. Allied to this is the issue of consumerism which seems to have burgeoned in proportion to the recent economic 'reforms' which have dovetailed the introduction of and dramatic increase in foreign cable and satellite channels.

What do these developments mean to the cultural identity of India? What is the nature of the relationship between these economic changes and media 'liberalization', and between consumerism and 'Westernization'? With the burgeoning of cable and satellite television channels and the co-presence of a multitude of news and current affairs channels and programmes interpellating audience groups in diverse ways, the time is ripe for the study of the Indian audience's interpretations of such popular non-fiction and fiction, along the lines suggested by Liebes and Katz (1990), but with a sufficiently sophisticated theory as the one indicated in this book, which would examine audience interpretations in the context of the developments sketched above. Given the current cultural-economic developments in India and the diverse ways in which citizenship is enacted in different social and geographic locations, such a task is both academically promising as well as politically overdue.

Bibliography

Alejandro, R. 1993. *Hermeneutics, Citizenship, and the Public Sphere.* Albany: State University of New York Press.

Alexander, D. 1945. *The Documentary Film.* London: The British Film Institute.

Allor, M. 1988. 'Relocating the Site of the Audience', *Critical Studies in Mass Communication,* 5.

Ang, I. 1985. *Watching Dallas.* London: Methuen.

——. 1989. 'Wanted: Audiences. On the Politics of Empirical Audience Studies', in E. Seiter, H. Borchers, G. Kreutzner and E. Warth (eds), *Remote Control: Television, Audiences and Cultural Power.* London: Routledge.

——. 1990. 'Culture and Communication', *European Journal of Communication,* 5 (2–3).

——. 1991. *Desperately Seeking the Audience.* London: Routledge.

——. 2001. 'Desperately Guarding Borders: Media Globalization, "Cultural Imperialism", and the Rise of "Asia"', in Y. Souchou (ed.), *House of Glass: Culture, Modernity, and the State in Southeast Asia.* Singapore: Institute of Southeast Asian Studies.

Apel, K. O. 1984. *Understanding and Explanation: A Transcendental–Pragmatic Perspective* (Translated by Georgia Warnke). Cambridge, MA.: MIT Press.

Appadurai, A. 1996. *Modernity at Large: Cultural Dimensions of Globalization.* Minneapolis: University of Minnesota Press.

Appiah, A. 1994. 'Identity, Authenticity, Survival: Multicultural Societies and Social Reproduction', in A. Gutmann (ed.), *Multiculturalism: Examining the Politics of Recognition.* Princeton: Princeton University Press.

Barker, M., J. Arthurs, and R. Harindranath. 2001. *The 'Crash' Controversy: Censorship Campaigns and Film Reception.* London: Wallflower Press.

Barnett, C. 2003. *Culture and Democracy: Media, Space, and Representation.* Edinburgh: Edinburgh University Press.

——. 2004. 'Media, Democracy and Representation: Disembodying the Public', in C. Barnett and M. Low (eds), *Spaces of Democracy: Geographical Perspectives on Citizenship, Participation and Representation.* London: Sage Publications.

Barnouw, E. 1983. *Documentary: A History of the Non-Fiction Film* (Revised edition). New York: Oxford University Press.

Bauman, Z. 1978. *Hermeneutics and Social Science: Approaches to Understanding.* London: Hutchinson.

Bazin, A. 1967. *What is Cinema.* Translated by Hugh Gray. Berkeley: University of California Press.

Benhabib, S. 2002. *The Claims of Culture: Equality and Diversity in the Global Era.* Princeton: Princeton University Press.

Bennett, T. 2007. 'Habitus Clive: Aesthetics and Politics in the Works of Pierre Bourdieu', *New Literary History*, 38.

Berger, P. and T. Luckmann. 1966. *The Social Construction of Reality: A Treatise in the Sociology of Knowledge.* Harmondsworth: Penguin.

Berger, P. L., B. Berger, and H. Kellner. 1974. *The Homeless Mind: Modernization and Consciousness.* New York: Vintage Books.

Beteille, A. 2003. *Equality and Universality: Essays in Social and Political Theory.* New Delhi: Oxford University Press.

Bernstein, B. 1973. *Class, Codes and Control, Vol. 1: Theoretical Studies towards a Sociology of Language.* St Albans: Paladin.

Bhabha, H. 1994. *The Location of Culture.* London: Routledge.

Biltereyst, D. 1995. 'Qualitative Audience Research and Transnational Media Effects', *European Journal of Communication*, 10 (2).

Bleicher, J. 1980. *Contemporary Hermeneutics: Hermeneutics as Method, Philosophy and Critique.* London: Routledge and Kegan Paul.

———. 1982. *The Hermeneutic Imagination: Outline of a Positive Critique of Scientism and Sociology.* London: Routledge and Kegan Paul.

Bourdieu, P. 1977. *Outline of a Theory of Practice.* Cambridge: Cambridge University Press.

———. 1984. *Distinction: A Social Critique of the Judgement of Taste.* Cambridge, MA: Harvard University Press.

———. 1989. 'Social Space and Symbolic Power', *Sociological Theory*, 17 (1).

Brah, A. 1996. *Cartographies of Diaspora; Contesting Identities.* London: Routledge.

Brain, D. 1994. 'Cultural Production as "Society in the Making": Architecture as an Example of the Social Construction of Cultural Artefacts', in D. Crane (ed.), *The Sociology of Culture: Emerging Theoretical Perspectives.* Oxford and Cambridge, Mass: Blackwell.

Brunsdon, C. and D. Morley. 1978. *Everyday Television: 'Nationwide'.* London: The British Film Institute.

Canclini, N. 2001. *Consumers and Citizens: Globalization and Multicultural Conflicts.* Translated by G. Yudice. Minneapolis: University of Minnesota Press.

Carey, J. W. 1975. 'Review Essay: Communication and Culture', *Communication Research*, April.

———. 1989. *Communication as Culture: Essays on Media and Society.* Boston: Unwin Hyman.

Chakravarty, R. and N. Gooptu. 2000. 'Imagi-nation: the Media, Nation, and Politics in Contemporary India', in E. Hallam and B. Street (eds), *Cultural Encounters: Representing 'Otherness'*. London: Routledge.

Clifford, J. 1997. *Routes: Travel and Translation in the Twentieth Century*. Cambridge: Harvard University Press.

Cohen, E. (ed.). 2005. *News Incorporated: Corporate Media Ownership and Its Threat to Democracy*. Amherst, NY: Prometheus Books.

Collins, R. 1986. 'Seeing is Believing: The Ideology of Naturalism', in J. Corner (ed.), *Documentary and the Mass Media*. London: Arnold.

Connell, I. 1985. 'Blaming the Meeja', in L. Masterman (ed.), *Television Mythologies*. London: Comedia/Routledge.

Corner, J. (ed.). 1986. *Documentary and the Mass Media*. London: Edward Arnold.

———. 1991. 'Meaning, Genre and Context: The Problematics of "Public Knowledge" in the New Audience Studies', paper presented at the fourth International Television Studies Conference, London.

———. 1995. *Television Form and Public Address*. London: Edward Arnold.

Corner, J. and K. Richardson. 1986. 'Documentary meanings and the discourse of interpretation', in J. Corner (ed.), *Documentary and the Mass Media*. London: Edward Arnold.

Corner, J., K. Richardson, and N. Fenton. 1990. *Nuclear Reactions: Form and Response in 'Public Issue' Television*. London: John Libbey.

Crane, D. (ed.). 1994. *The Sociology of Culture: Emerging Theoretical Perspectives*. Oxford and Cambridge, Mass: Blackwell.

———. 1994. 'Introduction: The Challenge of the Sociology of Culture to Sociology as a Discipline', in D. Crane (ed.), *The Sociology of Culture: Emerging Theoretical Perspectives*. Oxford: Blackwell.

Curran, J. 1990. 'The New Revisionism in Mass Communication Research: A Reappraisal', *European Journal of Communication*, 5:2–3.

Dahlgren, P. 1985a. 'The Modes of Reception: For a Hermeneutics of TV News', in P. Drummond and R. Paterson (eds), *Television in Transition*. London: The British Film Institute.

———. 1985b. 'Media, Meaning and Method: A Post-rational Perspective', *The Nordicom Review*, 2.

———. 1988. 'What's the Meaning of This? Viewer's Plural Sense-making of TV News', *Media, Culture and Society*, 10.

———. 1995. *Television and the Public Sphere: Citizenship, Democracy, and the Media*. London: Sage Publications.

———. 2003. 'Reconfiguring Civic Culture in the New Media Milieu', in J. Corner and D. Pels (eds), *Media and the Restyling of Politics*, pp. 151–70. London: Sage Publications.

———. 2004. 'Theory, Boundaries and Political Communication', *European Journal of Communication*, 19 (1).

Dallmayr, F. R. and T. McCarthy. 1977. *Understanding and Social Inquiry.* Notre Dame: University of Notre Dame Press.

Dalrymple, William. 2007. *The Guardian.* 24–30 August.

Das, S. and R. Harindranath. 1996. 'Nation-State, National Identity and the Media', Unit for M.A., Distance Learning. Leicester: Centre for Mass Communication Research.

Dirlik, A. 1997. *The Post-Colonial Aura: Third World Criticism in the Age of Global Capitalism.* Boulder, Co: Westview Press.

Dyer, R. 1977. 'Victim: Hermeneutic Project', *Film Form*, 1:2.

Eagleton, T. 1983. *Literary Theory: An Introduction.* Oxford: Blackwell.

Elias, N. 1978. *The Civilising Process, Vol.1: The History of Manners.* Oxford: Blackwell.

———. 1982. *The Civilising Process, Vol.2: State Formation and Civilization.* Oxford: Blackwell.

Eliot, T.S. 1970. *Collected Poems.* San Diego: Harcourt, Brav Jovanorich.

Ellis, J. C. 1989. *The Documentary Idea: A Critical History of English-Language Documentary Film and Video.* New Jersey: Prentice Hall.

Erni, J. 1989. 'Where is the Communication Audience', *Journal of Communication Inquiry*, 13 (2).

Evans, W. 1990. 'The Interpretive Turn on Media Research', *Critical Studies in Mass Communication*, 7 (2).

Fejes, F. 1984. 'Critical Communication Research and Media Effects: The Problem of the Disappearing Audience', *Media, Culture and Society*, 6 (3).

Fernandes, L. 2000. 'Nationalizing "the Global": Media Images, Cultural Politics and the Middle Class in India', *Media, Culture and Society*, 22 (5): 611–28.

Feyerabend, P. 1991. *Three Dialogues on Knowledge.* Oxford: Blackwell.

Fish, S. E. 1980. *Is There a Text in This Class?: The Authority of Interpretive Communities.* Cambridge, MA: Harvard University Press.

Fiske, J. 1987. *Television Culture.* London: Methuen.

———. 1991. 'Semiological Struggles', in J. Anderson (ed.), *Communication Yearbook, Vol. 14.* Newbury Park: Sage Publications.

Gadamer, H-G. 1975. *Truth and Method.* New York: Continuum.

———. 1976. *Philosophical Hermeneutics* (Trans. and ed. by David Linge). Berkeley: University of California Press.

Garnham, N. 1993. 'The Mass Media, Cultural Identity, and the Public Sphere in the Modern World', *Public Culture*, 5 (2).

———. 2000. *Emancipation, the Media, and Modernity.* Oxford: Oxford University Press.

Geertz, C. 1973. *The Interpretation of Cultures.* New York: Basic Books.

———. 1983. *Local Knowledge: Further Essays in Interpretive Anthropology.* New York: Basic Books.

Giddens, A. 1976. *New Rules of Sociological Method.* London: Hutchinson.

———. 1982. *Sociology: A Brief but Critical Introduction.* London: Macmillan.

Giddens, A. 1984. *The Constitution of Society: Outline of the Theory of Structuration.* Cambridge: Polity Press.

——. 1990. *The Consequences of Modernity.* Cambridge: Polity Press.

Gillespie, M. 1995. *Television, Ethnicity and Cultural Change.* London: Routledge.

Gillespie, M. 2000. 'Transnational Communications and Diaspora Communities', in S. Cottle (ed.), *Ethnic Minorities and the Media: Changing Cultural Boundaries.* Buckingham: Open University Press.

Gilroy, P. 2000. *Against Race: Imagining Political Culture Beyond the Color Line.* Cambridge, MA: Harvard University Press.

——. 2005. *Postcolonial Melancholia.* New York: Columbia University Press.

Giroux, H. 1994. 'Living Dangerously: Identity Politics and the New Racism', in H. Giroux and P. McLaren (eds), *Between Borders: Pedagogy and the Politics of Cultural Studies.* New York: Routledge.

Glasgow University Media Group. 1976. *Bad News.* London: Routledge.

Goldstein, L. J. 1961. 'The Phenomenological and Naturalistic Approaches to the Social', reprinted in M. Natanson (ed.), *Philosophy of the Social Sciences: A Reader.* 1963. New York: Random House.

Goodman, Nelson. 1978. *Ways of Worldmaking.* Indianpolis: Hackett Pub. Co.

Gripsrud, J. 1995. *The Dynasty Years: Hollywood Television and Critical Media Studies.* London and New York: Comedia/Routledge.

Grondin, J. 1990. 'Hermeneutics and Relativism', in K. Wright (ed.), *Festivals of Interpretation: Essays on Hans-Georg Gadamer's Work.* New York: State University of New York.

Grossberg, L. and C. Christians. 1981. 'Hermeneutics and the Study of Communications', in C. Christians (ed.), *Foundations for Communication Studies.* Iowa: University of Iowa, Centre for Communication Study.

Gupta, A. 2000. 'Blurred Boundaries: the Discourse of Corruption, the Culture of Politics, and the Imagined State', in Z. Hasan (ed.), *Politics and the State in India,* pp. 331–78. New Delhi: Sage Publications.

Gurswitch, A. 1970. 'Problems of the Life World', in M. Natanson (ed.), *Phenomenology and Social Reality: Essays in Memory of Alfred Schutz.* The Hague: Martinus Nijhoff.

Habermas, J. 1987. *The Theory of Communicative Action.* Cambridge: Cambridge University Press.

——. 1988. *On the Logic of the Social Sciences.* Translated by S. W. Nicholsen and J. E. Stark. Oxford: Polity Press.

——. 2001. *The Inclusion of the Other: Studies in Political Theory.* Cambridge, MA: MIT Press.

Hackett, R. and Y. Zhao (eds). 2005. *Democratizing Global Media.* Lanham, MD: Rowman and Littlefield.

Hall, S. 1980. 'Encoding/Decoding', in S. Hall, D. Hobson, A. Lowe and P. Willis (eds), *Culture, Media, Language.* London: Hutchinson.

Hall, S. 1990. 'Cultural Identity and Diaspora', in J. Rutherford (ed.), *Identity: Community, Culture, Difference.* London: Lawrence and Wishart.

——. 1992. 'New ethnicities', in D. Rattansi and J. Donald (eds), *Race, Culture and Difference.* Sage.

Harindranath, R. 1998. 'Documentary Meanings and Interpretive Contexts: Observations on Indian "Repertoires"', in R. Dickinson, R. Harindranath and O. Linne (eds), *Approaches to Audiences*, pp. 283–97. London: Arnold.

——. 2000. 'Ethnicity, National Culture(s), and the Interpretation of Television', in S. Cottle (ed.), *Ethnic Minorities and the Media: Changing Cultural Boundaries*, pp. 149–63. Buckingham: The Open University Press.

——. 2004. 'Battling Over the "Truth"', in A. Biressi and H. Nunn (eds), *Mediawar*, a special issue of *Mediactive* (issue 3).

——. 2006. *Perspectives on Global Cultures.* Maidenhead and New York: Open University Press.

Hartley, J. 1999. *Uses of Television.* London: Routledge.

Hermes, J. 1995. *Reading Women's Magazines: An Analysis of Everyday Media Use.* Cambridge: Polity Press.

Hermes, J. and Peter Dahlgren. 2006. 'Cultural Studies and Citizenship', *European Journal of Communication*, 9 (3).

Hesse, M. 1954. *Science and the Human Imagination: Aspects of the History and Logic of Physical Science.* London: SCM Press.

Hirsch, E. D. 1967. *Validity in Interpretation.* London: Yale University Press.

Hobson, D. 1982. *Crossroads: Drama of a Soap Opera.* London: Methuen.

Hoijer, B. 1992. 'Socio-cognitive Structures and Television Reception', *Media, Culture and Society*, 14 (4).

Howard, R. J. 1982. *The Three Faces of Hermeneutics.* Los Angeles: University of California Press.

Hoy, D. C. 1978. *The Critical Circle: Literature, History and Philosophical Hermeneutics.* Berkeley: University of California Press.

Hyden, G., M. Leslie, and F. Ogundimu (eds). 2002. *Media and Democracy in Africa.* New Brunswick, NJ: Transaction Publishers.

Jaffrelot, C. 1999. *The Hindue Nationalist Movement in India.* New York: Columbia University Press.

Jauss, H. R. 1982. *Toward an Aesthetic of Reception.* Brighton: The Harvester Press.

Jensen, K. B. 1986. *Making Sense of the News.* Arhus: University of Arhus Press.

——. 1987. 'Qualitative Audience Research: Toward an Integrative Approach to Reception', *Critical Studies in Mass Communication*, 4.

——. 1991a. 'Humanistic Scholarship as Qualitative Science: Contributions to Mass Communication Research', in K. B. Jensen and N. W. Jankowski (eds), *A Handbook of Qualitative Methodologies for Mass Communication Research.* London: Routledge.

Jenson, K.B. 1991b. 'When is Meaning? Communication Theory, Pragmatism, and Mass Media Reception', in J. Anderson (ed.), *Communication Yearbook*, Vol. 14. Newbury Park: Sage Publications.

Jensen, K. B. and K. Rosengren. 1990. 'Five Traditions in Search of an Audience', *European Journal of Communication*, 5 (2–3).

Jensen K. B. and N. W. Jankowski (eds). 1991. *A Handbook of Qualitative Methodologies for Mass Communication Research*. London: Routledge.

Keane, J. 1991. *The Media and Democracy*. Cambridge: Polity Press.

Kearney R. 1984. *Dialogues with Contemporary Continental Thinkers: The Phenomenological Heritage*. Manchester: Manchester University Press.

Keat, R. and J. Urry. 1975. *Social Theory as Science*. London: Routledge and Kegan Paul.

Kitley, P. (ed.). 2003. *Television, Regulation and Civil Society in Asia*. London: Routledge Curzon.

Kockelmans, J. J. 1967. *Phenomenology: The Philosophy of Edmund Husserl and its Interpretation*. Garden City, NY: Doubledays.

Komesaroff, P. A. 1986. *Objectivity, Science and Society: Interpreting Nature and Society in the Age of the Crisis of Science*. London: Routledge and Kegan Paul.

Kumar, S. 2003. 'Is There Anything Called Global Television Studies?', in L. Parks and S. Kumar (eds), *Planet TV*. New York: New York University Press.

Lash, S. and J. Friedman. 1992. 'Introduction: Subjectivity and Modernity's Other', in S. Lash and J. Friedman (eds), *Modernity and Identity*. Oxford: Blackwell.

Layder, D. 1990. *The Realist Image in Social Science*. London: Macmillan.

———. 1994. *Understanding Social Theory*. London: Sage Publications.

Liebes, T. and E. Katz. 1986. 'Patterns of Involvement in Television Fiction: A Comparative Analysis', *European Journal of Communication*, 1 (2).

———. 1990. *The Export of Meaning; Cross-Cultural Readings of 'Dallas'*. Oxford: Oxford University Press.

Lindlof, T. (ed.). 1987. *Natural Audiences: Qualitative Research of Media Uses and Effects*. New Jersey: Ablex.

Lindlof, T. and T. Meyer. 1987. 'Mediated Communication as Ways of Seeing, Acting, and Constructing Culture: The Tools and Foundations of Qualitative Research', in R. Lindlof (ed.), *Natural Audiences: Qualitative Research of Media Uses and Effects*. New Jersey: Ablex.

Livingstone, S. 1993. 'The Rise and Fall of Audience Research: An Old Story with a New Ending', *Journal of Communication*, Autumn.

———. 1999. 'Mediated Knowledge: Recognition of the Familiar, Discovery of the New', in J. Gripsrud (ed.), *Television and Common Knowledge*, pp. 91–107. London: Routledge.

———. 2005. 'On the Relation Between Audiences and Publics', in S. Livingstone (ed.), *Audiences and Publics: When Cultural Engagement Matters for the Public Sphere*, pp. 7–42. Bristol: Intellect.

Livingstone, S. M. 1990. *Making Sense of Television: The Psychology of Audience Interpretation.* Oxford: Pergamon Press.

Lowe, D. 1982. *History of Bourgeois Perception.* Brighton: The Harvester Press.

Ludden, D. (ed.). 1996. *Making India Hindu: Religion, Community, and the Politics of Democracy in India.* New Delhi: Oxford University Press.

Lull, J. (ed.). 1988. *World Families Watch Television.* Newbury Park: Sage Publications.

Madianou, M. 2005. *Mediating the Nation: News, Audiences and the Politics of Identity.* London: UCL Press.

Malik, K. 1996. *The Meaning of Race.* London: Macmillan.

Mankekar, P. 1993. 'Television Tales and a Woman's Rage: A Nationalist Recasting of Draupadi's disrobing', *Public Culture*, 5 (3).

—— 1999. *Screening Culture, Viewing Politics: Television, Womanhood and Nation in modern India.* New Delhi: Oxford University Press.

Minh-ha, T. 1993. 'The Totalising Quest for Meaning', in M. Renov (ed.), *Theorizing Documentary.* London: Routledge.

Mishra, V. 1996. 'The Diasporic Imaginary: Theorizing the Indian Diaspora', *Textual Practice*, 10 (3).

——. 2002. *Bollywood Cinema: Temples of Desire.* New York: Routledge.

Moores, S. 1990. 'Texts, Readers and Contexts of Reading: Developments in the Study of Media Audiences', *Media, Culture and Society*, 12 (1).

——. 2005. *Media/Theory: Thinking About Media and Communications.* London: Routledge.

Morawaska, E. and W. Spohn. 1994. '"Cultural Pluralism" in Historical Sociology: Recent Theoretical Directions', in D. Crane (ed.), *The Sociology of Culture: Emerging Theoretical Perspectives.* Oxford and Cambridge, MA: Blackwell.

Morgan, M. (ed.). 2002. *Against the Mainstream: The Selected Words of George Gerbner.* New York: P. Lang.

Morley, D. 1976. 'Industrial Conflict and the Mass Media', *Sociological Review*, 24:2.

——. 1980. *The Nationwide Audience: Structure and Decoding.* London: The British Film Institute.

——. 1981. 'The "Nationwide" Audience: A Critical Postscript', *Screen Education*, 39.

——. 1986. *Family Television.* London: Comedia/Routledge.

——. 1989. 'Changing Paradigms in Audience Studies', in E. Seiter, H.Borchers, G. Kreutzner, and E. Warth (eds), *Remote Control: Television, Audiences, and Cultural Power.* London: Routledge.

——. 1992. *Television, Audiences and Cultural Studies.* London: Routledge.

——. 1993. 'Active Audience Theory: Pendulums and Pitfalls', *Journal of Communication*, 2 (1).

Morley, D. 1999. 'Finding About the World from Television News: Some Difficulties', in J. Gripsrud (ed.), *Television and Common Knowledge*. London: Routledge.

Morley, D. and R. Silverstone. 1991. 'Communication and Context: Ethnographic Perspectives on Media Audiences', in K. B. Jensen and N. W. Jankowski (eds), *A Handbook of Qualitative Methodologies for Mass Communication Research*. London: Routledge.

Morris, M. B. 1977. *An Excursion into Creative Sociology*. Oxford: Blackwell.

Mouffe, C. 2000. *The Democratic Paradox*. London: Verso.

Mueller-Vollmer, K. (ed.). 1985. *The Hermeneutics Reader: Texts of the German Tradition from the Enlightenment to the Present*. Oxford: Basil Blackwell.

Munck, R. 2002. 'Globalization and Democracy: A New "Great Transformation"?', *Annals of the American Academy of Political and Social Science*, 581.

Murdock, G. 1989. 'Critical Inquiry and Audience Activity', in B. Dervin, L. Grossberg, B. O'Keefe and E. Wartella (eds), *Rethinking Communication*, Vol 2. London: Sage Publications.

Murdock, G. 1999. 'Rights and Representations: Public Discourse and Cultural Citizenship', in J. Gripsrud (ed.), *Television and Common Knowledge*, pp. 7–17. London: Routledge.

Nandy, A., S. Trivedy, S. Mayaram, and A. Yagnik. 1997. *Creating a Nationality: The Ramjanmabhumi Movement and the Fear of the Self*. New Delhi: Oxford University Press.

Natanson, M. (ed.). 1963. *Philosophy of the Social Sciences: A Reader*. New York: Random House.

——. (ed.). 1970. *Phenomenology and Social Reality: Essays in Memory of Alfred Schutz*. The Hague: Martinus Nijhoff.

——. 1970. 'Alfred Schutz on Social Reality and Social Science', in M. Natanson (ed.), *Phenomenology and Social Reality: Essays in Memory of Alfred Schutz*. The Hague: Martinus Nijhoff.

——. (ed.). 1973. 'Introduction', *Collected Papers, Vol. I*. The Hague: Martinus Nijhoff.

Nichols, B. 1981. *Ideology and the Image: Social Representation in the Cinema and Other Media*. Bloomington: Indiana University Press.

——. 1991. *Representing Reality: Issues and Concepts in Documentary*. Bloomington: Indiana University Press.

Nietzsche, F. 1968. *Will to Power*. Translated by W. Kauffmann and R. J. Hollingdale. New York: Vintage Books.

Oommen, T. K. 1992. 'Contradictions in language policies in independent India', *Media Development*, 1 (3).

Outhwaite, W. 1987. *New Philosophies of Social Science: Realism, Hermeneutics and Critical Theory*. Basingstoke: Macmillan.

Palmer, R. E. 1969. *Hermeneutics: Interpretative Theory in Schleiermacher, Dilthey, Heidegger and Gadamer*. Evanston, IL: Northwestern University Press.

Papineau, D. 1978. *For Science in the Social Sciences.* London: Macmillan.

Parkin, F. 1972. *Class Inequality and the Political Order.* London: Paladin.

Parret, H. and J. Bouveresse (eds). 1981. *Meaning and Understanding.* Berlin: W.de Gruyter.

Pattnayak, D. P. 1981. *Multilingualism and Mother-Tongue Education.* New Delhi: Oxford University Press.

Philo, G. 1990. *Seeing and Believing: The Influence of Television.* London: Routledge.

Platts, M. de B. 1979. *Ways of Meaning: An Introduction to a Philosophy of Language.* London: Routledge and Kegan Paul.

Rabinow, P. and W. Sullivan. 1979. 'Introduction: The Interpretive Turn: Emergence of an Approach', in P. Rabinow and W. Sullivan (eds), *Interpretive Social Science: A Reader.* Berkeley: University of California Press.

Radway, J. 1984. *Reading the Romance: Feminism and the Representation of Women in Popular Culture.* Chapel Hill: University of North Carolina Press.

Rajagopal, A. 2001. *Politics After Television: Hindu Nationalism and the Reshaping of the Public in India.* Cambridge: Cambridge University Press.

Reed-Danahay, D. 2005. *Locating Bourdieu.* Bloomington: Indiana University Press.

Renov, M. (ed.). 1993. *Theorizing Documentary.* London: Routledge.

———. 1993. 'Towards a Poetics of Documentary', in *Theorizing Documentary*, London: Routledge.

———. 2004. *The Subject of Documentary.* Minneapolis: University of Minnesota Press.

Richardson, K. and J. Corner. 1986. 'Reading Reception: Mediation and Transparency in Viewers' Accounts of a TV Programme', *Media, Culture and Society*, 8 (2).

Ricoeur, P. 1970. *Freud and Philosophy: An Essay on Interpretation* (Translated by D. Savage). New Haven: Yale.

Ricoeur, P. 1991. *From Text to Action: Essays in Hermeneutics, II* (Translated by K. Blarney and J. B. Thompson). Evanston, IL: Northwestern University Press.

Risser, J. 1991. 'Reading the Text', in K. Silverman (ed.), *Gadamer and Hermeneutics: Science, Culture, Literature.* New York: Routledge.

Roche, M. 1973. *Phenomenology, Language and the Social Sciences.* London: Routledge and Kegan Paul.

Rorty, R. 1982. *Consequences of Pragmatism.* Brighton: The Harvester Press.

Rosaldo, R. 1993. *Culture and Truth: The Remaking of Social Analysis.* London: Routledge.

Rosen, D. 1993. 'Document and Documentary: On the Persistence of Historic Concepts', in M. Renov (ed.), *Theorizing Documentary.* London: Routledge.

Rosenberg, J. 1981. 'On Understanding the Difficulty in Understanding Understanding', in H. Parrett and J. Bouveresse (eds), *Meaning and Understanding*. Berlin: W. de Gruyter.

Rouse, R. 1991/2002. 'Mexican Migration and the Social Space of Postmodernism', Diaspora 1 (1), Spring 1991, reproduced in J. X. Inda and R. Rosaldo (eds) (2002), *The Anthropology of Globalization: A Reader*. Oxford: Blackwell.

Rudolph L. and S. Rudolph. 1987. *In Pursuit of Lakshmi: The Political Economy of the Indian State*. Chicago: University of Chicago Press.

Said, E. 1986. 'An Ideology of Difference', in H. Gates (ed.), *'Race', Writing and Difference*. Chicago: University of Chicago Press.

Schutz. 1964. *Collected Papers Vol. II: Studies in Social Theory*. The Hague: Martinus Nijhoff.

———. 1972. *The Phenomenology of the Social World* (Translated by G. Wlahs and F. Lehnert). London: Heinemann.

———. 1973. *Collected Papers: Vol. I: The Problem of Social Reality*. The Hague: Martinus Nijhoff.

Seaman, W. 1992. 'Active Audience Theory: Pointless Populism', *Media, Culture and Society*, 14 (1).

Seiter, E., H. Borchers, G. Kreutzner, and E. Warth. 1989. ' "Don't Treat Us Like We're So Stupid and Naive": Toward an Ethnography of Soap Opera Viewers', in E. Seiter, H. Borchers, G. Kreutzner, and E. Warth (eds), *Remote Control: Television, Audiences and Cultural Power*. London: Routledge.

Sen, A. 1999. *Development as Freedom*. Oxford: Oxford University Press.

Seung, T. K. 1981. *Structuralism and Hermeneutics*. New York: Columbia University Press.

Seung, T. K. 1982. *Semiotics and Thematics in Hermeneutics*. New York: Columbia University Press.

Shapcott, R. 1994. 'Conversation and Co-existence: Gadamer and the Interpretation of International Society', *Millenium: Journal of International Studies*, 23 (1).

Silverman, K. (ed.). 1991. *Gadamer and Hermeneutics: Science, Culture, Literature*. New York: Routledge.

Silverstone, R. 1981. *The Message of Television: Myth and Narrative in Contemporary Culture*. London: Heinemann.

———. 1983. 'The Right to Speak: on a Poetic for Television Documentary', *Media, Culture and Society*, 2.

———. 1984. 'Narrative Strategies in Television Science: A Case Study', *Media, Culture and Society*, 5 (2).

———. 1986. 'The Agonistic Narratives in Television Science', in J. Corner (ed.), *Documentary and the Mass Media*. London: Edward Arnold.

Silverstone, R. 1989. 'Let Us Then Return to the Murmuring of Everyday Practices', *Media, Culture and Society*, 11 (1).

———. 1994. *Television and Everyday Life*. London: Routledge.

Silverstone, R. and E. Hirsch. (eds). 1992. *Consuming Technologies*. London: Routledge.

Sless, D. 1981. *Learning and Visual Communication*. London: Croom Helm.

Sontag, S. 1982. *A Susan Sontag Reader*. New York: Penguin Books Ltd.

———. 1982. 'On Photography', in *A Susan Sontag Reader*. New York: Penguin Books Ltd.

Strelitz, L. 2002. 'Media Consumption and Identity Formation: The Case of the "Homeland" Viewers', *Media, Culture and Society*, 24 (2).

Tagg, J. 1988. *The Burden of Representation: Essays on Photographies and Histories*. London: Macmillan.

Taylor, C. 1971. 'Interpretations and the Sciences of Man', reprinted in R. Beehler and A. R. Drengson (eds), *The Philosophy of Society*.1978. London: Methuen.

Thompson, J. B. 1981. *Critical Hermeneutics: A Study in the Thought of Paul Ricoeur And Jurgen Habermas*. Cambridge: Cambridge University Press.

———. 1984. *Studies in the Theory of Ideology*. Cambridge: Polity Press

Tomlinson, J. 1991. *Cultural Imperialism: A Critical Introduction*. London: Pinter.

———. 1999. *Globalization and Culture*. Cambridge: Polity Press.

Tsing, A. (2000/2002). 'The Global Situation', *Cultural Anthropology*, 15 (3), reproduced in J. X. Inda and R. Rosaldo (eds) (2002), *The Anthropology of Globalization: A Reader*. Oxford: Blackwell.

Tufte, T. (ed.). 2002. *Global Encounters: Media and Cultural Transformation*. Luton: University of Luton Press.

Vaughan, D. 1986. 'Notes on the Ascent of a Fictitious Mountain', in J. Corner (ed.), *Documentary and the Mass Media*. London: Edward Arnold.

Wagner, H. R. 1970. *Alfred Schutz: On Phenomenology and Social Relations*. Chicago: University of Chicago Press.

———. 1983. *Alfred Schutz–An Intellectual Biography*. Chicago: University of Chicago Press.

Warnke, G. 1984. 'Introduction', *Understanding and Explanation: A Transcendental-Pragmatic perspective*. Cambridge, MA: MIT Press.

Williams, C. (ed.). 1980. *Realism and the Cinema: A Reader*. London: Routledge and Kegan Paul.

Williams, R. 1981. *The Sociology of Culture*. New York: Schocken Books.

Wilson, T. 1993. *Watching Television: Hermeneutics, Reception and Popular Culture*. Cambridge: Polity Press.

Wimsatt, W. K. and M. C. Beardsley. 1954. *The Verbal Icon*. Lexington: University of Kentucky.

Winston, B. (1978/79). 'Documentary', *Sight and Sound*, Winter.

——. 1993. 'The Documentary Film as Scientific Inscription', in M. Renov (ed.), *Theorizing Documentary*. London: Routledge.

——. 2000. *Lies, Damn Lies and Documentaries*. London: BFI.

Wisdom, J. O. 1987. *Philosophy of the Social Sciences: 1. A Metascientific Introduction*. Aldershot: Avebury.

Wolff, J. 1975. *Hermeneutic Philosophy and the Sociology of Art: An Approach to some of the Epistemological Problems of the Sociology of Knowledge and the Sociology of Art and Literature*. London: Routledge and Kegan Paul.

Wren-Lewis, J. 1983. 'The Encoding/Decoding Model: Criticisms and Redevelopments for Research on Decoding', *Media, Culture and Society*, 5 (2).

——. 1984. 'Decoding Television News', in P. Drummond and R. Paterson (eds), *Television in Transition*. London: The British Film Institute.

Wuthnow, R., J. Hunter, A. Bergesen, and E. Kurzweil (eds). 1984. *Cultural Analysis: The work of Peter Berger, Mary Douglas, Michel Foucault and Jurgen Habermas*. London: Routledge and Kegan Paul.

Wuthnow, R. 1989. *Meaning and Moral Order: Explorations in Cultural Analysis*. Berkeley: University of California Press.

Young, R. J. C. 1995. *Colonial Desires: Hybridity in Theory, Culture and Race*. London: Routledge.

Zhao, Y. and R. Hackett. 2005. 'Media Globalization, Media Democratization: Challenges, Issues, and Paradoxes', in R. Hackett and Y. Zhao (eds), *Democratizing Global Media*. Lanham, MD: Rowman and Littlefield.

Ziff, P. 1972. *Understanding Understanding*. Ithaca: Cornell University Press.

Index

About the Author

Ramaswami Harindranath is Associate Professor in the Media and Communications Program at the School of Culture and Communication, The University of Melbourne, Australia. His previous publications include *Transnational Lives and the Media, Perspectives on Global Cultures, The 'Crash' Controversy* and *Approaches to Audiences.* He won a Commonwealth Universities Scholarship to do his PhD at the University of Leicester (1996), and has taught in several universities in India, the UK and Malaysia. He is on the editorial committees of the academic journals *Participations* and the *Journal of Postcolonial Studies.*